The Joy of
Being Human

About the author

Eugene Kennedy is the author of many best-selling books. Through his books, in the popular newsletters *You* and *Stress,* in articles in general and professional magazines, through lectures across the country, on television and in hundreds of personal consultations, Father Kennedy has become for thousands a source of inspiration and sanity in a troubled world. His rare gift for understanding and communication coupled with his vast professional experience as a psychologist has enabled him to reach out to contemporary Christians, to support the increasingly difficult struggle for personal and spiritual fulfillment. One of the best-known thinkers and prolific writers in the Church today, he is professor of psychology at Loyola University of Chicago.

About his other Image books

The Joy of Being Human

Reflections for every day of the year

By Eugene Kennedy

IMAGE BOOKS

A Division of Doubleday & Company, Inc.
Garden City, New York
1976

Image Books edition published by special arrangement with
   The Thomas More Press
Image Books edition published February 1976

ISBN: 0-385-00943-7

Introduction

Where are the secret springs of joy? Its headwaters are in the heart but life has recurrent dry seasons when our worlds crack like ancient bones under our feet and joy is a trickle rather than a flood. We are occasionally so parched that we are more mindful of our pain than of anything else. Joy can then seem a memory or an insubstantial longing, an occasional blessing rather than a regular experience.

That is why so many persons pursue pleasure and the easy promises of escape. As I write these words, a new television season has just begun. It is as good a commentary as we are likely to get on the abundant shallows in which we try to refresh ourselves. Americans deserve something better than to perish culturally watching "The Dating Game" or "Hollywood Squares." The escape entertainment of the day pulverizes meaning and so makes the discovery of joy more difficult. Perhaps there have never been so many people as well acquainted with the pain of life as today; personal and public sorrows abound. And perhaps there have never been so many people so poorly served by mass invitations to leisure and escape as today. Have you ever noticed the grim expressions on many persons bent on enjoying themselves? Joy is not found on the outside of pain; it becomes our possession when we learn to live in and with our sufferings.

Joy comes into our lives the same way that peace does —after we have made certain decisions about our goals and about the things that are of value to us. Joy is not for sale; it slips into the soul when we are serious about life's sources of meaning and when we are honest about our personal commitments to these. Escapes promise us a way out of life; meaning, however, is delivered only to those who find their way in. Joy stands at the entrance to everything that is ordinary; it attends us when we have the correct perspective on the commonplace. The real adventures of life take us to familiar places—back to friendship and the good things of life shared with somebody else, back to unselfish moments when we open our hearts only to find them filled rather than emptied by the gesture. These pages are meant to remind us of the everyday events and experiences that open rather than avert our eyes from the sources of joy that surround us.

Dr. Elizabeth Kübler-Ross, who has devoted many years to the study of the experience of dying, said once in an interview:

It's very interesting when you look back at hundreds of dying patients—young and old. Not one of them has ever told me how many houses she had or how many handbags or sable coats. What they tell you of are very tiny, almost insignificant moments in their lives—where they went fishing with a child or they tell of mountain-climbing trips in Switzerland. Some brief moments of privacy in an interpersonal relationship. These are the things that keep people going at the end. . . . They remember little moments that they have long forgotten and they suddenly have a smile on their faces. And they begin to reminisce about little memories that make their whole lives meaningful and worthwhile. I never understood in 40 years what the church tried to teach—that there is meaning in suffering—until I found myself in this situation (*Chicago Medicine,* Vol. 76, No. 17, August 25, 1973, p. 661).

This catches the perspective that is available to the believer long before death stands in the doorway. As we actively accept the sharp edging of suffering that is connected with everything worthwhile, we can face up to the deaths, separations, misunderstandings, and loneliness of life and come out whole everytime. Jesus has a simple message that tells us that joy and peace are the prizes for those who take on the flesh of their humanity with courage and love. We remember that best in the small moments when we have been truest to each other, when we have seen some difficulty through, when we have tasted bitterness without turning away. "Joy," Chesterton once wrote, "is the gigantic secret of the Christian." It flows from being human, from affirming our own incarnation, and from finding our way through pain together. There is nothing new in these pages; they are filled with old truths that loving persons know already. I hope that they will remind them of where their treasures are and encourage them to see them freshly each day of their lives.

Eugene Kennedy
F.S.

January

Winter seems a bad time to begin a new year; for many of us the weather seems more suitable for the end of the world than the start of another long-distance race against time and the Fates. We are usually glad to see the old year go—although its scars remain—but we are happy to have another chance at being or doing better. Most of us are like that, thank God, and, even as we climb out of the wreckage of the year past, we want to try again at doing the right thing about ourselves, our work, and our neighbor. The new year makes us think old thoughts about who we are and what we might become; it is a time to think about our promises even as we remember our failings—an interval for hope rather than regrets. And there are many things to think about. . . . Hope . . . where is it found and what is it like? It has gossamer edges in the oratory and sermons that urge us to wait expectantly for a coming sunrise of fulfillment; sometimes hope seems to be the commodity urged upon us by those people, in whatever profession, who cannot do anything for us in the present. The hints we get from the way we speak about hope make it sound like a vaguely fragile quality, something that can be dashed in an instant, something we are constantly told to be careful of lest we lose it. Hope certainly seems to be a mysterious thing, a wonderful heavenly force that usually hovers just above our lives but touches down to green the earth around it if we pray hard enough for it. The year cannot begin without hope, however, and it might be a good idea to mention some of the qualities of hope that make it both more understandable and available for us.

Hope, for example, is not something we can grab at on our own; it is not something we can earn or even pray ourselves into possessing. This distorted notion has been perpetuated by too many preachers who have fervently made hope the responsibility of their listeners, as though the congregation had the sole responsibility for its presence in their lives and that its absence was a sign of their spiritual imperfection. The Christian understands that hope does not work that way. You cannot demand hope of other people; you can only give it to them. When those close to us, be they family, parishioners, or patients, do not have much hope, the reason may be because we have failed to give them any. Hope is not actually a weak or easily destroyed phenomenon; it is just rare because it takes an investment (rather than a withdrawal) of ourselves in the lives and struggles of others. This active element is rarely present in those ecclesiastics who can only chide their people for lacking hope; in reality, the people merely display the kind of spiritual poverty they suffer from because the priest has nothing of substance to give. And it works the same way between husbands and wives, parents and children, and even old friends: Hope is the thing they give to each other in life, one of those precious elements that can only be given away, and the new year is a good time to remember this truth.

January 2
Hope Is Transferred . . .

only through human beings; hope comes when we are able to reach each other or it does not come at all. This is not to say that hope is other than the work of the Spirit, but it is to ratify in practice God's ways of working according to human ground rules. Hope is not the stuff of dreams nor of distant silver linings; neither is it the result of miracles that astound us as they blot out the tracks we necessarily make in our ordinary journey across the human condition.

Hope is not outside us; it sings in our bruised hearts when some person other than a mysterious angel of the Lord reaches out to us at the moment we feel like giving up. The Spirit works through the touch of the person who believes in us enough not to give up on us; this action of another makes the deadened filaments of the soul glow once again; it is through persons who give us their light when we are in darkness that we experience the power of Resurrection. Hope comes to life at any moment when one man reaches out sincerely to another.

January 3
The Beginning of the Year . . .

is a good time to shake hope down from the heavens where it has been thought to dwell for so long. It is also appropriate to reflect on our own responsibility to generate hope by responding to the needs of others. That is the kind of resolution that each of us keeps best in the circumstances of our own lives and relationships—in those intimate areas that only we can enter, the sacred places in the lives of those we love that are known only to us. Hope is what we plant in the lives of others; the more we plant the greater is the harvest. Hope is what makes the future for all of us. It is our best gift to an old world in a new year.

January 4
Commitment to the New

It is a curious truth that some people do not recognize or want to admit the essential commitment of Christianity to what is new, to the world that needs our hope, to the future whose shape is determined right now by our attitude toward it. The contemporary fashion, of course, is to be overwhelmed by the future, to stagger hazily in the grip of "future shock," almost enjoying the perilous tide that, we are told, is bound first to confuse and then to destroy us. That is part of the temptation described long ago by the German author Thomas Mann in his portrayal of persons with a "sympathy for the abyss," a dangerous and unchristian luxury. It is almost as bad as the well documented over-reverence of the past that has made tradition—shorthand for "the way we used to do it"—the sole model for the future. The beginning of the year gives us the chance to locate our own attitudes toward the future, toward the new world that beckons us as it forms before us. The following might serve as a check list of themes for our own self-examination.

The Gospels challenge us to be concerned not only with the last things, but, more urgently and practically, with the next things. Our beliefs were heralded in the testament of the new, and the great cry of the Book of Revelation gives the Christian a feeling for the saving dynamic that reaches out to the future: "Behold, I make all things new." The Christian is called to a life of hope, not just in longing for his own salvation, but in serving the world that is just coming into being. The greatest test the Christian faces—the one that draws the fibers of his being taut every day—is that of continuing to invest hope in others; the most ancient Christian temptation closes a man off in self-concern where he can forget the world of other men or simply say the hell with it. There is nothing more difficult, of course, than continuing to affirm others, especially when they seem so unconcerned or ungrateful for our interest in them and their lives.

January 5
Signs of the Times

Great changes are taking place but they do not portend the end of the world in our time. There are contemporary evangelists who are still scaring the lives out of people with their announcements that all the biblical signs are falling into place and that we will all soon be consumed in fire. Well, men like to be frightened now and then; it seems somehow therapeutic, no matter how short-term are the effects. The end, however, is not yet, and a far more demanding challenge presents itself than merely that of donning our sackcloth to await the gentle final rain of apocalyptic ashes.

There are indeed contemporary signs to be read, and some of them are in the sun and the moon, but their message is one of a world that we are just beginning to grasp, of a universe we are only now beginning to explore. The disorienting thing about the future is that it asks us to abandon old ideas in order to comprehend the truth about our life together in a redeemed universe. The reality of the interstellar age means that we can no longer apply a pre-Copernican template on our world; that is, we must finally surrender the notion that the earth is the center of the universe. The view of earth from the moon (that first glimpse of an earthrise) makes it possible for us to recognize that the earth is in the heavens rather than defined over against them. God's creation cannot be thought of as the earth below and heaven above, and we cannot enter tomorrow until we heal the terrible divisions that we have built on that presupposition. We cannot, for example, continue to separate the natural and the supernatural, the flesh from the spirit, or to imagine that there is a spiritual order somewhere outside of human experience. There is a new consciousness beginning to build in the world and it demands that we reaffirm the essential unity of our experience as God's creatures. This means that we have to drop the old self-complacent notions that have ruled our theological images of man and his world for so long. Light is showing through a crack in the twenty-first century, enough light to see ourselves a little more clearly, and to begin to sense our personal psychological and spiritual unity. We are beginning to drop the divided models of man which have so affected our efforts to live in the Spirit.

This adjustment to a better feel for the universe of

which we are a part will cause us to forge new and more effective religious symbols for a deeper, more comprehensive, and more mature faith. We are recognizing the unifying truth of our life in God and acknowledging that there can be no effective divisions of human experience into human and divine. A new year reminds us that we are just working out our understanding of this; the development of this awareness does not mean that we have become estranged as much as it means that at last we are finding our true way home in God's creation.

January 6
Faith Alive

The style of religious awareness that will be essential in the next century comforts us because it tells us that religion is not shattering apart as much as it is transforming its own understanding of itself and the world it is meant to serve. Man is on the verge of freeing religion from the exile in which it has somehow lived as a separate if important part of life. In the future man will need a religion that cannot be kept compartmentalized, reserved for churches, special occasions, or great catastrophes. As we begin to appreciate the intrinsic religious meaning of life, we will shed the symbols and habits of an age during which we thought that religion and this world were adversaries for man's soul. We will be wiser when we have accomplished this, of course, but we will also have to live far more truthfully and responsibly. Membership in an institution will not be enough to acquit us of our religious obligations because the realm of religious behavior will be as wide as man's hopes and dreams. We are all involved in working through this new religious sense of the universe. No one can safely ignore it because, whether we acknowledge it or not, we will feel its effects in our own lives. The quest for spiritual and emotional fulfillment will lead us over this ground into the future.

January 7
Well, What about Resolutions?

Our own checkered experience with resolutions, the changing times which no longer emphasize resolutions in the way they once did, and, perhaps most important of all, the difficulty in forging practical promises about our behavior —these combine to discourage even the inveterate resolution-maker. The following reflections are designed for the person for whom it is difficult to suggest resolutions.

The basic ground rules concerning resolutions call for choosing a new style of behaving that is neither too difficult nor too easy for us. Most of us have taken that trip before anyway; it is a favorite road because, when things are either too hard or too easy, we quickly excuse ourselves from taking the challenge seriously. We even forget it without guilt or regrets. This approach, by the way, is the one frequently chosen by the underachiever who does not want to give his powers a genuine test; real achievement occurs only somewhere in the middle range of action where the behavior called for makes him stretch himself but also includes the possibility of failure. When a man chooses something too hard or too easy he eliminates that terrible risk of failing. We cannot take the path of the underachiever if we are serious about using a resolution to further our own personal spiritual development.

January 8
A Few 'Suggestions'

A man might, for example, choose to work on an attitude rather than on a specific behavior. Instead of promising to act in this or that manner (not to smoke, to drink only a prescribed amount) he could try to listen more carefully to what is going on inside himself, especially in regard to

15

those relationships which so easily grow callous defenses over their sorepoints. This might be the best thing for a husband and wife, much better than resolving not to argue or to spend a certain amount of time together each week. It is wiser to begin to look gently into our attitudes: Why do I find it so easy to disagree with her every time something comes up? What is it that makes me feel so disappointed in him? Why do I find that I do not listen very carefully any more? The truth mined up through digging into our attitudes will prove far more helpful to us and to those around us in the new year. Indeed, it is only this somewhat difficult (but not impossible) self-search that enables us to keep ourselves from growing stale, dull, and finally all-defensive in our closest relationships with others. It is the modern way of removing the timber from our own eye before we go around observing the speck in the eyes of others. The greatest benefit of this kind of promise is that it removes the game-playing nature of resolutions and urges us to get more deeply into life itself.

Another area we might look into is that particular one we fight against inspecting. We all have such tender places in our psyches and, while we hardly need to probe them with the savage intensity of a misguided encounter group leader, we might just try to take a less hurried and more mature glance at the thing we like least to admit about ourselves. It is just damned hard to do, so it stays the way it is, a mild infection carefully bandaged but never getting much better from year to year. The greatest revelation of a braver look at what we hesitate to talk about even to ourselves is the discovery that the defense loses its power in direct relationship to our capacity to take a harder look in its direction. In other words, instead of trying to behave better in relationship to those around us, we might try to treat ourselves with a little more gentleness and compassion and a greater willingness to forgive ourselves for and to live with our prime shortcoming. Just a little progress in this regard will make the new year much easier for us and

16

for everyone we love. In case you have difficulty finding this area, listen carefully to yourself the next time you say "I don't want to talk about it," or "You'll just have to take me the way I am," and you'll find that you are standing right on home plate.

January 9
A Fresh Look

Probably the most vital area of general resolution concerns our attitude toward learning. It is never simple to begin to learn again after we feel that our learning days are behind us; a man grows tired of never ceasing to prove himself and his competence and he likes to settle into his niche with his own way of looking at and doing things. Old dogs resist new tricks, the coiner of proverbs tells us, and, while we like to apply that to all those other people (known universally as "them" and "they"), it really applies to most of us. If we are to break through to new learning, something has to die, and it is usually some adjustment that is comforting and comfortable. That applies to new understandings about the world, our work, and ourselves; the man of hope never finishes learning about any of these. It is the hopeful man who understands that his commitment to the future is not just a vague sense of confidence that all will eventually go well. He realizes that the price of concern for the future is a present readiness to look freshly at the emerging truths of life. The attitude of openness incorporates the Gospel ideal of dying to ourselves to give deeper and richer life and it holds true across all the human boundaries, from learning about the stars to learning about love. The new year begins best for the man who is not so afraid of new learning that he closes himself off from the uneasiness or pain that it generates in his heart; the open man already lives in the future where hope and hard learning go hand in hand.

17

January 10
A Life Without Surprises

A life without surprises would be a life without childhood
and one beyond joy—a commuter's dulled journey through
the grey monotony of the shambled sides of our cities, a
routine life, too controlled for men to bear. Oddly, however, some men would like to stamp out surprise in the
name of a better-run world; they want to eliminate all mistakes, somewhat in the way that a teaching machine does,
so that errorless progress up gently rising curves of knowledge becomes the rule rather than the exception. People
who like to make rules, of course, have always been the
enemies of surprise and novelty. Better, as they see it, to
trace the blueprints in advance and to design the properly
advantaged environments that will give birth to and nur-
ture successfully a marvelously controlled and totally un-
surprisable generation. Luckily, man outwits the social and
educational planners who fashion such patterns for him;
there is something in man's nature that makes him yearn
for and desire to generate surprises. It is one of man's
most engaging qualities, a close kin to his creative strength
—a sign, in a world weighed down with systems engineering, of the lively spark of life that endures in the human
heart. It is worth thinking about. . . .

January 11
Freedom Needs Surprises

A man cannot be human or Christian if he attempts to
eliminate the quality of surprise from his experience. He is
meant to live freely in a contingent world, where either
this or that—or some unsuspected third thing—might happen; he has to make his choices in this kind of environ-

18

ment where what he does has a distinct effect on the way his and other lives unfold. Crossroads are commonplace in the land of the free man and, as it was for the traveler in Frost's poem, the road we take does make all the difference. In a way, we are always choosing the pathway to surprise in life because, no matter how carefully we try to judge the trip beforehand—despite even the impressive forecasts we can gather to make our way easier—there are still shapes in the darkness that we do not or cannot see. When we make ourselves vulnerable to life by daring to be free, we choose to be surprised, knowing that we can rely on our capacity to handle situations as they arise. The great, and in many ways understandable, temptation of the age is to accept the security that well-worn paths offer to us, to play life cautiously in order to gain a measure of control over it. Living freely is indeed a dangerous business because it moves us into the world of self-responsibility where the falling shadows are filled with surprise. Roadmaps, weather forecasts, and college board scores have become so much a part of our lives that it is difficult for some people even to contemplate the unpredictable; they have conceived of it as an enemy for so long that they do not understand its charm until they are so involved in an overplanned life that they can do nothing about it. That is, they can do nothing but long for a little more freedom and a few more choices while they wonder whether they might not have followed some other road in life—a ripple of a thought, just a murmur in their consciousness that they can never quite answer or put to rest. That is why many men, even in mid-life and after very successful careers, decide to try something entirely different, to test themselves in an uncharted area of work or residence where surprise will wrestle with the gods of success or failure. But most men, because of family and financial responsibility, must keep moving through the dead calm of familiar surroundings untouched by the winds of surprise, or at least that is what they think. But is this necessarily so?

January 12
Growing from the Inside

A person may not be able to change his job or his lifestyle but that does not mean that he can never find the sweet savor of surprise. The reason for this is because the best surprises are within ourselves and we do not have to change our environments to find them. In fact, it is probably foolish for a man to manipulate his surroundings until he has attuned himself to his own best source of surprise, his growth from within. One of the fascinating things about growth is that it is not entirely predictable, despite the sophistication of our social science measuring rods. No educational specialist, for example, has had a very good batting average at spotting creative genius in the early stages of development; genius unfolds from within, delighting in the unselfconscious surprises that accompany the discovery of its strengths. Genius, however, is not a prerequisite for growth nor for the unpredictable discoveries that take place in our personalities when we seek the truth about ourselves. There are in each of us capacities for sensitivity and tenderness, for example, that many of us do not let surface; we are surprised, we say, when we experience them appropriately in life. We are thereby changed as well, and for the better. Life can never be quite so dull again for the man who lets himself be surprised by the deep strength of his need to love and be loved.

The relationship of a husband and wife will be only temporarily enlivened by reading something like *The Sensuous Man* or *The Sensuous Woman;* there are few surprises there anyway. Life does, however, become a more wonderful experience when a husband and wife can begin to tap and share other talents and activities that enable them to penetrate more deeply into mutual self-understanding. They will be surprised by the things they learn when they can shake loose the hardened but incorrect convictions that they have heard everything that each has to say. Couples can begin just by listening a little more carefully and they are almost sure to be surprised by what they hear. They will, of course, be hearing more of each other, sharing more of each other, and also discovering things together. The same holds true for a priest and his people or a teacher and his class: they are never the same old crowd, even though they may look that way. They are filled with the human surprises that spring from the fact that, at the bottom of it all, each of us is unique and the willingness to find them, especially in the company of others, causes us to come alive again, and to discover the wonderful quality of surprise that God built into all of life.

January 13
Who Doesn't Like Surprises?

Maybe, in the long run, it is the person who has never become very friendly with himself or with life itself. There are people like this and sometimes they cover up their uneasiness and fear with loud noises and large displays of bluster. The fearful man is not, however, malicious; he is just frightened and tries to do something about his fears in the only way that he understands—by sticking to what seems familiar, certain, and comforting while he erects defenses against the world around him. Fearful people hold back from life because of its dangers but they miss its beauty and much of its wonder at the same time. That is a high price to pay for not getting hurt. These frightened people cannot be coaxed into life; they can only be loved into life by those who can accept and understand them. Uneasy people must be assisted to take one step at a time toward fuller participation in life.

January 14
The Cynic . . .

is another case, although it is clear that he may be using his style of disbelief in human possibilities to protect himself as well. The trouble with the cynic is that he cannot see the possibility of anything being honest, true, or spontaneous. Love is a trap, faith an illusion, and so there is little room for hope at all. A cynical man would be genuinely surprised by the discovery of something that was not fake or flawed in human affairs. The tragedy is that, despite the amount of phoniness that the cynic accurately spots, he does it with a fevered heart that prevents him from recognizing man's chances for goodness and nobility; as a result, he does very little to promote these. Yet it is not enough to hold oneself together by expecting the worst so that one is never disappointed. That takes a man out of the context of life and renders him impotent in the worst and final way—he cannot enlarge the life of anyone else.

January 15
The Planners

We seldom question the contemporary planner who makes his blueprints for human behavior according to a theory of mankind that expects very little from man. Sometimes he is the city planner and sometimes he is the automobile planner (notable designers of environments uncongenial to human beings) but, more often, he is the architect of a pollution free world in which population growth will have reached zero, or of an antiseptic world in which venereal disease will have been wiped out. Don't misunderstand me; these are objectives that serious persons endorse as important for our future. I am not reflecting on the objectives as much as on the planning methods, few of which even suggest that tomorrow might best be entered by men who have achieved and increased internal freedom through old fashioned but durable means like self-understanding and self-control. Instead, the brave new world will open its gates to those who have been careful enough to prepare for or clean up carefully after any and every sexual experience. The place of sexual experience in human relationships is taken for granted, and maybe there is some kind of realism in this, but the possibility that man might put his sexual responsibility into greater perspective by attaining greater overall maturity is seldom ever raised. The planning, in other words, is all calibrated to the man supposedly liberated by the so-called sexual revolution; technology has freed him for greater pleasure but deeper concerns about the nature of love and the dimensions of human relationships are thereby avoided.

For example, in a recent book published by medically qualified people, the question of a man's sexual behavior during certain stages of his wife's pregnancy is discussed in terms of his need for some kind of outlet when the opportunity for intercourse with his wife is limited. There is no sign that the authors can see any other issue involved but the sexual freedom of the man (the word *outlet* has a strangely appropriate flavor since it refers to mechanical things) which evidently transcends any other aspect of the marriage relationship. This apparent toleration of extramarital sex at a time which in reality may call for increased sensitivity and fidelity is an example of the planner with an occluded heart. He cannot feel the real dimensions of the relationship between husband and wife; he can only emphasize the male role in a narcissistic and self-congratulating way. The other issues are not even discussed and the alternative behavior—that the man might have to acquire a new maturity as his response during this and other difficult times—is not even considered. This is a dangerously foreshortened view of the human person, one that registers all behavior as indifferent on the scale of Christian values, one that plans for more rather than less immaturity.

January 16
Living for Ourselves

This attitude can be seen in the many young couples who have bought without question the philosophy that their youth is the time to enjoy themselves and that having children can be put off, if it must be considered at all, until a later date. One does not have to have an ante-diluvian moral outlook to raise some questions about this kind of planning, a design for life that certainly wants to eliminate surprises. After all, we are told, the institution of marriage is changing and childbearing will be the responsibility of the few rather than of the many. And we can do so many things now, the reasoning goes. . . . But what, I wonder, happens to a relationship in which such clearly self-regarding decisions are made. They cannot be all wrong, of course, but what happens to love that does not grow beyond the boundaries of the man and woman toward giving and nurturing new life? What happens, in other words, if our planners let lovers think their love can ever be safely just their own possession? One of the reasons that the institution of marriage is under strain centers in our failure to deepen our grasp of the non-sexual issues involved in developing a relationship that has a chance of living beyond the exhaustion of novelty. These questions—concerning the growth of things like trust and tenderness which are too deep for tears—cannot be programmed out of peoples' lives in the name of giving them greater freedom. These questions return, perhaps as longings or doubts or the hunger for more meaning, and they must eventually be dealt with in any relationship that has human meaning.

January 17
Breaking Out

The problem all throughout history has been to help men to get out of themselves, to establish and develop relationships that break them free from the deadly self-concern of the narcissistic stage of growth. This is an imperative if we are really concerned with the future of the human race. Man's survival depends to a certain extent on clean air and clean water, on a planet that does not overpopulate itself to death: All this is true, but man's future also depends on taking himself and his deepest needs as a person seriously. The perhaps achingly slow maturity of the human race depends on those who remember what man is like and what he can be when he is at his best, when he is most fully human. Just being careful and avoiding the surprises of unwanted conception, venereal disease, or periods of inconvenient sexual abstinence is hardly enough; and the planner most dangerous to our future is the one who thinks that this is so.

January 18
If You Play God . . .

there are no surprises at all. That is not the reason given by those who take on the role of arranging and rearranging the lives of others, a dangerous but ancient game, now ready to be played again with new equipment and a new vagueness about the rules that are to be followed. The behaviorists are out to design whole cultures in order to preserve them and to improve the lot of man. Similar high purposes are spoken of by the genetic engineers who claim that we are on the verge of being able to more accurately design our own descendants. They are not issues to be

25

dismissed but neither can they be discussed without including the Christian viewpoints that help us to see ourselves and our human responsibilities more clearly. It is so easy to agree with the new plans for playing God; they seem aimed at eliminating so much pain and misery—the kinds of trials that go with the tragic side of surprise in illness, separation, and death. But will we ever outwit these completely, and what does it do to our lives when we try?

One thinks, for example, of the statements of playwright Robert Anderson who told a medical school meeting that he had not let his wife know that she had cancer even though he knew it for four years before her death. Instead, he said that he "played God . . . trying to arrange her life." He told the doctors that he thought he had been wrong. "It would have been easier, far, far less lonely, if she had known." Anderson touched a deep truth, one for all the planners to ponder as he went on: "I'm quite sure I deprived my wife of the right to share her dying with someone else. I played God for four years, trying to arrange her life in a way I thought she would want to lead it in her last years, but actually might not have led it if she had known they were her last years." For all we know, the loving ruse may not have fooled her; people have a way of knowing about sickness and death. What it did was to separate man and woman at the opposite ends of an experience into which they should have walked together. The decision eliminated surprise, but it destroyed the spontaneous realization of the last act of this couple's tender love for each other. By playing the Creator, even for the best of reasons, he denied them the full dignity of being mortal creatures whose love could only have drawn them closer to each other in the very shadow of death.

Life cannot be cleansed of surprise, even of the surprise of pain, if it means denying to people the opportunity to do the very thing which, through God's help, makes them most human—to learn to love each other more. To hide the surprise of death may be to lessen the chance for the full experience of life that comes to people when they have to face ultimate experiences together. And what else is there for human beings if we take away the trials and chance occurrences that make love the unlikeliest but the most available surprise for all of us?

January 19
Does Anybody Want to Be Holy?

That used to be a great ideal for man, the old vision of becoming a saint of some kind. Now the designation is used more sparingly; rarely does it describe an ideal we are all supposed to reach for. Where do you hear the saints spoken of these days? Hardly ever in church, not even in Catholic churches, from which their statues and relics have gradually disappeared over the past few years. Modern man clears his throat uneasily at the thought of the hagiographic details that once inspired his yearning to become a "pilgrim of the absolute"—unbathed old men staring out of their desert caves or off their isolated pillars, hardy ascetics rivaling each other in the now faded olympics of self-denial, beautiful and innocent young girls treated harshly by villainous and well-fed ecclesiastics—the roster is familiar to anybody with even a short memory. The term saint is still around, of course, and is applied by the pious to surviving models of heroic endurances—for example, to the wife who has managed a household for years despite an alcoholic husband ("She's a living saint!") or to a priest who still spends a lot of time in church ("Father's a very holy man!"). And there is secular sanctity as well, the list of the too-soon-dead heroes of contemporary life, the man whom, for whatever reason, we want to believe in because of the ideals they seemed to have. Once in a while a figure like Pope John walks out of history to be recognized as a saint by a quiet and undemonstrative universal acclamation that makes the process of canonization seem pretentious and demeaning in his regard. But, as a prospect for the average man, becoming a saint does not have the pull it once seemed so strongly to possess.

However, this does not mean that men do not want to be good or that they do not wish to do the right thing in their lives. Despite the pessimistic reports you are likely to hear about him, man wants to move in the right direction, wants, in other words, to make his life worthwhile. He just does not self-consciously perceive his goal as becoming a saint quite as clearly as did some of his Christian ancestors. That, in the long run, is a good thing: emphasis on the substance of one's life rather than on its heavenly accolades is a sign of progress. Men and women may not consciously strive to be called saints, but that does not mean that they are not or cannot be holy people in the best sense of the term. But what, literally in God's name, is the best sense of the term "saint" in our day and age? Maybe the following incomplete list will help us get the idea of being good into better perspective.

January 20
The Contemporary Saint . . .

is considered holy for what he does with people rather than for what he does in escaping from people. The present definition of being a holy man does not fit the hollow-eyed, desert dweller, or even the mountain-top guru, but rather the person who manages to be good and to be close to people at the same time. There is, as a matter of fact, nothing easier than to be thought holy because you stay at a distance from other human beings, and nothing harder than continuing to love them even as you get to know them better and they get to know you.

He is not the person, then, who is famous for long fasts and longer prayers as much as the man or woman who, whether engaging in these activities or not, is there when people need his response. The saint is not recognized by his heavenly glow but by his earthly presence at a time when we desperately need what only another human being can provide for us in terms of understanding, encouragement, or support.

January 21
Truly Holy People . . .

make room in life for you, that is, have a real rather than
a stylized relationship with you. Because he or she is truly
present to others, the saint breaks those bonds of space
and time which people are so aware of when they are dealt
with on a superficial plane and in a practiced way. You
have, as a result of truly being accepted and heard by the
other, a deeper experience of yourself and a better understanding of your own life. Another way to put this is to
say that anybody who makes you more alive in a lasting
manner does a sacred thing for you.

They do not scare you to death in the name of reform-
ing your life or mending your ways; hellfire and end-of-the
world theatrics are not their staples. Indeed, a modern
saint does not manipulate you in any way (and you can
tell when you are being manipulated or not) because his
scale of values does not make room for that kind of intimate sacrilege. The holy man or woman of today gives
you respect on every level, preferring to leave you free as
a complete individual rather than to have you pledge your
allegiance to God with only an intimidated part of yourself. This experience of being treated with regard for our
own personalities helps us to understand the genuine
meaning of redemption. Holiness means we become whole,
not that we cower half-grown in the shadow of an imagined sword of God's vengeance. The contemporary saint
gives us more of ourselves; he does not take anything away
from us.

January 22
The Person Living by the Spirit . . .

gives time, energy, and all the other human responses that
are appropriate to our needs—but does not make us feel

that we owe him anything. He may not seem "pious" by older standards, may not, in other words, have the mannerisms or otherworldly looks of supposedly holy people. That is all to the good because it helps others to recognize their own possibilities and frees them from feeling that being good demands more than being fully themselves.

He does not work miracles, talk in tongues, or seem in any way to need what we might with kindness call sensational demonstrations of his relationship with the Spirit. When promising to pray for us, he does not make us feel funny, as, in fact, many people who try to manipulate us into their own image do. These latter are not praying for our fullness as much as they are for their own. A contemporary holy person does not make you feel that he has plans for you as much as he helps you to discover your own.

He does not have answers for all your questions; in fact, he is just discovering many of the right questions himself. He helps us ask these questions and stays with us as we search out our own answers to them. At times the most he can do is to make hard questions bearable through his commitment to us as we try to answer them.

The contemporary holy man does not save us from pain, or make us look away from the agonies involved in everyday living; he helps us to recognize these as our experience of living in Jesus. He does not, however, get us involved in non-redemptive or unnecessary suffering; he does not, in other words, introduce extraneous suffering (e.g., new penances or promises) into lives which already have an adequate share of suffering.

There are saints operating in your life at the present moment although they are too close and too unself-conscious for most of us to recognize. There are saints all around us in the world, loving it and redeeming it with the gift they make of themselves in the service of others. Sometimes, as has been true of saints for centuries, they are in trouble with authorities, and sometimes they are involved in great controversy. That is because they have the most distinguishing mark that a holy person can possess, the mark of being truly alive both to eternal truths and to temporal affairs.

January 23
What Is Charism?

Well, it has been said that a charism is a gift from God, something like a talent, but the term has been used to explain a wide variety of behaviors lately. In fact, it has replaced "offer it up" as the interpretive phrase of choice for the philosopher of contemporary spirituality. "He has a special charism for this work," the saying goes, and sometimes it is even true, although the threadbare fruits of some alleged charisms make a man think the whole matter over carefully. You just cannot explain everything by invoking the charism rule, and it might be good to have some clear ideas about charisms before proceeding further.

First of all, charisms do abound. The world is filled with gifts that we have received freely from any number of sources. The more we recognize the lack of mystery about charisms, the better we will understand God's ways with men. He never overpowers them, or forces on them a talent or a challenge that totally defies their nature, their inheritance, or their cultural background. In fact, it is from these sources that our gifts flow; they have a human face for all of us. Everything that the rest of the human family has given to us is a gift to each of us, one that makes us aware of our responsibility to be equally generous to those as yet unborn. From the individual gifts plucked from our own family trees to the communal gifts of art, painting, and literature that belong to all of us, we are deluged with the charisms that equip us for our own work in life.

January 24
Charisms also . . .

are, by their very nature, free gifts. You cannot demand a gift from someone and no one else can demand that we accept a gift. Charisms are not subject to this kind of barter; they demand response on another plane of human activity where things cannot be forced or manipulated, a territory in which free responses are the only ones that count. The more freely a person affirms his own gifts, the more generous he is in sharing them with others; the more he is told that he must have a charism of some kind or other, the less freely and the less humanly will he be able to employ it. Charisms wither when they are made the subject of legislation.

Finally, charisms are available to us not just for ourselves but for the sake of the community of people around us; they only work when we remember this, and they shrivel in our hands when we clutch them to our own breasts. Gifts we have to give away, gifts that cannot be lost in the process, gifts that do not grow smaller but larger as we use them are charisms. The economy in which they flourish is located in the environment of human need around us, and the man who discovers that what he has been given is to be given in turn to others, has come close to discovering the meaning of life itself.

January 25
My Aunt Margaret

She knows more about life than most theologians, and, in a quite unself-conscious way, more about what goes into being what we used to call holy than a convention of Roman congregations. She is, despite her long dark hair, well into her seventies, and she buried her beloved bricklayer husband just a few Thanksgivings ago. She lives near the cemetery where he lies under the tombstone she had carved with little trowels and she misses him more rather than less, especially at holiday time. But, as long as I can remember, she has not taken much time to feel sorry for herself and she has never let other people enjoy the luxury of self-pity very long either. She is one of those loving ladies whose arms have always seemed big and tender enough to hold the world, arms in which small children have always felt at home. She has always looked at the world and at all of us with an earthy directness that neither attempts nor abides sham of any kind; she is, in a word, real, and everyone should have an aunt like her. Everyone always feels better when she comes into the room.

I think of the time when my father died and of the quiet numbness that filled our house until Margaret, still heaving sighs from her long journey, broke through it like a sunrise. Her presence, her instinct for the right human response to everyone's needs, made all the difference in those few days. She sensed when people needed her special kind of cheering and, with the openness that has always made her instantly available to everyone, she gave of herself simply and sensibly. It was no wonder that her grandnephews and grandnieces crowded around her, elbowing each other out of the way to get a place by her at a meal, probing her with questions on every subject just to hear her laugh and, as she had done for as long as I remember, tell them just what she thought.

It is difficult for a family—no matter how many of them there are, no matter how deep their faith or how prepared they are for a parent's death—while waiting in the limousine after the last goodbye at the funeral home before the cortege heads for the church. It is a moment for remembering and regretting, a moment for feeling the pain of loss that the rush of events has obscured until then, a moment badly in need of the intervention of an Aunt Margaret. She began to speak of her late husband, not to get attention, but to challenge the gloomy and unchristian silence that had enveloped all of us huddled together. "Mr.

Gleason," as she referred to her ruggedly handsome husband who had worked at his trade for over sixty years, "Mr. Gleason bought a cemetery plot with another bricklayer back around 1915 when the two of them were friends. Then his friend, Pat, died about ten years ago but they hadn't been friends in years; you know these Irishmen could get into fights with each other. Well, Mr. Gleason, who hadn't spoken Pat's name for years, suddenly wanted to go to the wake. I couldn't understand it but he had that set look of his and I knew he meant business." The god of morose thoughts was already gone from the limousine as she continued: "So I said to him, 'What the hell are you going to Pat's wake for?' But he just put on his hat and headed for the door. On the way, I asked, 'Would you like to stop for a Mass card?' but he just glared at me and said 'I would not!' and off we went.

January 26
More on Aunt Margaret

"Well, we get to the funeral parlor and there's the old widow by the coffin and everybody around and he walks right up to her and in that loud voice of his says, 'You cannot bury Pat in that cemetery! I hold the deed we bought years ago and I'll not have him lying there!' Well," and by now Aunt Margaret had us all imagining Mr. Gleason, his thatch of white hair above his reddish face, acquitting an old grudge as only an old Irishman could do, "Well, if that's not enough, he looks down at Pat and says, 'He's so crooked he won't lie straight in his grave, the old cheat!' With that, he turns and over his shoulder says to the undertaker, 'If you try to bury him, I'll dig him up!' and out he strides like the fighting bantam he was. That evening the undertaker calls me up and says, 'Mrs. Gleason, you'll have to speak to your husband; we're afraid to bury Pat because he says he'll dig him up. Can't you do something about it?' They were all upset," and her voice warmed with the recollection of an eighty-year-old man still capable of raising so much stubborn hell. "So I said to him, 'You can't do that,' and he said to me, 'Like hell I can't. I'll have him out of there an hour after they get him in.'" Margaret paused again, smiling a bit herself as the tone in the limousine was transformed around her, "I said to him, 'Mr. Gleason, where's this deed you say you have?' and he went right upstairs to find it. He was up there a long time and when he came down, I could see that the wind had gone out of him. He was quiet and subdued as he gave me this faded old deed to look at. Sure enough, Pat had never put anything but his own name on it; Mr. Gleason didn't have a legal right in the world to the plot. 'He's cheated me again from the grave!' Mr. Gleason said, but he looked old and kind of beaten now. I said, 'You thick old Irishman, you should have looked this up first before you scared them all to death!' But he was in a mood and got very quiet. Finally, I said to him, 'How will I bury you now? Shall I get a new plot for us?' But he just looked at me and said, 'Oh, Mrs. Gleason, just stick a bone through my nose and let the dogs carry me away.'"

By this time the hearse was ready and the procession began, but we had much lighter hearts than we had had a few minutes before. It was an unlikely tale, this story of an old bricklayer whose long-held grudge suddenly evaporated after fifty years of waiting, but it was a story of true life told not to get a laugh but to give a smile in a dark moment. That is the way Aunt Margaret has responded to people all her life, with something down to earth in the way of human medicine at times when all other medicines were too bitter to take. Aunt Margaret, with her sure sense of when to tell a true story, had taken us all in her arms for a few moments, even as she had when we were small boys, and hugged us and put us down to walk on our own again. Only people who are truly alive can work that kind of magic—people whose piety is too unvarnished to resemble the strange masks of some of mankind's isolated ascetics. There is a lot to learn from women like my Aunt

Margaret; one is tempted to say that there is everything to learn from them about loving one's neighbor in an age that is short on neighborly love.

January 27
Look in the Corner of the Picture

It has recently become the fashion in movie and television plots to hinge the unraveling of the mystery on photographs taken at or near the scene of the crime. Not that the photographer sets out to take a picture of the murder or robbery. Unknowingly, he just happens to include the evil deed while taking a shot of something else. In his darkroom he notices something in the background, the criminal event he had not observed when he first trained his camera on the scene. You have seen this happen any number of times; it is an appealing gimmick of surprise because it seems like the kind of thing that could happen to any one of us. If the device served Hitchcock, it ought to serve us as well.

The resolutions we made a few weeks ago tend to make us focus on ourselves and this, in itself, is one of our chief problems. Self-concern, anxiety about the way we look or the way we perform or what others think of us—these feelings undo us for two reasons. Always putting ourselves in the center of our mental concern may seem natural enough but this kind of concern makes it more difficult to live a spontaneous and free life. Furthermore, looking mostly at ourselves also complicates our efforts to love; it becomes harder to see or make room for others in our lives. We might start the year by looking at ourselves in a new perspective, by viewing ourselves in the background of some activity with which we are associated. This is not an imaginary scene, mind you. It merely means that we shift our angle of vision so that we are no longer center stage but, as in the detective stories, we happen to be included merely as a figure in the background. It is something like changing the Mercator projection of the world, that flat schoolroom map with which we are so familiar. Whenever we see it, the United States is right in the middle, a result of the nationality of the map makers. If we move some other continent into prominence we suddenly have a very different view of things. So it is with ourselves and our examinations of motives and plans with which we are concerned at the start of a new year. In addition to several values to be found in this, it is also fun, something self-examination is not noted for.

January 28
A New View

First of all, we will see ourselves more accurately and without the distortion of self-interest or excessive self-concern which ordinarily affects our views of ourselves. Look at yourself, for example, as a participant in a meeting which you are not running. Focus on the chairman and you will get a surprisingly new look at yourself and the way you interact with him and the others around the table.

January 29
And More Besides

When we are not saying "cheese" we are not so self-conscious. That is why it is better to look at ourselves when we are not so self-preoccupied that we lose the context within which we lead our lives. Pictures of people when they are not thinking of themselves are called candid for a good reason: these pictures get at the truth of a man or a woman. The same truth comes out in many of our activities—when we are least thinking about ourselves and our position in the picture. This off-center focus helps us realize that it really doesn't matter where we are standing or

37

even which profile is showing as long as we are doing our best and doing what is right for ourselves and for those around us. You never see this very clearly as long as you insist on top billing in the examination of your life.

The achievement of a healthy identity, according to the experts, marks the difference between the person who is able to break out of himself and share himself with others and the person who is so lost in himself that he wanders through life in suffocating self-absorption. Getting a new look at ourselves helps us to grasp our own identity more securely. This is true even if what we see is not entirely flattering or is not exactly the picture we would want extra prints made from. A sense of who we are comes out of such new self-perceptions. You recognize it, for example, in the offhand comments someone might make about you, or perhaps in the way someone imitates you, or gives you a nickname. Those are all good leads, enabling us to say within an acceptant brand of wisdom: "Yes, I guess that is the way I really am when I am being myself." This is not a bad thing to learn and it is a very good beginning on a new year.

Seeing ourselves off-center can make us more self-confident. Sometimes when we bear down on ourselves too much we not only enlarge our faults but we diminish our strengths so that they are all out of proportion in our picture of ourselves. It is important to believe in ourselves; an off-angle view of our personalities may enable us to see that, although we are not the world's greatest saints, neither are we its greatest sinners. We do have something we can give honestly and sincerely even though our gifts may be modest in themselves. Such a vision may enable us to love ourselves a little better, to forgive ourselves a little more for our store of failings, and to carry on with a more realistic sense of ourselves and our potential. Start the year by seeing yourself in the overall setting of your life. The change will do you good in many unsuspected ways—not the least of which will be your capacity to see not only yourself but other people much more clearly.

January 30
Now Is the Hour

Unlike Olympic athletes we do not have a sports official to fire a starting gun at the beginning of the enterprises we undertake. We must start by ourselves and follow through on our own if we are going to achieve anything—either as a friend, a worker, or a neighbor. And, although it is up to us to start, we often throw wrenches into the machinery of our decision process, delaying even when we know that an opportune moment has arrived. The problem for most of us is not to decide *when* to act. It is far simpler: We must decide *to* act, to get something going, to perform the physical functions or to speak the words which make operational the fancied commitments of our hearts. We must release some healthy aggression to achieve any goals and this applies to everything from saying our prayers to saying I love you. Putting things off is an enemy to life and growth, a demon to be exorcised as the year begins. Recently, a business consultant said that the hardest thing to get salesmen to do is to make the calls that get them the business they need to be successful. It is not a question of wondering who to call or when to call; it is simply a question of doing battle with the reluctance that enables us, for a variety of reasons, to postpone the things that we know we should do and that we are quite capable of doing. There is a lesson in this for all of us.

January 31
The Demon of Reluctance . . .

eats away at our New Year's resolutions like a bird of prey on a fallen beast in the desert. By February 1st there is not much left but bones. Not that the resolutions were poor or unsuited to us; we did not take into account that strange human uneasiness about following through on what we know is the right thing to do. This phenomenon is often connected with a fear of being embarrassed or of failing in some way. Those are the sticky issues that give us pause. By delaying we do avoid embarrassment, of course, but at the same time we miss the chance to achieve. Faint hearts have never won fair ladies, and people who are afraid to reduce their resolutions to action just get lonelier and more discouraged with their lot in life. It is part of an old mystery that St. Paul described as his own difficulty in doing the good that he wanted to do. The year that is a month old bids us to face the small fears that cause us such large problems in both living and loving more fully.

February

February 1
What Do You Do for Fun?

A psychologist colleague of mine once asked that question of a number of professional people only to find that they were hard-pressed to give much of an answer. These people all had serious responsibilities in life and the idea of having fun for its own sake seemed strangely remote from their experience. Fun could be earned by a hard day's work, they felt, and satisfaction came from a difficult job well done. But the idea of spontaneous enjoyment seemed difficult for them to justify for themselves; they did not feel free just to have fun. They were not speaking, mind you, of the superficial kind of fun and games that lonely people look for in singles bars and nightclubs—not even the strenuous leisure time activity that has people hauling skiis and snowmobiles hundreds of miles on a weekend to have fun with the equipment they owe too much money on not to enjoy.

Maybe it is a good question for each of us to ask himself. Fun, after all, need not have a mortgage on it. Young children do not have to earn the spontaneous enjoyment that is so much a part of their lives. Lovers do not have to pay interest on the joy which they can experience just being in each other's presence, doing the simplest and least expensive of things. Fun yields its secrets to those who have not lost sight of the fundamental values that still work in the same paradoxical way in all of us. That is, values demand an in-depth commitment on our part— especially to each other—and, even as they demand this, they give us a sense of great freedom. It is precisely for

this reason that many people do not have much fun—
because they do not feel free to have it. The answer is not
to be found in grabbing at pleasure but in returning to the
human truths about ourselves that must be accepted before
we experience liberation for a fuller life. Growing up, in
other words, is a necessary step toward the rediscovery of
the wonderful freedom for fun that we knew in childhood.
That is why Jesus said that the kingdom opened its doors
to those who were like little children; having fun, believe it
or not, gives us some insight into the real nature of that
kingdom.

Well, what do you do for fun? If you're trying awfully
hard and enjoying it less, maybe you need to explore yourself and the values you live by a little more closely.

February 2
The Faces of Happiness

People have known for a long time that happiness does not
seem to have much to do with things. However, it does not
have much to do with the contemporary effort to peel
away the things of this world either. It is well to remember
Henry David Thoreau's warning: "Beware of all enterprises that require new clothes." Well, college students and
others have taken this idea to heart, but the simplicity of
faded jeans and army jackets does not seem to make them
more happy. You have to live with the world as it is and
according to the way you are; that, in fact, is the path to
true simplicity of spirit, one of the states called blessed by
the Lord in the Beatitudes.

Although happiness is not the opposite of sadness nor
the absence of pain, it can coexist with these. Its real opposite is fear, the kind that robs us of the chance of living,
the enemy that takes our breath away as it makes us shrink
back from the possibility of hurt. Happiness only comes to
those who face life straightforwardly; then it is mostly as a
by-product of the fact that these people do live that way.

February 3
Suppose I'm Still Unhappy?

A good question, because most of us have learned to accept, if not to embrace, the blahs and the blues as unfortunate but necessary parts of life. Most of us realize that our moods are as regular as the tides and that sometimes we just have to wait it out until the winds and the water change for us. Being able to live in such a world is one of the ways of being happy; trying to be smilingly happy all the time is, for most of us, just a way of being silly. The people who think everything is wonderful all the time just haven't heard the news yet. But if a person cannot shake off the weight of melancholy after a reasonable time, then he ought to listen to this message from his inner self. When a person cannot deal constructively with depression then he ought to do something about it, and I don't mean just to pray about it either. He should get some professional help because depression is one of the sensitive signs of problems that need resolution in a person's life. That is what professionals are for—to assist persons with the emotional problems of living. When the unhappiness hangs on like a heavy fog, then it is time to get that kind of assistance.

February 4
Modern Moods and Myths

These are no better than the old-fashioned ones which everybody decries as part of the moribund Protestant ethic. As a matter of fact many of them have considerably less validity than the notions about hard work, faithfulness and fair play that seem like quaint and cracked family album pictures in the era of the goof-off, the make-out,

43

and the rip-off. Modern man is no longer a slave to the old compulsions always to do his best; he is liberated from those notions and he is free to let himself go as he gorges himself on the forbidden fruit of life. But is he happier? Or just lonelier and sadder on the thousand next mornings that always follow the heady quest for new sources of satisfaction? Yes, and maybe a little more worldly-wise and cynical as well.

The gateway to happiness is through new sexual celebrations according to many of the modern myth makers, the ones who can paint premarital and extramarital sex in such romantic shades. But people do not look noticeably happier to me in the age of sexual liberation; some look a little worn-out and many others a little intimidated, but a lot of them just look grimmer. Maybe that is because you really cannot separate sex from human relationships and the institutions that are meant to serve them best, at any rate not with the hope that this will lead to a greater share of happiness.

Even research seems to bear these notions out. The couples who report the greatest happiness in marriage are still those who did not indulge in premarital sexual experiences. This is a consistent finding, one that makes a person think about the combination of character traits—some of them with dreadfully old-fashioned sounds like *self-discipline*—that go into the making of an enduring and satisfying relationship. Other research has consistently revealed that the factors that relate to happiness in marriage are associated with the happiness of the marriage of the couples' parents. Happiness is not inherited, of course, but it seems clear that what people learn about life from loving others is profoundly significant in shaping their own personal happiness.

Happiness has never been the brass ring that you get by chance or dumb luck; it is a phenomenon, a mysterious one in a way, that arises when people actually try to do their best with each other and with their work in life. Pleasure is another story, and for many it is all too often a very short story indeed. Happiness, however, does not have anything like an ending when it flows through the life of a person who has given the best of himself in his love and his labor. It may rise and fall but it cannot die nor be destroyed completely because, like breath and spirit, it is a function of the kind of person you are much more than the kind of circumstances in which you find yourself. That is why the modern myth makers keep getting it wrong, sending people on expeditions to territories that are too separated from what is really human to be the source of lasting happiness.

The saddest part of all this lies in the frustration and longing that gradually crowd everything else out of the lives of people who are misled by new myths into blind alley searches for something they can only find if they turn back to taking their own personalities seriously. Happiness surprises the man who learns again that it is in coming home to lasting values that he finds the raw material of his own joy.

February 5
More Faces of Happiness

Happiness is not self-conscious, does not advertise itself, is not, in short, a leisure time activity. There is no way to demand or to attack happiness directly; happiness gives itself not to those who seek it directly but to those who find it when they are trying to lead good lives.

Happiness is often recognized only later on. People are forever looking back to when they *were* happy, sometimes mourning their apparent loss, sometimes overwhelmed by their present challenges. Most of the studies reveal that happiness is associated with struggle rather than with final achievement, with being on the way to someplace rather than with arriving there. So the widow of the famous automaker, the 100-year-old multi-millionairess, looked back and said that she was happiest "when I used to pack Mr. Dodge's lunchbox everyday." This is one of the most common faces of happiness and one of the most reassuring to people who feel themselves in the grip of life's struggles. To be alive and to be engaged in something worthwhile, to love and to be loved—these are the unself-conscious elements of happiness that are seldom fully recognized when we most deeply experience them.

Part of the nature of happiness and one of the ways in which we can recognize it when it is truly ours is that happiness does not stand still. It slips away even as we realize its presence, not like a phantom which tempts us and then never returns, but as an experience that stretches us out of ourselves and bids us to continue to seek the things that matter in life. And there are no freeze-frames of happiness; its essence lies in finding it when we are trying to give ourselves away, of feeling it when we are involved in doing the right thing with our lives.

In a special and imperishable way, happiness belongs to those who love and who continue to work at loving, despite disappointments and discouragements. The Beatitudes remind us that happiness belongs to those who have loved enough to mourn, to those who work for peace and justice despite war and hatred, to those who have not turned cynical about love and its possibilities. In the long run, these people are the source of happiness for the rest of the world as well, the people whose love is stronger than death, and who light the way to joy for the rest of us.

February 6
The Twilight of Self-denial

That seems to be the time of the day on the contemporary clock that men read to regulate their lives and enterprises. To deny something to the self in a world whose economy pivots on our willingness to indulge ourselves seems secular sacrilege at its worst. "You only go around once," the antiphon of the beer commercial goes, "so you have to grab all the gusto while you can." This theme, focusing on the here and now pathways that lead to the door that closes on death, recurs in books, films, and even in casual conversations these days. Well, is it worthwhile to enter a season of self-discipline, or is it an old-fashioned madness that has no place in the life-affirming, take-it-while-you-can attitude of today? The Christian ought to ask the question even if he is not completely sure of the answer.

February 7
The Facts Tell Us

We have come a long way from the penitential ages in which cathedral squares echoed with the wailing spirits of sack-clothed men busy subduing their bodies; we no longer accept the body as a natural enemy that is always ready to betray us nor do we think that the body must be done to death in order to clean the soul of its trappings. That treacherous crack across the image of man has been filled in by generations that have rediscovered his personal unity. We have come out of the shadows of what people refer to as dark ages and the sun feels good on our backs; we like life and we are even beginning to like ourselves, even parts of us, like our sexuality, that we never thought we would be able to affirm at all. Man is trying to get himself together, an important job, and, for the moment at least, the old disciplines that urged him periodically to tear himself apart for the good of his soul have been retired.

This journey to friendliness with the self has been long and difficult. If it left behind old dangers in our understanding of man, it has uncovered new perils along the way. It is a good thing not to practice self-denial for its own sake in the ruthless and unforgiving ways that seemed favored in other times. But can man survive only on affirmation in life when he still has to deal with the problem of death? Is he enjoying the affluent society or burdened by its weight? Is he sure of himself anymore? Columnist James Reston, summing up a departed year in *The New York Times*, feels that he is not. He writes that man has failed at success: "Adversity we have conquered with perseverance, but prosperity has been too much for us.

47

The old gods may have failed, but the 'bitch goddess, Success,' was no substitute." So it seems for the country and so it seems for many individuals who look up from the plentiful life in search of the secrets of the good life.

February 8
No Is Part of Yes

This statement may sound like some Far Eastern or far-out philosophy, but it is only Christian common sense. You cannot say *Yes* to life unless you are able to say *No* to yourself. This starts early in our development as persons—this long and fascinating struggle to master words and muscular movements, the almost miraculous passage to self-consciousness and independence that goes with being an independent human being. Like love, or anything else good, it is filled with hard learning, with lessons that cannot simply be memorized and tests of existence that allow for neither guesswork nor cheating. A person must give up certain things in order to get other things of greater importance and higher value; he must give up being cared for and being carried and cleaned by others. Gradually he must surrender the viewpoint that makes him the center of the universe if he is ever to take his proper place with others. A great many *No's* go into being able to delay gratification, but this is one of the essential marks of a person who has learned to affirm himself in life.

The rising and falling tides of self-discipline and celebration flow from headwaters deep in the heart of man; they reflect truths that are not changed by time—not even by future shock—truths that are built on man's gradual way of growing and his need to understand the healthy *No's* that are inevitably part of any worthwhile *Yes*. There is, in other words, something deep in the pattern of man's personality that rejects a life that has no resistance built into it, that balks eventually at a journey without headwinds. The achievement of maturity depends, to some extent at least, on developing our capacity to handle the hard things in life constructively, to discover the intimate and necessary relationship between joy and suffering, affirmation and negation, responsibility and self-control. A man may be bar mitzvah'd or confirmed but he does not pass to manhood unless he has been bloodied by life; he may never work out the mystery of the relationship between learning to say *No* to himself in order to say *Yes* to his true personality, but dealing with it is an adult and enduring task.

This same pattern is at the root of the Gospel call to fuller life for all men. Yes, a bountiful life is promised by Jesus—good measure, shaken down and pressed together, and flowing into your lap—but there is a big condition built into this promise. A man must be ready to die, and that means to die to himself, in order to reach the resurrection experience of a fuller life. To be born again demands that we let the old man (that locked off, narcissistic self about whom St. Paul wrote) die first. The Christian metaphor of life-death-resurrection is not an easy invitation. Accepting this means that we commit ourselves to a life of saying *No* to our selfish impulses.

February 9
Important Things

There is a difference between the Christian who tries to lead the Gospel life and the neurotic person who enjoys self-punishment on some level of his uncharted psyche. The latter person is forever creating situations that generate some kind of punishment for imagined guilt; he is not growing toward a fuller realization of the person he really is as much as he is punishing the inner ghosts that he has never looked full in the face. An example is the man who is consumed with thoughts of his unworthiness and spends his energies in atoning for his deficiencies: he holds back from life in the process so he never really gets the chance to do anything that he could honestly feel unworthy about.

49

All the time, of course, he is as unhappy as he is un-developed, but that is precisely the reward that his dim view of himself demands. Far better, in the long run, the lusty sinner who has something genuine about which to feel guilty—and who has real wounds to heal in himself and others. At least he is alive and his guilt is that of a man who knows that he is responsible for what he does to himself and to other persons. There is a person who can take atonement seriously. But taking atonement seriously is not the same as self-punishment or self-denial.

February 10
Healthy Self-denial . . .

or dying to the self is that which is required in the deepest and most significant human activities that we know. Ask somebody who has really loved another person and you will learn something valuable about the amount of dying that goes into keeping even the richest of loves alive. Sometimes—and probably because lovers live at such close range—there seems to be more dying to self involved in making love grow than anything else. It takes dying to the self to listen to another, especially when we think we have heard everything that the other could possibly have to say. A man or a woman must sacrifice to keep each other in focus as separate human beings whose rights and needs demand constant care and respect if their relationship is to flourish. Love does not take care of itself the way blue-chip stocks do after a one-time investment; it demands constant re-investment of the self with no interest charges at all. Love does not just lie there; it needs life breathed into it at every moment, life that comes only from those who embrace the thousand private deaths of intimacy.

The same thing goes for having faith in other persons, or hoping in them. These are the vital parts of living, the only experiences that enable us to recognize ourselves as human beings—the pain that is the price for relationships that sing of the best that is in us, that is the suffering that redeems, that is worthwhile because it increases life while neurotic suffering only deforms it.

February 11
The Big Problem

It has always been a big problem to help people to recognize the meaning of the pain that is so much a part of just being alive; it is the willing embrace of this pain that smoothes off the uneven aspects of our personality as it frees us from the consequences of unredeemed selfishness. The suffering that accompanies the effort to love is our own personal experience of living in the mystery of Jesus. You do not need to construct artificial penances when there are so many real ones all around us. The great *Yes* to genuine living includes all the *No's* that the real world forces upon us all the time.

Authentic, redemptive suffering about important things is almost always connected with our relationships to other persons. The most significant pains of life for the common man are those that come from loving and everything that goes into it. Be wary of pains that have nothing to do with others. That may mean that our lives have nothing to do with others. Strange practices of self-denial usually come from strange persons. People who dramatize or like to get reactions to their self-denial fall in this same category. Redemptive suffering is real but unself-conscious. It arises from and is part of the effort to live at a more than superficial level. It is also mixed with hope and joy, the signs of life in persons who incorporate their self-denial into living in a healthy and constructive way.

Rather than imagining or inventing some problems of your own, it would be better to try to share in the struggles and suffering of somebody else. It is difficult to look at the problems of others or to stand with them as they try to weather them or figure them out; we all know the temptation to look away or to change the subject; maybe the dying to ourselves that goes into genuine compassion is the most redemptive suffering we can share in.

February 12
Who Owns Love?

Sometimes the headlines make us feel that all love dies somewhere just short of middle age, that it can only be the property of the young who have, at most, a tenuous grasp on it. Tragic love seems best of all, especially if it contains a *Love Story* ending in which the couple is separated before they have fallen out of love with each other. The hazards of seven year itches, middle-age crises, and disillusioning divorce statistics make us wonder whether there is any such thing as enduring love any more. Better the way of the cynic, making what he can of the new stock of love's supposed refreshments—serial marriage, refreshing "affairs," or what have you—and staying clear of the bittersweet waters of love. It just seems too hard, or too impossible to keep working at it throughout a lifetime.

As we approach Valentine's Day it might be worthwhile to recall that love does not belong to any particular age group, although one would hope that the young would have plenty of it—enough, indeed, to last beyond a lifetime. We need, however, to recall that many people stay in love through poverty and riches, sickness and health; their example gives courage and hope to us all. The old couple chronicled in a *New York Times* piece on the loneliness of the elderly defy our disbelief about the enduring wonder of love. Writer John Corry describes them:

> The couple down the hall have been married 63 years. He is 87, and she is 80, and rather beautiful. "We are really blessed," she said. "You must live long enough to enjoy your retirement. We like nature. We walk. We went to the flower show . . . ." "If people live alone," he said, "it is not good, but when you have someone it's

different." The owner of their building has watched the old couple for some time, and he is entranced by them. "I see them," he said, "and they're out walking, and they're holding hands. Holding hands. My God, I think to myself, I know what it is: They're in love."

Love becomes simple only in the lives of those who have used their years together to deepen its promise, in the lives of people who have learned to understand and forgive, in the lives of those who know that fidelity has a special fulfillment. The world is filled with bad news, of eras ending, institutions crumbling, and days that will never be the same again. It is helpful to everyone to have some news that love can survive, that it responds when men and women work at it, and that it is God's best blessing to us all.

February 13
Love Is Stronger Than Death

That is what St. Paul wrote in a phrase that puts our two most important concerns in relationship with each other. The wonder revealed to those who take love seriously when it comes to them is that love is also stronger than life. Love is powerful enough to challenge life and its thousand outrages as well as death and all its mysteries; it enables people to withstand and overcome the worst that life has to offer in terms of illness, hurt, and disappointment. Death, after all, can only strike once, but life can have its way with us over and over again, wrestling us to the earth and testing the strength of our spirit to respond; indeed, the strength of our spirit to respond comes precisely from love rather than from an unredeemed stoicism. One cannot deny the staying power of some stoics, of course, but love lets you cry rather than just grit your teeth; love lets you feel even the worst of things and survive while stoicism braces the emotions into place against the shocks of life.

February 14
Only Lovers Understand

Perhaps only the person who loves has a real chance to understand life or death; they are not easily understood by any means. The loving person—the person fired by the Spirit who is the source of all love—experiences time in a different way. It is a strange thing that love should shift our rooting in that dimension of existence that is so curiously saved and spent on the clocks of the universe. Lovers are not the victims of time; their presence to each other takes them out of its conventional measures. This is why they never grow bored or why, without anything else to do, they can enter so fully into just being together. Love breaks the locks of time and gives us a precious insight into the meaning of eternity, a concept so attached to the sweeping passage of time that we cannot imagine it. That is why love is stronger than either life or death: It means that man has a hint within his own experience of the things that eyes have not seen and ears have not heard, a sign, in the love he has shared, that neither death nor earthly time with all its meanness can have final dominion over him.

February 15
Is Peace a Gift?

Where does the deep peace that Paul lists as a gift of the Spirit come from? The Christian might indeed ask something about these gifts in general while he is trying to understand peace in particular. Are they showered randomly on the world with some people spiritually more lucky than others? It has always seemed grossly unfair for spiritual writers to explain the presence or absence of certain rich Christian values with the close-to-a-cop-out notion that some people have the gift (from that of faith to that of tears), and others do not. That makes the Christian life sound like it has a genetic basis, involving the same method of transmitting talents as one finds with the gifts of musical or artistic skill. Such randomness may fit the personality of a moody king but it does not match what we know of a loving God. His gifts are always available to us; we just have to make ourselves ready for them. The blessing of peace, along with joy and patience, comes quietly but fully to those who open themselves to life and, in the process, to the working of the Spirit. Peace, like happiness, is a byproduct in a life that has a Christian center of gravity; the person who lives by the Gospels can walk through the contemporary valley of the shadows (which may now be a scene of urban terror rather than the psalmist's pastoral loneliness) strengthened and supported by the Spirit.

These gifts of a loving God are not sometime-things or grab-bag surprises; there are certain basic conditions which we must meet if we are to receive them in our lives. These are not strange or exotic demands on our attitudes or behavior; they are rather the simple and straightforward giving of ourselves to the things that count in any human life. We must try to use our energies in productive if not compulsive work and we must not grow weary of loving others even when this is an apparently disheartening business. In other words, we must move into the mystery of life, taking life on the uneven terms which are its chief characteristics. To be alive means to be vulnerable and to find our peace in the unity that marks those who realize that dying and arising are the inevitable elements in a life that means something. Peace is denied to those who only shield themselves from the dangers of a life lived with and for other persons; such compromise agreements with life are treaties that are always broken.

Peace is called a gift not because it comes unpredictably but because it is something that cannot be bought or bargained for; it comes freely to those who do not look directly for it at all, but who find it because they have learned to lose themselves.

February 16
We All Want Peace

But for a worn-down world, peace seems like something that exists more in the imagination than in our own experience (remember the gold at the far side of the rainbow and childhood visions of heaven?). What would it be like, we wonder, to live in a world cleansed of wars and the rumors of war, where the dying had ended and a great calm, like that of a summer afternoon, had settled on us all? It is hard to imagine; we almost feel that we would be uneasy rather than peaceful, half expecting the sounds of bugles or gunfire that have been the background music of our growing up, and feeling, for a few moments at least, unsure of ourselves without them. We would, of course, grow accustomed to peace and we could learn to relax in a world where nobody wanted to hurt us; but war has been so much with us that we do not even remember the feel of peace.

February 17
Peace Is a Journey . . .

more than an achievement, a condition rather than a goal, something man must continually strive for even if he only partially attains it. We must think about our ideas of peace and wonder deeply about something we want so much but seem to experience so fleetingly. Our uncertainty as we reach out for personal and public peace tells us a good deal about the human condition. Man may never completely end his wars, but that does not mean that peace is a cruel illusion or something, however real, that will always be just beyond him. The difficult search for peace raises questions about the meaning of life and our share of responsibility for ransoming the times in which we live; it also invites us to re-examine our ideas about man and the possibilities of his redemption. Peace makes us take a long look not just past the edge of war but into the mists that make it hard for us to lay hold of all the loose ends of life.

February 18
Is Peace Something to Pray for . . .

as though it always comes from somewhere or someone else? Is prayer, no matter how fervent, a cry for deliverance or a commitment of ourselves to the active making of peace? Before one even begins to answer these questions, however, it is important to inquire into the nature of a peaceful world, especially in view of some of the new utopian formulas which distinguished men of science have offered to us lately. Dr. Kenneth Clark, president of the American Psychological Association, for example, has proposed that peace be maintained through chemistry, that the world's leaders should be kept pharmaceutically calmed to prevent them from leading us into one final Armageddon. And Dr. B. F. Skinner, in his much-publicized book *Beyond Freedom and Dignity,* says that the world will know peace only when it has sloughed off the coils of autonomous man in an environment where all behavior is under the careful control of benevolent leaders. Neither of these men is a stranger to the long and troubled history of utopias whose promise of earthly gardens fit for the lying down together of the lion and the lamb has been piped to men for centuries. Both Clark and Skinner are criticized because most people are uneasy about delegating the technology of control to any committee, no matter how sophisticated or enlightened its members may be. Besides that, the nirvana committee would disintegrate in endless inconclusive meetings anyway. Perhaps Clark and Skinner are easy marks even though what they suggest is probably prophetic of the way men will try to manage us into the next century. There is something deeper, something in the dark heart of things, something just beyond our words about the mystery of redemption that makes us pause at accepting the guaranteed engineering of peace.

To put it simply, we must wonder whether we can ever fully achieve peace any more than we can fully expect the final perfection of man. In other words, our many expectations of a final plateau of history graced by men all turned good is not only naive politically and psychologically, but theologically as well. Man's long struggle to find and fulfill himself, his slow but persistent progress toward some kind of internal and external harmony—these will never be completed in this world and those who hope or even pray for these things are trying to tame a reality far stronger than they are. The alternative to the vision of a new Eden is not hopelessness, not some selling-out of the self to the solemn-looking social scientists already prepared to condition us back to innocence. Rather, it is to enter into the mystery of salvation which is worked out not with saints but with sinners, not in an ultimately perfect world but in one whose waters wash over constantly drifting continents that defy fixed and final measurements. A man's life is too precious to be lived out in a world where friction and resistance have been erased, and his individuality is too great a treasure to confine to the perfectly clean pathways of the civilization-sized maze that Skinner has designed for him.

February 19
The Story of Man's Redemption . . .

is not one of his totally overcoming his shortcomings or his sinfulness; it lies in his finding his life even as he loses it, in his capacity to go beyond but not to overturn the cruel limits on his being, in his ability to love truly with a heart still cobwebbed with minor hates. There is a long crack running through our history; it proclaims how imperfect we are, but, in a way that passes understanding, it lets the light in as well. Our faults are inseparable from our dignity and our continuing promises; we are saved not when we are perfect but when we put a trembling (rather than a tranquilized) hand into the fires of life. It is precisely through the acceptance of our mortality that we begin to understand our place in the raveled scheme of things; it is in living with our frailties and failures that we reach the meaning of healing and forgiveness; in sensing how closely linked are our deepest passions to do right and to do wrong we identify ourselves as human beings. Life yields its meaning inch by inch to those who do not grow weary of the world's narrowing mixture of beauty and terror, and peace comes only to those who keep working for it in a world that works against it. Our contemporary return to the puzzle of death is a sign of our effort to make sense out of a pattern of existence that is cross-stitched with internal contradictions; we sense, in some deep religious wellspring of our being, that death, which seems to be the enemy of life, is actually a part of it and that the embrace of a mortal and imperfect condition is essential to the Christian who seeks for the gifts of wisdom and peace.

There is an irreducible tension between these contrary elements in the lives of persons who try to redeem rather than just escape this badly scarred but painfully beautiful world. The Christian vision of the world does not call forth utopia or an environment made bland by behavioral control; it sees salvation as the outcome of struggle just as healing comes only after hurt, and resurrection only after death. The ridges in the heart of man are not to be smoothed over or cosmetically disguised; they are to be accepted as a strange source of human identity and saving energy. No man can find peace or beseech God for it unless he first understands that the peace he seeks must match his true nature. Peace cannot be identified with the highly tooled control that blinds man to the mystery of his own jagged edges while reinforcing what some psychologist decides are socially desirable responses. That kind of future may be marked with the absence of war but it will not sing with the presence of peace. Peace means something only between men who love each other while they retain the power to hurt each other; it is nothing if their vulnerability has, like an evil spirit, been exorcised from them. Indeed they are no longer men if they are purged of their restlessness, their curiosity, and their spontaneity; they may not know sin in that far off day but they will not know joy either. Peace, peace, they may moan with Jeremiah, but there will never be peace in a world in which men have had the strength to achieve it bred out of them.

February 20
The Pursuit of Peace . . .

whether it is in our own lives or in the world at large, demands a sense of realism about man and a willingness to work with him as he is even as the light fails around us. The Spirit comes when we actively struggle to reach out to each other rather than when we are just trying to avoid the pain we are liable to inflict on other people. Peace is a gift to lovers who live on the shifting edge of a world that never loses its power to betray them; love means little if it is just "adjusting to" or "getting along with" others; love is stronger than death for those people who know that life itself has the power to kill you. The economy of Christianity is ill-ordered and its mysteries are still written with crooked lines. Peace, like love, is only achieved by those who understand this.

February 21
A Work for Sinners

Redemption is the work of sinners more than of saints. It is achieved by persons willing to make themselves seem foolish as they search out a higher wisdom, by persons whose very weakness makes it possible for God's power to reveal itself through them; the witness of these Christians cries out against those who think that the future can be designed so that cloudless tomorrows will roll in shiny perfection off the assembly line of psychological conditioning. The meaning of the Christian life is made most clear wherever people commit themselves to saving each other in the midst of the real and asymmetrical world; peace comes from people like that because they continue to hope and love despite the heaving and buckling both within and without them. We finally learn the lessons of profound peace from those who are not afraid to live in an ultimately unpredictable world.

February 22
Disturbers of the Peace

There is little doubt that some of us are vulnerable to the experts in interpersonal guerilla warfare, the skilled assault troops who know just what buttons to press in order to get us into a tropical storm—if not a full-fledged hurricane—of fury. Example: The child who knows just how to scrape a file across the taut nerves of the older generation in order to get some attention. We know we should not take the bait, right? We have been through this before, grown practically hoarse and apoplectic in responding to the classic maneuver, right? But we go for it again almost every time, hurtling harmless thunderbolts and uttering entertaining oaths at the child whose half smile in the midst of our rage is the tip-off that he has gotten just what he wanted out of us. It may take years and considerable self-observation to learn how to stay out of this game in which you can only lose once you get started. The young have no monopoly on providing this contest, although some of them have almost preternatural skill at it. The answer is simple and we can even bow to B. F. Skinner as we give it: If the child's reward is our anger it is obvious that he will keep it up as long as we reward him; the minute we no longer follow the old game plan—the moment, in other words, when he no

longer gets a kick out of it because we do not get mad—
that is the moment when the game begins to end and peace
of mind begins to return.

We all learn that lesson sooner or later in life; after all,
we may have done the same thing to our elders when we
were young. There are other, more adult disturbers of the
peace whose activities may not be so apparent. They are,
of course, more subtle, but they are just as effective. I refer
to those persons who adjust to life not by growing up—
they are incapable of mature give-and-take relationships—
but by playing with other people. They are often as unaware as you are of the ways in which they do this; in fact,
they are sometimes so skilled that you can hardly notice
that the earthquake all around them can be traced back to
a hairline fissure in their own personalities. It is worth
thinking about these characters, however, both to be on
guard against them and so that we can relate to them in a
way that prevents them from disturbing us even as it
demands a more mature response from them.

February 23
Some Examples:

The Man in the Eye of the Hurricane: You may not get
to recognize him for a while, not until you notice that
whenever there is tension or big trouble this person is
somehow present. It is like the old sci-fi story by Ray
Bradbury about the reporter who noticed the same woman
in the background of all the photographs of auto accidents,
an ominous and barely noticeable presence connected—
but not quite connected—with disaster. Such people do
exist all right and there are probably a few of them inside
your life space at this very moment. They exercise a powerful influence on us even when we do not seem to be
aware of them and they ordinarily look as innocent as clergymen, however innocent that is these days. The next time
the peace is disturbed in your school, your club, or your

community and you cannot quite put your finger on its cause, start looking for the person who, like the sci-fi lady, always shows up in the background at the event. You will find it hard to prove anything because this disturber of the peace knows all the moves very well, but you may be better able to address the whole situation once you can see his possible relationship to it. Look for the man who enjoys the tension, the shattering of the peace as an end in itself, and you will take a big step toward restoring your own peace of mind. The best tactic, of course, is the same one you would use with a child: do not reward him by getting upset.

February 24
The Man with a Cure . . .

for the Problem You Do Not Have: This person is found in many places these days. He is a fixer, especially of other persons' problems, whether they think they have problems or not. The "Fixer" is a man of seeming good will; he only wants to help, oh, say with something like "the communication difficulties" between husband and wife, business colleagues, or a pastor and his curates. The problem is that what he styles as a cure is actually an infection. The "Fixer" to whom I refer is usually an amateur in human relationships who has taken a course or two or heard a lecture about group dynamics somewhere along the line. Because he is unaware of his own needs he moves forward to creative, ultimately disruptive, situations in the lives of relatively normal people all around him. Do not take a treatment from this type of practitioner unless you check his credentials and have a little insight into his motivation. Never let anyone manipulate you into becoming his patient or client when you do not need his ministrations. You will be putting him out of business and saving yourself a large helping of grief. And there are not many days on which you can accomplish that much.

February 25
What Takes Our Peace Away?

If we confine our reflections to our personal lives, each of us has to take responsibility for part of the answer; what diminishes my peace of mind may hardly disturb yours at all. There are some people who never seem to get upset, but most of them are either asleep, tranquilized, or living in another world. There is no such thing as perfect cool, although it is a desirable pose in many corners of the country. Cool, of course, keeps you beyond the sharp edges of caring; it is a self-invented and strenuously maintained sanctuary where a man can keep himself from getting hurt. So William Buckley in his book, *Cruising Speed,* tells us somewhat sadly of how and why he keeps a cool exterior in his hazardous role as a public debater: "It is very hard for me to appeal, without protective covering, directly to an audience, because the audience might turn me down. . . . I must not give the audience the power to believe that its verdict matters to me. There is my failure as a public figure; and my strength." And, in one way or other, we may all use similar maneuvers, even when we are not on public view in the way Mr. Buckley is, in order to preserve something of our own calmness and dignity when the world in general or somebody close to us in particular has hit us where it really hurts. We will not give away any ground, we tell ourselves, and nobody is going to know how much this cuts, and certainly nobody is going to see me cry. Well, of course, there is something to be said for that kind of holding ourselves together, for going through our duties even numbly, in order to keep our lives from shattering and falling apart completely. But those hurts, among many other things, are the ones that take away our peace in private even when we make a pretty good show of it in public.

There is no shame connected with feeling deeply about

things or finding out that we can be hurt by life; indeed, the quality of the things that hurt us tells us something about whether we are connected with life in any way that counts. The person who finds that he is hurt by other people is much better off than the man who can only be disturbed by the variations in a stockmarket ticker. It is, in the long run, much better to care about the pulse of men than just that of industry, better by far to react like persons who have known something of love than to have kept ourselves safe from all that. It is not a bad thing that our peace can be shaken by the course of our friends' health and fortunes, because this provides evidence that we are humanly alive, that our hearts are in the right place. It may not be so wise to try to push that discomfort away or to pretend that it does not exist. We can only be friends, at times, by drinking a bitter cup with those who mourn or with those who are lonely; we have no life to give if we are, like the characters in so many modern movies, desperately past genuine feelings of any kind.

February 26
The Trouble Is . . .

that, for most of us, these are the things that stalk us in the night, holding sleep at bay, and filling its edges with bad dreams; these are the events that distract us when we should be giving our attention to something else; these are the emotions that make our hearts feel like lead in our chests. There are a thousand signs of anxiety, including everything from facial tics to Freudian slips, but none are as important as the signs that come to us from the heart of our relationships with others. Instead of plastering these over with self-reassurance we might well inspect these feelings more closely. If we have the courage to hold our gaze steady, we may discover that they are more intricate in their weave and design than we at first thought. For example, we may find that concern about a friend's illness may reveal mixed feelings, sometimes contrary in nature, that disclose a strain of self-concern which runs neck and neck with compassion. Or we may discover a discordant note of gratification blended with our concern, a strange gladness that our friend is finally having a measure of comeuppance. There are numberless variations possible here, and we do not always feel much like taking a close look at all of them. Salvation and more peace of mind come to the individual who can confront the coat of many colors in which his soul is wrapped. That is what we discover when we look into ourselves during the moments when our ordinary calm has been disrupted—that we are quite complicated emotionally, and that the better we understand and accept this truth the deeper will be the peace that we have in our lives.

There is a kind of peace that mature people are able to maintain not because they do not have troubles but because they are no longer strangers to themselves. They are not totally destroyed by life because they have an understanding of and patience with its crooked paths and dead ends. They are saved from cynicism because they have a feeling for the human condition that neither over-romanticizes nor underestimates it. The man who wants peace of mind does not try to avoid looking at himself; in fact, he knows that a deep and forgiving look builds more peace than the sterile coolness in whose shadows he is constantly tempted to hide.

February 27
Some Lessons of Love

It is all very well for love to last in the lives of a blessed few, a casual observer might note, but what can I do to keep it alive in my own? There are, of course, some powerful lessons to be learned about love; if they seem to have been mastered by the old, that does not mean they did not have to learn them at some time in their lives. Love does not consist in waiting to be loved. This is a widespread illusion which, incidentally, affects all age groups. Indeed, it may be difficult, for example, for some very young people to understand this because they have been the receivers of love from their parents for such a long time. They get the idea, at least unconsciously, that to be cared for by the other is the important thing. This passivity distorts the whole idea of love, of course, because it destroys a genuine relationship between growing adults and recasts it in the familiar terms of parent-child. One of the reasons that many young people have so much difficulty with love is that they have not come to terms with this reality; they are unwilling, in other words, to learn one of the basics of love. That, of course, is that the lover reaches out to the other, even when he or she experiences the love of the other. The love that redeems and endures is built on giving and not so much on receiving, although receiving follows automatically. This sounds simple but it is extremely demanding and takes a long time to understand.

February 28/29
A Willingness to Listen

Closely related to giving love is the necessity to develop an ever increasing sensitivity to the person you love. A willingness to listen and still to hear the other as a separate person, a commitment to an ever finer appreciation of the reactions of the other—these are the challenges to a man who wants to stay in love. Deepened sensitivity to the other resists the forces that make persons give up or tune out on each other; this sensitivity demands a death to the self if it is to grow, but it is the secret of the loving communion that guarantees a flourishing communication between the couple. The worst enemy of love is the conviction that you have heard everything the other has to say, that you know him or her so well that all you need to do is to make a check mark and pass on. As soon as you begin to feel that way, you had better start asking why, and, in a very practical manner, begin doing something about it.

March

March 1
Winners or Losers

Americans have a thing about winning or losing, qualities which seem to define the very essence of life. Hardly an hour, much less a day, goes by that we are not checking the figures on some aspect of our experience. And this includes presidential elections, super bowls, and the Nielsen ratings of television programs. Our interest is not just in the candidate or the team that comes out ahead. Our passion now turns us with equal concern to which network wins the largest share of the audience or which computer wins the race to predict the election outcome ahead of everyone else. If that's not bad enough, there are stock-market reports on the radio that insist on reporting, whether you care about it or not, how much an average share gained or lost on a given day. It is enough to give a person an old-fashioned complex. In fact, many of us suffer from one already. It is the Dow Jones of the self, the constant cost accounting of our every move so that we can place it properly on the scoreboard of life. We nod smilingly at Grantland Rice's famous lines about "how we play the game," but we still want to know the final score. It is a way of looking at life that gradually dominates our imagination, tempting us to believe that life resides in numbers.

St. Anthony is the benign holy man who has a reputation for finding things that we lose. He has turned up a large number of earrings, plane tickets, and bank books in his day. Man, however, continues to lose things, so it is good to know that there is heavenly help still available to aid us. There are, however, things we are destined never to find again, things that are lost in the pursuit of life. We lose, for example, *beats of the heart and breath* in the moments in which we suddenly feel the intensity of life itself. These may be moments of danger to the body, but they also come with challenges to the spirit. They come, for example, when we are asked to believe or to trust more in another individual, be he spouse, child, friend or student. A man can lose his breath at a time when he realizes better what God seems to expect of him, even as Jesus sighed in the garden as he contemplated the suffering climax to his own life. Life attacks the heart constantly and our lost heartbeats are the measure of whether we have any pulse at all.

March 2
We Have to Lose Some Things . . .

like familiar ways of life. This is not often discussed but it is a familiar American experience, one that has even come to affect those who live deeply inside the relatively stable structures of monasteries and other religious houses. Americans are always on the move, so they are always leaving something behind. All people try to set down roots wherever they go; it's cutting them off that is the hard part and the common kind of loss. It is difficult, for example, to give up a neighborhood, friends, or the closeness of other members of one's family. It is hard to lose a pattern to which we have become accustomed, to face the loss of routines which comfort us precisely because they are familiar. A lot of longing occurs because of these losses and yet there is nothing—except perhaps loneliness itself—that occurs more often in our human experience. Even devoted religious have found the greatest challenge in their lives in losing the schedules, Latin prayers, or the rhythms of existence that have been transformed by change. These are necessary losses, however, and they demand something more than moans from those who would adjust to new times and new places successfully. Sometimes a loss like this tells us something we did not understand about ourselves. It wakes us up to opportunities for growth we might otherwise never have known. There is always pain with the loss, of course, but it seldom kills us and it may even make a new and richer life available to us.

March 3
Gain or Loss?

Many other inevitable losses come to those who take life and other persons seriously. We lose energy, for example, if we have any responsibility or care at all for other people. We lose some measure of our health—or think that we do—through the headaches, churned stomachs, and other physical aggravations that go along with concern for those around us. Time slips away as quickly as anything else and we can almost feel ourselves growing older in some of the experiences that are most significant in life. Lovers feel it all the time, not because the passing years threaten them, but because time vanishes so quickly in the atmosphere of their affection. The loss of time has a familiar look, of course, as we know from thinking of how much time goes by just waiting for people to come home, or to return from a trip, or to make up their minds. Losses, yes; but they are blocked out of our lives only at great expense and at the risk of losing any feeling for life itself in the process.

Furthermore, we also lose arguments now and then, and the sooner we admit it the better off all of us are. The truth endures even when we are too stubborn to admit that we do not have a complete grasp of it. After all, it is not the worst thing in the world to discover that we have not as yet learned everything. This discovery may even be the beginning of wisdom.

March 4
The Urge to Evaluate

A person must step back and reflect for a moment about his compulsion to make judgments—many of them of a moral nature—about so many things in life. Is it really necessary to categorize people and events under the heading of good or bad, sinful or virtuous, winners or losers? That this evaluation is common does not mean that it is necessary or beneficial. Indeed, the urge to pin a price tag on ourselves and others is so deeply rooted that we take it for granted and seldom examine our judgmental processes at all.

There is an old saying that we do not see the world as it is but rather that we see it as we are. Out of the brewing kettle of our own needs we impose on our own perceptions a pattern which makes us think that the world outside of us corresponds to the way we would like it to be or according to a psychological necessity of our own. The individual who constantly judges whether what he does is sinful or eternally meritorious may be so preoccupied with winning or losing that he misses the heart of life's meaning. The judgmental tendency abides in all of us. Just listen to yourself or to your friends in the ordinary conversations of a day. We constantly ask for evaluations. "What did you think of that?" is the constant inquiry made after classes, movies, lectures, or almost any other form of human activity. But does the habit of judgment allow us to see or hear clearly? Why are we so confident in our judgments, especially when our viewpoint may be limited by narrowness of experience or by other factors which we hardly recognize?

A better question might be, "What is he trying to say?" This is the searching phrase of the individual who is more interested in understanding life than in evaluating it. For this kind of question is asked by a person who does not

71

suffer from the compulsion to brand the labels of sin or virtue into everything in sight. The understanding question opens events up rather than closes them off under the titles of judgment. The capacity to understand—to search out the inner nature and genuine significance of what occurs in life—makes a great difference in our appreciation of ourselves and other people. Neither we nor they need be on trial every moment and our heads need not be miniature jury rooms populated by bedeviled veniremen trying to pass urgent verdicts on everything and everybody in sight. Life seems gentler and less threatening to the person who tries to understand rather than just judge. Freed from the compulsion to judge himself as good or bad, a person has a better chance of becoming himself and enjoying life far more. The world reveals itself as beautiful only to those who try to understand it.

March 5
Understanding Begins at Home

Fundamentalists love to judge, marking off increasingly large herds of sheep and goats. It takes a truly religious individual to look at humanity with the kind of understanding that deepens a feeling for individuals' differing life histories, motivations, and opportunities. The understanding person can see people as they are because he has overcome his need to see them according to unseen needs of his own.

We can apply this to ourselves as well. Instead of adding up the wins and losses, the points of virtue scored or the debits of sins and semi-sins, we might just try to look at ourselves from the viewpoint that surrenders evaluation in favor of understanding. Understanding provides the only mature way to confront our true selves. At the same time it provides the best light by which to identify who we really are. To understand is a kind and good gift to prepare for ourselves and others. We can now appreciate the scriptural warning that we are not to judge if we do not want to be judged. The positive side of this advice tells us to understand and we will find that others understand us. There is an added advantage to the gift of understanding. It is one of those wonderful qualities we cannot lose even though we give it away. Half the time people are worrying that they will never find love and the other half is consumed by the worry that they will lose it. Of course, we need to work at love constantly if it is going to remain fresh and alive for any of us. It simply does not take care of itself and, if it is lost, we can look to ourselves rather than to fate for an explanation. Love is never lost by those who give rather than demand things of it. Love, some people think, is supposed to take care of us as though it were a mysterious force independent of our lives, attitudes, and feelings. A person with that attitude will never have enough love to notice its loss. He will spend a time grasping for it because he looks at himself outside of the simple secret that brings love into our lives.

The loss we must face is the loss of ourselves, of our own concerns and our own inclinations to keep private places in our lives into which we allow no entrance. The person who would stand close to another must open all of the doors of his heart. He must relax the controls that make him secure in the same way an artist does in order to make his creative energies available for his work. It is the great secret of the kind of dying that Jesus tells us about, the readiness to surrender ourselves in response to others. Lovers lose something of themselves each day, killing selfishness in order to find and share more life. The loss that lovers know is never permanent; this is one of the reasons they are prepared to face death without any fears that it is final. Something more comes of their mutual surrender.

Are we winners or losers? Sometimes it is hard to say, unless, of course, we examine our attitudes in the light of the New Testament. Jesus said that those who lose their lives end up finding them, while those who desperately try to hang on to them lose them—and everything else worthwhile at the same time.

March 6
What Do You Do with Regrets?

"Regrets," Charles Dickens wrote in *Martin Chuzzlewit*, "are the natural property of gray hairs." This may be a good line but it is not necessarily true. Although the young have a certain resiliency, they are as vulnerable to regrets as anyone else. Regrets can come at any time in life after we are old enough to have made decisions (Yes, Harvey Cox, not to decide is to decide) that define ourselves in life. Big regrets come, for example, when we have wagered a portion of ourselves on a certain course of action, the decision for which was, whether we like it or not, under our own control. You do not have to be old to have regrets, just human.

March 7
A Case History

A young man recently came to me complaining about feelings of anxiety and depression; as a matter of fact, he was feeling these things because of regrets that were just too painful to face and call by their right names. He was graduating from school and was just beginning to realize that he had not used his talents very much; he had, as a matter of fact, skimmed along on cleverness, living by his wits rather than by acquiring much wisdom. And he got by—at least part of him did—enough to get a diploma, but hardly enough for him to feel that he had done even a small percentage of his best. His depression during the last school-term was a reaction to the things he regretted about himself—the irretrievable time he had wasted, the mileposts he had forever ridden past. This is a typical way in which we all deal with the things we regret; when the episode is too painful to look upon, we unconsciously develop other symptoms which make us uncomfortable but which also protect us from seeing the real source of regret. Of course, this young man has everything on his side; he is young enough to do something about his life and smart enough to look beyond his depression in order to understand correctly the nature of his regret. He cannot relive the past but he has a large supply of future events to draw upon to set things right.

March 8
Other Ages, Other Regrets

The middle-aged person, on the other hand, is painfully aware that what the young man has in abundance, he has in a more limited and rapidly dwindling supply. Essentially, this means time, the treasure we begin to appreciate only when we have begun to use it up; time, that great factor in regrets, is the desperate ravager of middle-aged hearts. The midlife siege of regrets has many faces but the same basic mechanism: A man or a woman, hovering at the point of no return, looks back and wonders whether he or she has done the right thing in life. And now there are children, mortgage, and other responsibilities to reckon with—the face of reality, without any make-up, scowls at our sudden surges of regrets so that we dare not speak their names. Yet many persons experience the symptoms of unresolved regret—the restlessness, the unexplained hostility, the defensive cynicism about all things human—the telltale signs that their lives are not what they might have made of them. Regret is the heavy weight springing the hangman's trap to squeeze the breath out of men and women in midlife. And middle-aged regret is not, as it may seem in youth, a realization that always follows upon a great error in living; it can just appear, as unannounced as it was unexpected, perhaps at a time when the person had expected to begin enjoying some of the harvest of a well-spent life. Thus, some parents begin to ask questions about their children and what it all means now that they are more or less grown and educated. They wonder if things might not have gone better in some other way. It is a strange and vague feeling, an impacted regret that nobody can do anything about.

Married persons are not the only ones subject to midlife regrets, however. Clergymen and other dedicated religious personnel can have them as well; in fact, this is an almost commonplace experience at the present time. The world and the church are changing irrevocably around the middle-aged priest and religious; what they knew and committed themselves to seems as far gone as pre-Civil War plantation life. Was their sacrifice worthwhile? Is there time yet to adjust, or perhaps even to change and make a new life of some kind? This latter question comes to every person who faces regrets and it is an inquiry that nobody else can answer.

The older person runs the danger of adjusting to advancing years by feeding on regret, drawing a peculiar energy from a past that never seemed happy and which cannot now be refashioned. The regret of old age is as bitterly cold as the end of a bad year when the early darkness of December comes filled with snow. Depression and discouragement are almost old friends to persons who have come to their last years without coming to terms with their own lives. But time runs out on the elderly and despair can be an open sore in their souls. They are deprived of the feeling of wholeness—that sense of integrity which older persons feel, like the warmth of the sun, when they have lived with a sense of purpose and direction.

March 9
Avoiding Regrets about Regrets

It is clear that regrets can fall like rain on the just and the unjust alike. What are some of the things to avoid if we are to lessen the burden of regret and live decently and honestly with ourselves? There are, as a matter of fact, some things to watch for in our own lives, little signals which indicate that we may be piling up regrets later on because of the way we handle our problems in the present.

Beware if you find that you are blaming other persons for your own difficulties in life. This may be the chief sign by which to diagnose an imminent case of personal regret. The individual who continually justifies his or her own lack of initiative by accusing everybody of duplicity or bad faith in not giving the recognition he or she deserves is almost certainly going to end up bitter and regretful. This is not to say that injustice does not exist; it is to point to a pattern of passivity which puts the burden for our success or achievement on others rather than on ourselves.

Be careful if you find that you are emotionally unwilling to take any risks in life. The person who will not expose his talent to criticism out of fear of failure places himself next in the line of succession to the throne of regret. The most abiding of regrets comes not from things we have done wrong but from our failure to do the things we could have done if we had been willing to risk ourselves.

March 10
And Be Careful . . .

if you find that your lifestyle is one characterized by waiting for something to happen to you. You will regret what happens. I remember, for example, visiting a seminary about five years ago; it had been designed for 250 students but it had only 26. I said to the rector, "Well, what are you going to do?" He replied, quite seriously, "We thought we would wait and see what happens." I said, "Didn't you see it? It happened." Such persons, like Mr. Micawber waiting for something to turn up, find out too late that only regrets come to those who fail to make things happen for themselves.

Be careful about living in the past. Nostalgia crazes are part of the way in which man deals with the regret potential of life. But nostalgia does not change the present nor soften the future despite the undeniable pleasures of recalling what seemed to be happier moments. Happiness is not something that happened long ago; it is not to be mourned as though it could never be found again. The individual who can deal with his life realistically—even in old age—can always find enough happiness to fend off unrelieved regret.

Be careful if you find that you get sick whenever a big challenge comes into your life. Illnesses can be part of a language we use to tell ourselves about deeper and more significant difficulties in our personalities. The one who has enough bad health to be excused from life's most difficult moments is already in the first stages of terminal regret.

March 11
Faith and Regrets

Regrets have little power over the person who lives by faith. I do not mean a mere reliance on God's goodness, although this is obviously important in framing our lives with the kind of meaning that goes deeper than the chances of fate or the dictates of the stars. Even faith in God grows from our ability to invest ourselves in other people and in the significance of our own work. Through faith we believe in what is possible in ourselves and in other persons; faith is a commitment of ourselves to our own truth and a promise of our energies to the fulfillment of others. Faith is not just a leap in the dark. Faith is a leap made toward life, for the sake of living things, in the very shadows of the regret that always menaces the possibility of our failure in any of these ventures. Believing in ourselves and in other persons is not an accident or a luxury. It is very much at the heart of a loving life, of working at reaching others even when we have been hurt or when we are tired or our strength seems all used up. Faith lies in sticking with life and growing against death and decay. Faith is caring when we would rather say the hell with it.

Faith, in fact, is our response to our potential for regret.

It is deeper than positive thinking and more lasting than the posturing in the bullring that passes for manliness in the fantasies of so many. Faith means that we take a deep look into the bewildering glass of life, that we see it all—wars, deceit, loneliness, and broken hearts by the score—and yet we can still believe in life and the goodness of man. Faith is the power by which a good man lives even when he knows full well the treacheries of the human condition. This is what makes faithfulness—to ourselves, to our word, to our beloved—so important. Through faith we may not cure the sick or cleanse the lepers, but we do commit ourselves to the life that God has given us. We have, then, the power for small but significant miracles: To open the world to the young, to encourage those at the midday of life, to breathe hope back into the elderly who are on the edge of despair.

Faith is what we need in our lives if we are serious about love; when a man announces that he no longer believes in anything, he is merely telling us that he has boarded up his heart against love. This kind of loss of faith is a prelude to the kind of regrets that kill us long before we die. If we want to know what to do with our regrets, we might take a closer look at our present life. As long as we can believe and love, we can solve our problems—and do something that gives lasting life to others at the same time.

March 12
The Decline of Friendship

Although it seems as unlikely as the cancellation of Christmas, something has happened to friendship. Men have craved more of it ever since they first laughed heartily at the sparks that showered from the twigs and sticks they rubbed together; women have had an interest in and a claim on it as well. In fact, friendship—that luminous and enlarging move out of the self and toward another—seems to be recognized by everybody as one of the first great mysteries of growing. Despite all this—yes, despite the banners that reassure us that friends divide our troubles and double our joys—despite Kahlil Gibran and the longings of all the world's lonely people, something has indeed happened to the market value of friendship. If it is a growth stock of limitless potential it has also become a highly speculative issue, not long guaranteed by even the most humanitarian underwriters, and not bought up by the huge mutual funds that specialize in secure but superficial leisure-time activities. Why have people become suddenly wary of friendship? Three contemporary attitudes are worth inspecting: friendship is (1) **impossible, (2) too dangerous, or (3) just possibly grounds for indictment as homosexuality.**

Some have come to believe that friendship is impossible because they think that no relationship of any lasting consequence can be achieved between persons. To support this viewpoint the nay-sayers cite the complicated psychological reality of man, noting that the best of persons spend a lifetime sorting out the false from the true aspects of their personalities. People often build bridges from a phantom and unreal self that they do not acknowledge or understand to an equally vague surface image of another. They do not meet; they just get entangled in each other's webs and they are blinded even as they are bound together. Only after months or years of thinking that they know each other do these supposed friends discover that they do not even know themselves very well, and that what they thought to be present was more illusion than reality. Novels and movies are filled with such groping men and women, people who seem to fall into friendship or love, and then grow bitterly out of it, convinced by the cold stone of alienation that weighs down their hearts that man can never really share, that life, in some poignant and final sentence, condemns us to walk its long corridors alone. This is the painful conclusion of many observers—even of some participants—in life: Friendship is a snare for the naive and the overoptimistic, something we would all like but something none of us is ever destined to possess.

March 13
Friendship Is Ruled Out of Bounds . . .

as too dangerous for most mortals, even by those who admit
that it is possible. The danger springs, oddly enough, not
from the illusion but from the reality of friendship. People
may become friends all right; they may even come to love
one another. But inevitably, they will kill each other off
with the hurts they exchange once they live at close range.
That is why so many friendships fall apart: The risk is just
too great, and if you let somebody see you as you really
are, he is bound to take a shot at you while your guard is
down. Even lovers do it, the scarred and weary will tell
you, and it is small wonder that so many friends, even in
marriage, drift just far enough out of each other's range to
prevent any damage from the gunfire that goes along with
intimacy. What you must do, consciously or not, is adjust
to each other rather than work steadily at being genuinely
close to each other. It is like the incredulous response of
the parents in the recent motion picture *Lovers and Other
Strangers*. Asked if they are happy, they respond heatedly:
"Happy? Who's happy? We're not happy. . . . Content?
Yes, content, but we're not happy." This represents the
manner in which many people make a truce with life and
their chances for love—by not expecting too much, by
learning how to minimize conflict and by living a kind of
affable coexistence which, if it is not deep and reaffirming
friendship, is at least free of the wounds which this dangerous commodity visits on those who take it seriously.

March 14
Can You Control Friendship?

There are also those within the church who, in their fervent quest for community, try to control the possibilities of

81

friendship in order to restrict it, for example, to what they look on as the reasonable and proper realm of religious or clerical life. Their grounds for doing this are that friendship is just too dangerous to permit or encourage on a free and unlimited basis. Such friendship, sometimes between the sexes, is obviously dangerous, they tell you, and, after several confused years of renewal with innumerable priests and nuns falling in love and marrying, it is time to get this back under control. Friendship seems indeed too dangerous, too much a threat to community life, ultimately too uncontrollable to encourage, too unpredictable to tolerate, too Christian to contemplate.

March 15
And, in Case You Have Not Heard . . .

the predictive aspects of our culture—the arts, letters, and cinema—have been telling us for some time now of the growing suspicion that homosexuality runs like a river through even the best same-sex friendships. The current socially acceptable view suggests that there is no friendship like that between a man and another man; that after all the paens to the man-woman relationship have been sung, the boys must still band together to become fully masculine. All this good fellowship in bars and duckblinds is to some avail after all; men finally redeem each other, backslapping and bullshooting in the all-male atmosphere of ultimate masculine invigoration. But, perched like an expectant vulture on a limb high above all this, a close-eyed bird clucks that such brotherhood is bonded by homosexual motivations; that men, of all things, are secretly meant and long for each other. Well, this has given men a little pause about their *bonhomie* and introduced a note of suspicious caution into their feelings about friendship.

There is another aspect to this issue of homosexuality, of course, one that capitalizes equally on the American tremors about being thought queer. The latest thing is the use of homosexual accusations in the running battle between certain women's lib leaders and their male chauvinist counterparts. Why else, the indicters ask, should these men and women be so defensive about their gender? There is something sneaky in all of them—at least that is the way the slurs run. It adds to the charged atmosphere about human relationships, closing people off rather than opening them up, making the accusation of latent homosexuality the *coup de grace* that finally destroys discussion altogether. The charge of homosexuality has, in other words, become an assaultive weapon in a psychologically-minded age; it is better to be on guard against it than, through too much spontaneous friendship, to lay oneself open to the charge. Well, what about these charges? What does a Christian who believes in friendship have to say?

March 16
Is Friendship Impossible?

In a way, friendship is impossible, or unlikely, between human beings who are well known for their capacities to disappoint and hurt each other, for their positive genius at times in betraying trust and homing in on each other's jugular veins. In many ways, friendship is the least likely thing to find in an inconstant world; and yet it is part of a larger understanding of love that, in fact, heals the wounds of the embattled universe and makes life possible. Friendship would have little significance if it were an easy goal or a simple and effortless achievement. The wonder of friendship is that it is God's gift to a broken world, a truly "amazing grace" that defies the laws of likelihood and challenges the charges that it is impossible. People who believe friendship is impossible because of man's psychological complexity forget that friendship is tailored expressly for psychologically complex man; friendship fits man as he *is* rather than as he might ideally be. In other words, friendship is not reserved for persons who, after

83

years of analysis, are keenly aware of every one of their psychic kinks and deceptive motivations. Being friends would be an icy business in a landscape of personalities forever freed from the emotional earthquakes and flashfloods of the human condition. Friendship is available not just to the perfect but to every person who is willing to work at it and not be afraid of spills and hurts now and then.

March 17
It Can't Be Forced

Friendship is impossible for those who, perhaps to avoid some of its potential painfulness, try to make it happen instantly or without effort. A man cannot dodge the hazards of learning to be a friend; he cannot eliminate his own need to die to selfish things inside himself if he is going to break through his own self-containment. There is a large measure of delusion in the promise—made by a variety of groups, from those who practice sensitivity to those who pray together—that friendship can grow out of a mere few hours or days together. Cervantes wrote long ago that "a man must eat a peck of salt with his friend before he knows him," and that still holds true today. The kind of friendship that is truly impossible is that which people try to accomplish by short cuts, the painless *Reader's Digest* version of what is essentially a continuing story.

March 18
Is Friendship Dangerous?

To this charge, of course, friendship must plead guilty, if dangerous is the correct word to describe the state of lowered defensiveness that must develop. Friendship is dangerous for the very reasons that life is dangerous:

take it seriously and something is liable to happen to you. Not all the possibilities of life or friendship are, however, sinister; the person who tries to avoid all dangers had better live in a museum than in the real world. Running risks, however, as we are forever reasserting intellectually, is essential for any kind of life; the trouble is that the risks are emotional—that's where you get hurt in the guts, not in the head. And hurt is the biggest danger in a phenomenon as sensitive as friendship. You just cannot have friends without this dangerous possibility any more than you can have an ocean without water. Eliminating or attempting to overcontrol the possibilities of danger just kills off the substance of friendship altogether. But friendship is also quite durable when it is real, and it offers strength and protection against danger even as it makes us vulnerable to it.

Friendship is most dangerous to those who expect it to be so. Friends, after all, support each other much more than they hurt each other. But individuals who overplay their concern about the dangers of friendship reveal an uncertain outlook in themselves that almost surely makes friendship dangerous for them. The question that must be asked of these persons is this: What are you afraid of? This is a particularly good question when the individual who expresses concern is actually meddling in the lives of other persons. It takes more self-confidence than most of us possess to pass judgment on where, when, and how persons can be friends to each other. Good example is better than bad advice in this regard. As a matter of fact, the best thing that anyone who is preoccupied about the dangers of friendship could do is to emphasize the development of solid and mature friendship in his or her own life. People learn more about friendship and the way to handle its dangers successfully from observing the manner in which genuine friends get on with each other than they do from an armful of warnings. Friendship is dangerous in the way that all precious things are; it may be misused, misunderstood, or even lost. This does not change its value, however. It merely emphasizes the essential importance of our active commitment to friendship.

March 19
Is It Homosexual?

You must wonder, in this day of abundant amateur psychologizing, whether there is anything that cannot, by some strange logic, be branded as homosexual. This charge, formerly hinted at discreetly, is now made against many persons, places, and things, as the ultimate put-down. It is like finding out, in the flurry of reports about all the harmful ingredients in our food and drink, that everything is contaminated, that nothing is pure or safe anymore.

People who get too shaken up about the hidden homosexual implications in their relationships will become very self-conscious and, if anything, more, rather than less, unsure about themselves. The homosexual accusation bit has been quite overdone; it is a sign of emotional immaturity to consider the charge of homosexuality as a bludgeon to use against others anyway. And it is a sign of the fatal brand of romantic homosexuality to insist that all friendship that is noble must, in fact, be basically homosexual. Persons should not be surprised to find that homosexual feelings are part of life for everybody, but they should not be thereby appalled nor unnecessarily defensive as a result. Man is a complex reality and he takes a long time to grow; the easily-generated spectre of ever-present homosexuality can only make mature growth more difficult for the great middle range of healthy persons. It is obvious that shying away from friendship because of a fear of homosexuality only reflects a deeper set of personal uncertainties in those who take the threat too seriously.

March 20
Christians Cannot Cop-out

In friendship, that is. A Christian may not feel like marching in picket lines, working in the Third World for a couple of years, or giving some other public witness to his faith; that is understandable because not everyone is expected to man the barricades, or be in the forefront of Christian activity. But no Christian worthy of the name is exempt from being a friend, not just to man in general but to men in particular. The ability to share friendship with others, despite the perils involved, is the distinguishing mark of the Christian. The Lord called us to be friends rather than servants, to reach out in love rather than to hold back in fear, to conquer rather than be overcome by the difficulties of living. Friendship is a sign that the Spirit is still at work in the world, joining people in the closeness through which they redeem each other. The Spirit fills friends with the life that sustains them as they exchange vulnerabilities, progressively becoming more fully present to each other. In the long run, the Christian is called to spend his life making friends, not in a superficial or merely self-satisfying way, but as the signal that God's power is revealed in people who draw lovingly close to each other. The Church is a sign that friendship is not impossible and that human beings are not fated to continually fail each other.

March 21
A Sign to the World

Friendship, like no other sign, tells the world that there is hope for human beings, that the universe is not a cruel isolation ward where there is no exit and no future. The community that Christians build does not set itself off from other men; rather, the Christian community is constantly expanding circles of friendship. The old walled city has indeed collapsed and in its rubble Christians are becoming aware that they are meant to build a church in which men can truly say, "We have been friends together." Building such a community is not creating a world in which some elite may pursue a specialized vision of perfection; neither is it calling together people who plan to be friends only to each other. The church is ultimately a place of friendship in which all men may recognize that what makes them brothers is richer and deeper than the fears and uncertainties that set them against each other. Heaven will be no surprise for those persons who have learned how to become friends here on earth.

March 22
The Future Is Too Much with Us

Modern man is so preoccupied with the future that he is beginning to lose his sense of the present. He used to say that he wanted to be "where it's happening" or "where the action is." Now, carefully marking his place with finger in a copy of *Future Shock*, he is waiting for something to happen, although he is not quite sure what will happen. Around the world men already feel the rumbling in the ground that tells them that a new century, like a volcano in the sea, is taking shape out there in the dark. Men are fascinated with the future, excited by its science fiction possibilities and seemingly intrigued with the fact that its problems will be even more insoluble than the ones we have at the present time. If you wonder why people have a faraway look in their eyes it is because they have focused into the vague years that are yet to come, a stance in life that is aided and abetted by the increasing literature on the future.

Whatever your interests, you can read about what they might be like in a generation or two. Everything falls under the wand of the futurist: marriage, the churches, the stock market and, of course, sex. If you feel bewildered it may be because it is so difficult to find an anchor in the present moment. Everything has happened already or has not happened yet, and it is difficult to be a truly contemporary person. The old adages about living from moment to moment or getting through one day at a time are increasingly difficult to follow: "You ain't seen nothing yet" is the barker's cry as he holds the tent of tomorrow slightly open for us. It does not do much good to say that there is nothing new under the sun, especially in the age during which we have put something new on the moon. All this future orientation has a healthy side, of course, but there is no path to the future except the one we find in the present. The future, whether it is of ourselves, our country, or our religious faith, does not hang like a blossoming fruit waiting to be plucked. The future, in fact, seems to have a life of its own, as though it were a locality into which we would travel as we might into a bordering state. The future, already formed, is not out there waiting for us. We are generating it even now; the best preparation for it lies neither in unbridled enthusiasm for its delights nor in uncontrolled shudders over its potential horrors. The future for each of us depends on the decisions we make here and now.

This understanding of the future has a special meaning for us because we can be tempted so often to wait things out—be it a change in the weather or a change in the temperament of our boss. We have become estranged from the fact that what we once rigidly termed "the will of God" is really something we give substance to ourselves by the quality of the choices we make in the course of our own lives. It is not just Rotarian heartiness that bids us to focus again on the present; it is plain Christian common sense. We bear the future inside ourselves and we understand it not so much by looking into the darkness ahead as into the depths of our own being.

March 23
The New Perfectionists

Men are making plans for us, you can be sure of that. Even now, if you listen carefully, you can hear the tiny squeals of joy in laboratories where enthusiastic scientists are planning the faultless man of the future. He is practi-

89

cally within their grasp, as indeed so many earlier utopian visions of man have also seemed to their creators. Now, however, it seems different. The future of man will not be the outcome of political moves or theological theories; it will flow from the perfect calculations of scientific planning. Scientists are having a new look at man and they are out to eliminate all the small shocks that this flesh is heir to. A generation of noble and heroic humans will emerge.

In *New Yorker* magazine Mike McGrady relates his interviews with some of these planners. He quotes Dr. J. K. Sherman: "Frozen human semen banks can offer a wide range of material for selection at any time during an indefinitely long period—we have only to look at improvements in our dairy herds and their products to appreciate the merits of utilization of select donors." As McGrady notes: "It is possible, without further delay, to begin breeding a race of men who look like Paul Newman and John Lindsay, men who will all stand 6'2" and smile through baby-blue eyes and whiz through Cal-Tech in three years. We are finally able to rid ourselves of the mentally deficient, of the hunchbacks, the weaklings and the troublemakers, the stammerers and the poets. I have had a glimpse of the future. It doesn't look as though there is going to be room here for everyone."

March 24
A Race of Supermen?

McGrady's irony is almost too subtle for the problem at hand. The decision makers do indeed foresee a perfect generation and there may be a great deal to be said positively for genetic engineering. Before we get too wrapped up in the subject, however, it might be well to remember that superman will always be beyond our grasp. There is something imperfect about man which will never be overcome, even by the most sophisticated scientific techniques. All praise to those who can remove problems which result

90

in a crippled life for some people. But beware of the planners who honestly feel that they can usher man into a golden era. There is more to man than his body and you cannot plan the proportions of his spirit with a slide rule.

March 25
The Trouble with Planners

Some future planners, with copies of B. F. Skinner's books under their arms, are already mapping out the subdivisions of Walden II. In this vision, men will beat their weapons into ploughshares and peace will come at last. All of this will be accomplished through reinforcing the right responses of individuals who, thereby, always succeed, never know failure, and never slip off the prescribed pathway of behavior. Even now, however, other experiments have shown the complications that arise when a person is raised on a regime in which he always succeeds through repeating the reinforced response. Constant success leaves people unable to deal with failure, conflict, or ambiguity—elements which make up, for good or for ill, a large part of real life. There is probably little to worry about in thinking of B. F. Skinner's future anyway; it will be left in the hands of a committee, the final graveyard for good as well as grandiose ideas.

There are also new perfectionists at work on the most important of our human relationships. Not only do people give us advice on how to win friends and find marriage partners; now the whole way is made smooth by the marriage manuals that promise sexual success as well as by the matrimonial contracts which are written to guarantee the success of a man and woman's new equal partnership with each other. All of these developers, including the genetic and the psychological planners, make the same mistake which was once made on such a great scale by the ascetic writers of the church. They felt that perfection could be captured in planning, that it could all be written down, that all man had to do was to follow the directions and he would not only be saved but he would also climb high on the ladder of perfection. That old framework came tumbling down years ago, but the corrupted vision that made it possible lives on in these new planners. The marriage contracts read, in their immense detail about human behavior, like the religious rules of olden days. There is a right way to do everything, and conflict can be avoided by careful planning. The difficulty with this, of course, is that avoiding genuine human conflict means that we avoid life itself, that we never get very deeply into it, and that what the overdetailed plan sets out to preserve it manages to destroy.

The problem with the new perfectionists is that in their focus on the future of man they have forgotten much of his past. They may have looked toward a broad new horizon but they have not looked very deeply. Man the imperfect will always outwit them, no matter how carefully they lay their plans. That is the wonder of the fact that man can be distracted, can have new thoughts that challenge the patterns of his conditioning, and yet he gropes toward a genuine feeling for himself even when others have decided what he should be like. Man at his best is not necessarily man as perfect; there is reassurance for all of us in that.

March 26
Praying

Breaking free in a healthy way in life is, as many a weary Christian knows, both an achievement and a hazard; it is the right thing, yes, by any measure the right thing, to move out of constraints and controls toward taking more responsibility for oneself. But the price of this heroic vision has never been frozen and goes higher every year. The documents of Vatican II, according to some people who have tried to take them seriously, should have been labelled with some sort of warning like this: *Reading these may be dangerous to your old convictions, your feeling of being securely saved, and your peace of mind.* No surface of the formerly smooth mosaic of the Christian life has been webbed more with the cracks of strain than that of prayer. This is true for the Christian community and for the individual; prayer is given in the tradition of the church, something a man feels guilty about questioning in the present because he was always so sure of it in the past. It is as if a great pianist suddenly discovered that the elementary scales were a code that he could not crack and that, although he could still deftly flip his tuxedo tails out of the way as he placed himself at the keyboard, he could no longer even begin to play. Many a Christian feels the same way about saying his prayers these days. He should be good at it, God knows, and he remembers how to kneel; but where does he begin and how can he tell the middle from the end? The Spirit may be groaning inwardly for him through all this confusion, but he wants to speak the old petition: Lord, teach us how to pray.

Prayer is part of the problem in more ways than one. It is difficult enough to be sure about how to pray, but it is even more disconcerting to face the question of whether a man should pray at all. Many of the arguments for a definition of prayer which hung in undisturbed rectitude along with board of directors' portraits in the marbled foyer of the old Church Militant are hidden in its broken-columned wreckage. Now a person must ask whether, in fact, he should pray, and, if the answer is *yes,* whether he needs to stir out of his house to do it. Complicating this somewhat depressing brace of questions is an additional wonder, perhaps the most unsettling of all, namely that many a Christian went along accepting the old verities about prayer without question for a long period of time. Many, then, are not only confused but angry that they have come late to so many questions which other men struggled with long ago. Some of those rebels and freethinkers seem to have been way ahead at a time when they were perceived with the kind of smugness that only the surely-saved Christian could muster up. Now many of these persons seem less villainous and more sincere, and that discovery, in itself, makes a man wonder at the illusion of certainty that a former age in the church generated. If those pepole did not have the answers, at least they seem to have had some of the right questions. These questions hang on, and recognizing their right to exist does not make it any easier to respond to them.

March 27
The Growing Christian . . .

usually discovers that prayer is often not a solution but rather part of the problem of Christian life. This is a common and widespread difficulty. Prayer, once accepted as a curiously but generally healing blend of duty and consolation, now seems elusive and somewhat extraordinary if it can be located at all. The searching Christian looks at prayer and wonders at the contradictions, past and present, that have attended it. On the one hand, many people who formerly did a lot of praying did not seem to enjoy it much; it fell into the category of unpleasant wholesomeness, its benefits rising in direct proportion to the self-denial involved. On the other hand, there are presently segments of the church who say that prayer is the best trip of all, and that smiles of joy should go along with the various gifts—such as tongues and healing—that flow from being "baptized in the Spirit." The average person feels genuinely estranged from both of these viewpoints. Yet he also feels that he should pray, or that he would like to if he could, but he is not sure about the deepest reasons why or the best ways how. And he is made cold rather than comforted by the all-weather aphorism that prayer is a mystery. That answer is no more acceptable now than it was when Augustine used it to explain the obvious lying and deceit in the biblical story of Jacob and Esau: "It is not a lie; it is a mystery." This kind of explanation is not very satisfying to the Christian who wants to know why prayer, which presumably ought to be so much a part of his life, should always be just beyond his grasp. These are good days to meditate on the subject.

March 28
A Human Activity

This means that prayer, or any experience that deserves that name, matches the human condition. It is something peculiarly human, the kind of thing that a man does when he is truly maturing. Prayer, of course, contributes to his development even as it also expresses it. In a profound way, prayer is what a man does when he is in touch with himself and the world around him; and he does it whether he knows it or not. Essentially, prayer is much closer to the activities man inevitably engages in as he becomes aware of and uses his powers than it is to the awkward negation of self with which it has frequently been associated. This is not to say that genuine prayer is easy; but deep thinking is not easy either. Both are the sort of challenging and profoundly human tasks to which men give themselves when they are mature. They are not the kind of activities that go against our possibilities; rather they make us realize them. Prayer, in other words, is appropriate and necessary for the filling out of personality. The man who does not pray—no matter what name he gives it—has not yet learned what it means to be a man. And prayer that fails to move a man toward self-discovery—no matter who names it—is not prayer.

March 29
Something We Need

Man needs to pray even if God does not need to hear him; God, after all, is not diminished because we have failed to pray. However, we are diminished because we have stifled the soundings in ourselves that tell us of the far reaches of reality in a redeemed universe. Prayer is one of the means through which we achieve our specifically human identity, and this on at least two levels: through the special awareness it builds in us, we see ourselves as we are far more clearly, and we perceive our relationships to God and to others much more accurately. Prayer helps us to find our place in the cosmos, not as a curious speck falling across the face of the sun, but with that sense of significance that comes from recognizing ourselves in God's love and taking our responsibility for sharing that love with other persons. Prayer, in other words, never takes us out of reality; it plunges us into it, giving us the saving light, like that which a painter or a sculptor needs, to see things as they are.

Prayer is the answer to the stirrings inside of every man when he feels that what he sees and knows in the world around him falls short of what it might, on some unimagined day, be like. Prayer is in the pain that a person feels when he dares to enter the human situation where doubts and cruelties, burning in the same howling forge of history, first char, then purify, and finally reshape an earlier kind of faith. Prayer is hard, not because it is unnatural, but because it fits the battered yet pulsing spirit of the man who remains faithful to his promises in a world that seems to break all of its own; it is hard, in other words, because life is hard, and there is no way, except by wishful thinking, to meet it except on its own terms. Wishful thinking and fantasy, drugs and dreams—the commodities that promise the unsuspecting a deep, even a religious or mystical vision of reality—take a man away from the world that prayer enables him to see much better.

It would be a sad thing, a tragedy of sorts, if a man were to turn away from contemplating his experience of reality to try to find some better ground on which to pray. Man prays on his home grounds, earthquake-ridden though they be, or he does not pray much at all. Prayer is the right name for what a man does when he seeks the truth about himself and his need to respond to rather than hide from the world where his roots are tangled and deep.

March 30
Alive to Self, Alive to God

It is hard to know how a man can respond to God's presence unless he has tried to be alive to his own best possibilities. The man who avoids this most humanly demanding experience cannot bring much sense of life to prayer. If, however, a man breaks out of himself in order to reach another in a relationship of love, he enters, even if his heart is bruised in the process, into life more fully. The same must be said for hoping, whose difficult lessons are not learned by whistling into the winds but by challenging them. So it is with loving; long prayers to ask God for the gift of love are no match for long months or years of giving love steadily to the heartbreakers all around us. A man does not pray in order to find his way into life; he enters life and finds out how to pray.

March 31
Praying Together

Liturgy becomes the meeting ground for Christians who recognize each other more for their common scars than their religious medals. Liturgy is not to be thought of as that which produces Christian experience as much as that which symbolizes it; it makes people more keenly aware of the full reality of the lives which they bring to the public worship of the church. Individuals who expect the liturgy to create Christian community independently and of its own power, separate from the living experience of the people, are making magic of it, looking for it to overwhelm and supplant its own context in life itself. Liturgical reform, joining priest and worshipers together in rituals that speak much more clearly the truths of Christian faith, cannot be successful as a performance. Liturgy witnesses to the fundamental reality of our relationships to each other in the mystery of Christ; it proclaims the church as alive in and through the relationships of people. Worshiping together makes us deal with the truth that authentic religion is not a private affair, so our coming together is not a matter of indifference but a question of response. Drawing together in a corporate presence is essential to our full realization of the church as a People of God, right down to the jostling crowds, babies' cries, smokers' coughs, and sometimes-wandering sermons. We come together to recognize ourselves as the church—not as a perfect society of laws as the authors of the *lex fundamentalis* would have it —but a gathering of essentially imperfect people who cannot be Christians or human beings without each other. Worship, then, is not for obligation but for responsibility. It is perfectly fine to close one's door and pray in private; but it is also essential for people to recognize each other in the breaking of the bread if they care about sharing the Christian message with the world. The church as servant arises from the presence together of flawed people whose mingled weaknesses, touched by the Spirit, are a stronger and more constant kind of prayer than those that echo in the big, lonesome, bureaucratic Christianity.

April

April 1
The Season of Resurrection

Resurrection is one of those theological words we have
known since our childhood; it describes a saving and continuing event that is at the center of our consciousness during Eastertime. Like a great many good things, however,
resurrection has been discussed so much in a technically
theological way (count if you can the debates about the
physical resurrection of Jesus that you have heard during
the past few years) that the event itself has come to seem
quite remote from our own experience. We have lost touch
with the continuing dimension of resurrection, the manner
in which it is still an urgent part of our own lives. It is
easier, of course, to debate the historical resurrection than
it is to rediscover its dynamic power in our own day-to-day
experience.

The wonder of Christianity lies in the way it con-
tinuously alerts us to the mysteries of ordinary living; it
helps us always to see reality freshly, to perceive, in other
words, how laden with truth and beauty our lives with
each other really are. We are so accustomed to the various
sore spots of everyday living that we find ourselves estranged from the marvels of living in a redeemed universe.
Mysticism and spiritual fulfillment always seem just
around the bend or across the farthest border of our existence; our faith in the resurrection, however, enables us to
come alive again to the spiritual riches and opportunities
that are close at hand. That is why the Lord said, in what I
am told is the most accurate translation of the phrase, "the
kingdom of God is in the midst of you."

Resurrection completes the circle of our Christian experience. We are never left abandoned in the daily pain that makes us aware of the shadow of the cross in our lives. Suffering is not the end of things for the believer. Our faith helps us into our separate futures, bridging the moments of suffering with hope and giving a sense of meaning to our sacrifices as well as a sense of direction to our lives. A life lived for others empties us and scars us as well; but the reality of the resurrection in our human experience fills us up again and heals us. We are never left gesturing against an empty sky or contemplating the darkness that has fallen around us. We need not grit our teeth and live as though life had no meaning at all. Resurrection, you see, is not just an intellectual promise, nor a historical event, but a daily experience for the Christian who knows that his faith lies not in remembering but in living here and now. How do we sense the ongoing mystery of resurrection in our own lives?

April 2
Moments of Resurrection

We have only to recall those moments in which we have felt enlarged or the times in which our lives have been deepened because of what somebody else has meant to us. We locate the resurrection experience in our own lives by identifying those moments in which we have become more of ourselves; they are almost always related to the action of someone who has loved us enough to make the power of resurrection a reality in our own lives. This happens, for example, when somebody else trusts us, allowing us to find our own way or to test our own powers, perhaps for the first time. We are aware that the trusting person has not abandoned us and that, in fact, by giving us a vote of confidence he gives us some of his strength to help us find the way that is right for us.

100

The power of resurrection may become a reality in our lives when somebody, sometimes a stranger, responds to us with a genuine understanding of us and some trial we may be experiencing. The understanding person does not necessarily agree or disagree with us, but he sees into our lives in a way that enables us to see more of ourselves at the same time. Just to understand another does not seem like much to the person who feels that he must be busy altering and planning the lives of others with the intensity of a do-it-yourself home hobbyist. Just as home hobbyists sometimes make doors and windows that don't quite fit, so too the amateur activist's plans for others frequently do not quite work out. Indeed, to understand another person is a great thing—perhaps, in certain circumstances, the greatest experience of resurrection that we can offer to another.

April 3
Someone Enlarges Our Lives . . .

by honestly letting us see into his own. We do not even need to know the people who do this for us. Frequently this is the gift given to us by the writers and artists or filmmakers, by the persons who are working at the frontiers of all human experience, trying to understand it and translate it into some form that enables all of us to know ourselves and our lives better.

Our lives can also be enlarged when somebody inspires us to become more ourselves. We do not speak much of inspiring people lately; the fatalist and the cynic have convinced us that history kills its heroes too soon. But there are still inspiring figures all around us who do, in fact, breathe new life into us, just as the word *inspire* suggests. Each of us still responds to a personal hero in some way or other. Who is it in your life? And why is it that he or she gives you courage and strength to keep going or to keep trying to do better?

April 4
How Do We Resurrect Others?

The first lesson we must recall is that to enlarge the life of another person we must allow some of our own life to get out; we must, in a truth as old as anything we know, let others into our personalities, make room for them in that inner space which we can so jealously keep very much to ourselves. The person who would make the lives of others fuller begins by relearning the lessons of dying. Something in us must die if something of the power of our own life is going to get out to transform the suffering and hopelessness of another. There is no other way for the Christian to hand on his own life if he does not learn to make those small surrenders that put an end to his selfishness. When the Christian has learned this he understands what Paul spoke of when he wrote to one of his communities that "death is at work in us but life in you." The Christian transaction has always exacted this same price, although it is seldom counted in very dramatic forms. Perhaps it would be helpful to look at some of the more common forms of Christian exchange, the human modes through which the Spirit makes passage from one to the other.

Sometimes it is as simple as giving up our own daydreams and reveries in order that we may pay more attention to others. It is strange how much of our time is spent in worlds other than this one even when we are surrounded by persons in need. The surrender of our distractions enables us to move closer to others.

Listening well requires us to die to our own needs and curiosity, to give up what we wish to speak about so that we can truly hear the message another wants to give. All too often our periods of supposed listening to others are merely intervals in which we wait for the chance to speak again. The death that enables us to give our full attention to another is, in the long run, as unseen as it is lifegiving.

Being with others—in other words, making ourselves consciously present to them even when we are at a great distance from them, or when there is nothing that we can say—requires a death to our own feelings. Staying with those in grief or illness is a special sacrifice of ourselves to become partners with family or friends in the struggles of their lives. It is one thing to say that we are interested in others but it is quite another to dispose ourselves so that the power of the Spirit reaches through us to strengthen and give added life to others.

Sometimes it is in giving our best performance whatever our work in life is. All too often routine and boredom rob us of the creative strength that reaches through our work to make a difference in other persons. Sometimes we settle for cleverness, and this is the death of integrity in our dealings with other persons. The teacher, for example, who never revises his lecture notes stopped giving life to his students a long time ago. The preacher who uses the words of others instead of finding genuine ones of his own has forfeited the possibility of enlarging the life of his parishioners. It is a difficult thing to take each performance—or whatever approximates it in our profession—as a new and separate experience. It is, however, the way to give the best of ourselves and so it is the clear path to providing a resurrection experience for others.

April 5
Clues for Resurrection

A double vulnerability is involved in letting people be free and allowing them to have their own lives in their own time. They may disappoint us or cause us pain because they use their freedom poorly or because they grow old when we wish they would not. We are, then, prompted to overprotect our children or isolate our loved ones from any opportunity to taste life itself. But controlling the lives of others or attempting to eliminate the necessary conditions of life are strategies that almost always diminish rather than enlarge the possibilities of the other. What individuals need most is the kind of freedom in which we stand by them and the kind of time which we are willing to enter into at their side, so that they can find and live by the truth of their own personalities. Freedom and time can seem like masters to us if we are afraid of them; they are on the side of those who have truly learned to love.

This is the problem with people who have no patience with the good things that insistently demand an investment of time. They want things immediately, and the delay of gratification seems sinful to them. What is it, after all, that you can have right away in this world of wonders? A radio station that, thanks to the miracle of transistors, comes immediately to life to tell you the news that you have already heard two or three times before? A television set, bursting into color at the touch of a dial, to show you a rerun of a game show? Man's marvels of communication only make life more painful, filling him with a greater yearning rather than satisfying him. The things we can have instantly are often shallow and insubstantial, commodities that cannot last and that quickly dissolve the very quality of time they have tried to overcome.

What is timeless and lasting is a life to which we give ourselves freely in the knowledge that we will have to learn to deal with time if we are going to live as God's children. There are a thousand deaths involved in meeting life on its own terms, yet this is the way to go deeper into life and to discover there the richness and the values of loving and believing that outlast all the clocks of the universe. The Christian commits himself to the human condition, acknowledging his mortality, and exposing himself to the hazards of real living that are understood by those who are afraid of freedom and time.

April 6
All This Can Be Done

In what is surely one of the more marvelous aspects of Christian reality, each of us can resurrect others without becoming perfect. Even the most flawed of us, as I will observe later on, can still give life to others. Perfection has never been a requirement for loving; indeed, love does not exist except in the lives of ordinary, imperfect people like us; this is one of the most reassuring things we can understand about it.

Without totally giving up our own individuality, our own interests, or our own lives, we enliven other persons precisely because we do remain separate from them with our own obligations and life situations. Enlarging the lives of others does not demand that we leave no time for ourselves, our own families, or our own interests; it only asks that we be willing to pull away from these personal interests at times in order to share our own strength with those who need it. In fact, our strength to resurrect others comes from the roots that reach down, sometimes tangled, into our own imperfect lives.

April 7
A Part of Everyday

Resurrecting others is so much a part of our ordinary existence that one can hardly claim credit for any larger-than-life heroism. People who like to feel self-righteous about religion are disappointed by the fact that the essence of resurrecting other persons is simply not dramatic enough to inflate them or to inspire tall tales which they can tell their friends about. When we give life we do it in simple exchanges that are so remarkable that we sometimes do not recognize them—in listening to the troubled, in standing with the oppressed, in winking, as H. L. Mencken suggested, at a homely girl. Many times it does not take much to give a lift to another; it takes thoughtfulness and time and a loving if imperfect heart.

April 8
Better a Lively Sinner than a Dull Saint

Saint Thomas once asked whether, in a certain time of need, it was better to have a timid or a proud man. His answer was to choose the proud man because the timid man would be overcome by his fears and would end up doing nothing, even though it might seem that he accomplished this with becoming modesty. The proud man, on the other hand, might be overconfident in his powers and might, in fact, choose to do the wrong thing; but at least he would do something which, in the great philosopher's opinion, was always better than not doing anything at all.

What is it about the human family that so often makes the slightly roguish more attractive than the self-consciously saintly? Would we, along with Mark Twain, decide to visit hell rather than heaven because the company in hell seems more sprightly? Why is it that religious behavior has so frequently been equated with a dullness to the things of this world, a detachment from anything that could make the human heart happy or make the human spirit sing? Does being holy really require being so grim and so unflinching in one's determination to avoid the contamination of pleasure? This is an old theme, but it is worth recounting when we are trying to understand how the power of resurrection persists in our lives, incorporating us into the mysteries of Christ exactly in proportion to our willingness to incorporate ourselves into the human family. It seems, on balance, that lively sinners offer us more promise of resurrection than do the supposedly

saintly but deadened models that have been held up to us
for so many years. The reason, of course, is that the sinner
has been involved enough in life to have stumbled and
fallen; he bears the scars that tell us that he is not a
stranger to trouble or mistakes. He seems like one of us,
and when, with undiminished spirit, he can throw himself back into life he makes it seem possible that we
too can do the same. The plaster saint—and surely these
have never resembled real saints—seems to stay too close
to the edges of life, having mortgaged himself to an ideal
that is so beyond most of us that we can only get discouraged in contemplating it. The essence of Christian teaching
lies in the fact that sinners can save each other, that the
Spirit of God is poured forth in the hearts that have been
cracked and broken by the pressures of the human condition, that the power of the Spirit can only be glimpsed in
the wonderful liveliness of people who know very well that
they are the weak things of this world. We are all the sick
to whom Christ came in preference to those who are well;
because we know the strains and shortcomings of living we
have the power to breathe life into each other. This is the
thing to remember in the season of the Resurrection; this
is what the alleluias are all about.

April 9
Life Is Also Renewed When . . .

someone stands by us, even though he or she says very little, perhaps nothing at all. In fact, at those times when we
just have to be alone in order to pull ourselves together,
we need friends who are sensitive enough to give us the
privacy, the time, and the place to resurrect ourselves.
They are there when we need someone within reach, providing that human presence that acknowledges everything
and demands nothing from us. The power of resurrection

is in such presence because it is such a powerful sign that we are never truly alone.

April 10
It Is Good to Remember

Each of us can make his own list of times when we have known the power of the Spirit through the presence of someone else who has responded to our needs at a difficult time in our lives. Occasionally, the knowledge that there are people who would so respond to us—if we could be with them—is enough to strengthen us for the continued long haul of life. Friends, in other words, have the capacity to resurrect each other even when they are not together, even when they do not immediately know each other's difficulties. And this is one of the magnificent aspects of Christian reality. The power of attentive love is not diminished by either space or time. We move on, however, from recalling our own experiences of resurrection to the question of resurrecting others.

April 11
People Do the Damnedest Things

Something in man, like the frozen ground swell in Robert Frost's celebrated poem, does not like a wall; sooner or later, and against all odds and predictions, man wriggles out of expected patterns, mocking them even as he celebrates his freedom. This, indeed, is a far more interesting truth about man than the fact that he can be so thoroughly conditioned in so many aspects of his behavior. Man, you see, is full of surprises; he is forever doing exactly what he said he would not do and omitting what he thought he would do. Man, in fact, does the damnedest things all the time; and by man, I mean you and me. . . .

We are always telling ourselves and others what we are going to do, but then we never do it. And this kind of resolution-making covers a broad range of behavior. So we start diets and fail to follow them almost immediately. We learn hard lessons just about ordinary eating and drinking —about how much is too much, for example—and, along with the sadfaced man in the television commercial, we go ahead and eat the whole thing anyway. There are two odd parts to this strange behavior. First, we know we are going to suffer for deviating from our resolve, but that does not stop us; and second, we not only break our resolve, but we sometimes brag about it in sophomoric celebration of our own nonheroism.

We commend the benefits of exercise and then, with keen memories of the sore muscles and aching joints that come, we tend to overdo our calisthenics anyway. This follows the same pattern as eating and drinking, and it is just as predictable and regrettable.

We get frustrated with some situation at home or at work and express the home frustration at work and the work frustration at home, doing nothing constructive about either but making ourselves feel worse about both conditions. This situation gives rise to more frustration and more sidestepping, and this type of vicious circle is hard to break.

We claim that once we get out of a certain situation—say, paying off a debt or fulfilling a certain burdensome work obligation—we will never again let ourselves get involved in the same way. But, before we can congratulate ourselves on escaping, we get involved or committed in exactly the same manner again. Try it; you won't like it, but you will usually do it.

April 12
Why Does It Happen?

Nobody can give you a complete answer for why we are always painting ourselves into familiar yet uncomfortable corners. The following are some of the suggestions that people have made about our self-defeating habits. In human affairs the effect of a reward, no matter how small or infrequent, is very powerful in motivating behavior. A reward, even an unpredictable one, outweighs a predictable subsequent punishment in many situations. In other words, what we get in pleasure at a certain moment is enough to support us through the pain which we know will inevitably follow. We settle for that as a kind price; we even make parables about pipers who must be paid in recognition of this common occurrence. So a man drinks or eats at this moment because the reward—which may be very complex in its nature—seems to be enough for him to face the headache or stomachache that is sure to follow.

Many of the patterns of our behavior make more sense than we think they do on first inspecting them. Everybody knows that Doctor Freud applied this principle to slips of the tongue, but not many of us apply the notion seriously to what we ourselves do everyday. The fact is, however, that many of the strange sequences of our activity—those little hitches that identify us all as a little neurotic now and then—have been learned as carefully as the multiplication tables. In other words, some of the roundabout, inefficient, and sometimes painful personal strategies we follow in life are in reality paths we have hacked out in an effort to solve some more central conflict. We make our way around it—a straight line is not the shortest distance between two psychological points—as we can sometimes notice ourselves doing in conversation. We go to great lengths, for example, not to discuss a certain topic; sometimes we even take the polar route in conversation to avoid using certain words we may have difficulty in pronouncing. The point is that at some level of consciousness (which is not too deep down) we are making a strange kind of sense to ourselves. We have learned a way of handling some of life's conflicts and we hold onto our solution even when it proves disadvantageous from many other viewpoints.

April 13
And Sometimes . . .

we engage in self-defeating behavior because of the attend-
ant excitement of the activity, because, in some way, it
matches our needs for keeping on the move and keeping
ourselves distracted in fever-pitch America. Pulitzer Prize-
winning reporter David Halberstam wrote in *Harper's Ba-
zaar* of this common wrinkle in the psyche of contemporary man: "The truth is, in fact, that we would be lost
without the pressure. We are more afraid of getting off the
treadmill than staying on. We cannot resist: Knowing that
we are already overloaded, we accept more—not less—
work and commitment. . . . We become, in little ways,
quirky—a gentle description at best. And we seek, in many
ways, escape."

This is not, of course, the adjustment that leads to peace
of mind; it directs us, instead, to doing the darndest things
day in and day out because doing the darndest things beats
not doing anything at all. It beats having to come to terms
with ourselves, our work, or the long-range meaning of
our lives. And it is exhausting into the bargain; it speaks of
our loneliness and our need to return to thoughtfulness if
not some form of contemplation. One thing is clear:
Frenzy is self-perpetuating, hooking us as surely as heroin
would, and deflecting us just as surely from a better grasp
of ourselves. This feeling—that we cannot get off the
treadmill or the merry-go-round—may be the best signal we
get to tell us that it is time to look deeper into ourselves.

April 14
Blind to Ourselves

When we do not pay attention to these clues we are as self-
destructive as the rioters who, out of unnamed frustrations,

burn down their own businesses and homes. We are as blind to what we are doing to ourselves as the people in badly polluted communities who deny the medical findings about what the smoke and soot are doing to their children and merely shrug off the problem. There is a time when the balance sheet is drawn up on each of us, a time when the treadmill stops whether we like it or not. The person who has not understood himself and his need for constant motion will discover the cruelest self-defeat in the loneliness and uneasiness of the years whose quiet he has never prepared for.

April 15
Will Perfect Man Remember How to Love?

The fundamental question about the perfect man of the future is will he still be man at all. One wonders whether future man, genetically pure and behaviorally correct, will be able to love anymore. The planners, no matter how scientific, often leave something essentially human out of their calculations for the future. It is easy for planners to make mistakes, like the proud group of engineers who opened a beltway around a great eastern city for which they had forgotten to provide exit ramps. You could go round and round but you could never get off. Maybe man in the future will find himself traversing the same kind of circles, never able to break out of the perfect arcs and into the middle of life, that dangerous place where he can find out what it feels like to be himself. It is hard, you see, to build the unpredictable quality of love into the mathematical logic that is supposed to make all the rough paths smooth in our common future. But without the possibility of love, will man's spirit die despite the perfection of his new body?

Love seems to arise only in imperfect conditions, in adverse tides and winds, when there is always the chance that everything can go wrong and that pain will be the reward of our efforts. Love goes along with human limitations; it is difficult to imagine how love could survive in a world where, due to mistaken utopianism, we try to remove all limitations. Love, after all, would not mean much unless we knew the bittersweet feeling that comes with nightfall on days that we want to last just a little longer; love would be hard to recognize without the separations that fill our splintered hearts with yearnings; love would have no test except for death, the door that threatens to open to nowhere; love would ask little of us if we did not know the hurts that even the truest of lovers can inflict on each other.

Love is the response to all that is flawed about the human condition. Its strength enables us to face and triumph over our failures and shortcomings rather than just be devoured by longing and guilt. It is not a sentimental thought to realize that genuine life lies largely in our efforts to reach out and to share things with each other. Even in the shadows of pain and death man becomes himself through loving; if his newly engineered perfection removes the challenge of growth will he ever be able to find love again or even to remember what it is like? Marriage contracts written against conflict and hurt still do not deliver the gift of love that, like a buried treasure or a distant goal, must be sought after. And the seeking is as important as the finding. The overperfect man of the future may never feel the need for another person and so he will only be able to love himself. He may be more healthy, but at the same time he may be lonelier than ever with no one to reach out for, no one to miss when they have gone, nothing to make up for, nothing to transform by the power of his love. The icy sameness of perfection quick-freezes the hearts of lovers because it takes away that longing which makes them beat wildly and warmly with the very rhythm of living.

April 16
Does the Person Fit a Perfect World?

Like so many people who decide how man should be, some of the designers for our future mistake the regulation of behavior for that which is really best for human beings. A world in which no one gets sick or lost, a world in which lover's quarrels are worked out in legal briefs—this is the world to beware of because it will be cold and empty for its lack of love. If he is to survive as we know him, man needs freedom and that dangerous realm of vulnerability in which everything can go wrong at any moment. He needs chance meetings, the pain of separation, and the challenge of learning better the lessons of love in order to move toward anything we could regard as an adequate human destiny. Otherwise the future will not be a world in which the machines have become more like men; the men will have become more like machines, clattering out letter-perfect exchanges which eliminate pain but destroy love at the same time. Man needs the freedom to be his playful self, to let himself go, to commit himself to the unknown; he will not survive long with the manuals for the new perfectionism.

April 17
"Be Ye Perfect"?

In this regard, one might well remember that Jesus did not give a new list of detailed regulations to human beings through which they would fulfill their religious duties. He did not even tell man to become perfect, despite the Gospel verse about being perfect as the heavenly Father is. This verse means, according to Scripture scholars, that man must try to be everything that he can be. Jesus saw man as growing but never, in this world, completely

114

outgrowing the human condition. That is why Jesus said that we find and redeem ourselves through the mystery of love. This is the commandment that leads us to life; it is the only commandment that can save us in the restricted homesites and planned communities of tomorrow's perfect world.

April 18
The New Asceticism

Rituals and fasting have been out of date for some time now; you hardly know when Lent occurs, and not too many people miss the fish on Friday. The relaxation of self-imposed penances does not mean, of course, that pain and suffering no longer exist in the world. In fact, the relaxation of the ideal of self-inflicted asceticism allows man to see the trials of his ordinary life as they were always meant to be perceived—as his share of redemptive suffering and as a quite adequate source of ascetic purification. We need to recognize and perhaps affirm the little deaths of every day lest we resign ourselves to the caricature that the cross of Christianity comes with a foam rubber covering these days. In other words, the things which are painful in real life are not meaningless; they are the stuff that redemption is made of. Among the items on the agenda of the new asceticism we might note the following:

The Asceticism of Meetings: Management consultant Peter Drucker once wrote that a man either goes to meetings or he works. We all recognize some truth in that statement, but we also know that, for some reason or other, one's work is more and more involved with meetings of one kind or another. Maybe it is a by-product of the age of dialogue, but I think you know what I mean. And there is plenty of suffering connected with almost any meeting— along with an almost endless list of virtues from patience and fortitude to forbearance and understanding—which is required in order to survive it constructively. To make oneself participate in a difficult or boring discussion

115

requires a kind of incarnation that admirably fulfills the requirements in anybody's book of asceticism. It does more than that, however, because the meetings of today, which seem to interfere with our own work, may also be better settings for the action of the Spirit than pentecostal revivals. When people are really trying to reach each other, despite the difficulties that are always involved, then the conditions for Christian growth are present. Maybe meetings are part of the modern day understanding of the scriptural phrase: "Where two or three are gathered together . . . there I am in the midst of them."

The Asceticism of the Generation Gaps: We may be more conscious now than we have ever been of the complications of remaining in healthy relationships with both our children and our parents. The oft-cited strain on the middle aged from this two-sided pull is familiar to everyone. It was all much simpler in the days when it seemed that this difficulty did not exist, when parents' words still bore the weight of finality, haircuts were shorter, and the older generation conveniently had a shorter life expectancy. The new asceticism lies in the human effort to listen to the young without romanticizing them while caring for the old without isolating them. It is no easy task and it is filled with the kind of death to self that the Gospels identify as redemptive. The persons who are earnestly engaged in these activities need no extra penances at any time.

April 19
Then There Is . . .

the Asceticism of Dealing with Change: This affects everyone in some measure or other, requiring a willingness to give up something of themselves in order to bring about changes that are beneficial for mankind. Most adults have had to face the pain of saying goodbye to a world in which things seemed to run better or at least less hurriedly; they have had to face and try to absorb the implications of changes in almost every aspect of their lives. It is no wonder that we are surfeited with nostalgia crazes. We would like to go back, yet we have to forge ahead even when we are not at all comfortable with the idea. There is a genuine asceticism associated with accommodating ourselves to change, a death to the self involved in every healthy step forward. These lessons are hard to learn; indeed, some people reject them bitterly and miss an understanding of one of the chief sources of transforming suffering in our contemporary experience.

the Asceticism of Being Uncomforted: Many modernday people lament like Rachel, who could not be comforted at the loss of her children; they are undergoing sufferings which are in some way or other a participation in the sufferings of Jesus, and they have not been helped to recognize this. Included in this category are the unvisited people all around us—in short, the widows and orphans, the sick and the crippled of Gospel times. In fact, the uncomforted are sometimes lovers and friends who, sometimes at least, fall out of tune with each other and wonder whether anyone in the whole world understands them. Life is filled with uncomforted moments; it is just too hard to admit to ourselves that we need comforting for fear that we will seem weak or will have to face the loneliness of our own tears. Battling back against this feeling requires all our energies, lest we fall into the quicksand of self-pity. However, the struggle is as redemptive as ever, especially if we try to make ourselves more sensitive to others who need our comfort rather than just moan to ourselves, merely becoming more isolated and miserable.

April 20
Dealing with Ourselves

The men and women who want to live by the Gospels know that life cannot be put off forever—that, sooner or later, if they are to achieve any measure of lasting happiness, they must get better acquainted with themselves. We are literally never too old to find out about ourselves; we can, in fact, learn new and useful tricks that will help us to possess a firmer identity and a surer sense of ourselves. This is part of being a Christian because unless we understand and possess ourselves we cannot mean anything in a lasting way to other people. It is much harder to bring all of ourselves into being—to rid ourselves of the adjustments to self-defeat, for example—than it is to crush ourselves under the rubric of an ancient and unfriendly asceticism. At this time, however, we need the best of each of us involved in the business of living and in the solution of the enormous problems all around us. To come more alive, then, requires, among other things, a little prayer and contemplation, a willingness to assay and redirect the forces of our personalities.

April 21
Where Do You Listen?

We should listen carefully to ourselves as well as to others. We are constantly giving ourselves very clear messages about our likes, dislikes, and conflicts. But we are not accustomed to listening for or to these messages. However, they are there, usually beneath our feelings. Any man who wishes to learn a great deal more about himself can do so by attuning himself more sensitively to them.

We should be a little more patient and forgiving of ourselves, even of the never-ending discoveries about the darndest things that we manage to do or to get into. This is a first step toward a generally more constructive handling of life and its problems. "In your patience," the scriptures tell us, "you will possess yourselves." That insight has never been improved upon. It leads us back to our true selves, to the center of gravity that allows us to move out into life according to the best things that are in us. And that, in the long run, is the darndest thing of all to do in life.

April 22
I Want to Be Happy

These words are made sadder by a tinge of longing for what the afternoon soap operas refer to as a "brighter tomorrow" or something like that; words sung and danced to again in the recently revived Broadway version of *No, No, Nanette;* words through which we look back to the twenties as the time when everyone not only wanted to be but, in fact, was happy. Just remembering Warren G. Harding and Calvin Coolidge would seem to be enough to challenge the nostalgia that glows, like sunlight in the next valley, from that patch of years.

Well, man still wants to be happy; perhaps he remembers the twenties as a time when happiness seemed a goal that was more within his grasp, when, in other words, man had a little more hope than he now possesses. About happiness, of course, there are many theories, and most of us have been tempted to try them all, at one time or another, in our own quest for the brighter tomorrow. For example, let's consider:

Minimalists, who say that a little happiness, or a little less misery, is about the best deal a person can arrange with life, and that he had better settle for this. It is much in fashion now to approach happiness in this way, with rhetoric and ideals as slim and expressionless as a fashion model. These people speak of *making do* with life, of, as a movie essayist in *The New York Times* wrote, "eating chocolates on the afternoon my lover doesn't show up." There is a fragile sadness in approach and an almost quiet sense of defeat; yet many people live this way, afraid to hope for too much because the hurt is so great when nothing comes.

Cool Ones, closely related to the Minimalists, who are able to cover up their vulnerability completely. There is here no admission of entanglement in the human condi-

119

tion, no conscious making peace with it on its own severe terms. By pretending not to care they raise a shield of protection against the fates and call it happiness. This is, of course, unrelated to happiness because it eliminates the necessary condition for happiness—the exposure of the self to the uncertainties of life. These people have actually anticipated the cryogenic experts who want to freeze us until cures can be found for our fatal maladies; they freeze their hearts against life rather than death and count themselves lucky to survive in the uncaring cold. Warmth has terror for them and they live by the words Robert Frost spoke to the orchards, "Fear fifty degrees above more than fifty degrees below."

Illusionists, second cousins to all of these, who distinguish themselves by denying the real possibility of happiness at all: for them, it is a quickly vanishing ghost, one that slips away when you look at it too closely. The Illusionists have a philosophy of life, but being happy has a small and not very significant place in it. They often sound as though they were speaking for effect, telling us the way in which they make do themselves. Thus the great De Gaulle, who certainly never looked happy in public, said to his friend André Malraux (quoted in *Esquire*): "On the whole, women think of love, and men of gold braid or something of that nature. Beyond that, people think only of happiness—which doesn't exist." Close to this kind of viewpoint, of course, is that which tells us that life itself is a species of illusion in which our imagination supplies notions about nonexistent things like hope, love, and trust which torture us because they are always just beyond us.

April 23
Then There Are . . .

Escapists, who, only in their most extreme form, advocate flight from the cutting edges of existence through drugs

120

and other quasi-mystical means. They are ordinarily found in more subtle forms—for example, some Escapists gradually withdraw their investment in people and events in an effort to move back from the flow of time in a search for happiness. Jorge Luis Borges describes such an old lady, a woman who had not been out of her house in Buenos Aires since 1921:

> The last pleasures left her would be those of memory and, later on, of forgetfulness. She recounted historical happenings, but always using the same words in the same order, as if they were the Lord's Prayer, so that I grew to suspect there were no longer any real images behind them. Even eating one thing or another was all the same to her. She was, in short, happy.

This type of withdrawal from everything that is new, from everything that can hurt or stimulate, turns the mind into a shuttered and dusty movie house showing revivals in the darkness that keeps out the day. There was a time when much was made of this as a kind of detachment that was supposedly a sign of advancing sanctity. That is probably why so many saints and heroes—like De Gaulle himself—have looked so serious in the misrepresentations of them that have come down to us through the years.

April 24
And Also . . .

passivists, whose ranks are daily increasing because of man's documented feeling of powerlessness in the face of life's blind and inexorable ways with us. Whatever the reason, these people choose passivity rather than activity as their method of handling life and achieving some measure of happiness. There have always been persons who wait for happiness to come to them, whether in the form of the recognition by others, or the big break, or something of that nature. Happiness seldom arrives or stays very long with the passive person, of course; and the new breed of them is not very happy either. They tend to think that nothing can be done about anything, that you just have to let people be, whether they are your children, your friends, or even your enemies, because to intervene would be to go against the rights or freedom of the other. It is through this brand of passivity that a man supposedly frees himself from concern and reaches a kind of contentment. It is, however, a deadly state in the long run, more of an illusion than some other people make happiness out to be. But, surprising as this may be, there is an increase in this attitude, perhaps out of simple exhaustion, among many persons today.

April 25
What about Happiness Anyway?

What, indeed, can be said about a subject which, like love and longing, is a distinctive experience of human beings, a sign of what we are like and what we need as much as water and sunlight for any kind of life at all? Does a man have a right to happiness in a world in which he will settle for that which gets him through the night? Can he even dream of joy in a world that hardly speaks the word anymore? The answer to all these questions is in the affirmative, of course, especially for the believer who has a clear vision of the meaning and relevance of faith. Religion has seemed anything but good news, preached, as it has been, by the grim and avenging orators who have blistered church ceilings for generations with fiery and fearful visions. I am reminded of Groucho Marx's story of meeting a priest in a hotel; the priest shook his hand and said, "Thanks for putting so much happiness into life," and Groucho, sloping away, replied, "Thanks for taking so much out of it." Some forms of religion have exercised control over men by scaring them to death by translating their urgings toward happiness into temptations to wickedness. This type of religion is falling apart today because it was never religion at all, not so much because it affronted God but because it affronted the dignity of man himself.

Religion is fundamentally *Good News:* that God understands and accepts us in our human condition, and that he wants us to find and to fulfill ourselves in it. This is another way of saying that God wants us to be happy rather than miserable in life and that the practice of religion is meant to support the former rather than the latter option. The basic problems connected with the pursuit of happiness do not have to do with things but with each other. Religion is connected with happiness because it lights up the way we walk with each other in life. It does not point toward a mountain peak of detachment that must be climbed single file; it says that everyday life—the common and homely search for friendship and love—is the source of both revelation and redemption. And these are essential elements of anything we call happiness.

April 26
Revelation . . .

is not something out of long-dead history, a story told long ago in a time we can hardly imagine, much less remember. Revelation takes place and continues in any relationships in which people meet and begin to share life with each other. As friends reveal themselves to us they provide the light that enables us to see ourselves better. Revelation is the kind of human exchange that enables us to learn with each other the deep truths about life that we can never learn separately. This is undeniably a risky business, filled with false moves and small hurts even in the best of us; it is, however, one of the ways we get deeply enough into life to experience what it means to be happy.

Coupled with this, indeed sown deeply into it, is the experience of *redemption*. We stand close enough in everyday life to hurt each other, but, through God's faithful help, we can also heal each other. Jesus has enabled us to reach through the mistakes and misplays of life, to find each other even when we seem to be hopelessly lost, and to make each other whole again. Redemption goes on all the time in the lives of people who love each other. It is never without pain, but it leads to the kind of happiness the Gospels speak of as a treasure that cannot be taken by thieves nor corroded by rust.

This kind of happiness is present in the lives of those who know where their heart is. These people, in other words, have developed a set of values which are deeper and stronger than the pains and apparent limitations of life. The values that are realized in our relationships with each other help us to understand God's ways with us; they also break through the very elements that pose such a threat to less profound contentment. Time, illness, and death destroy what is only superficial pleasure, but they are themselves outwitted by people who have entered deeply enough into life to experience revelation and redemption with each other.

April 27
A Happy Man

Feeling sorry for ourselves is one of the major obstacles to laying hold of more happiness in our own lives. Perhaps no man ever had more reason for self-pity than the famous "elephant man" of last century London. Hideously deformed, rejected by a society in which he could not appear except wearing a shawl-like covering that obscured his features completely, he was befriended by a physician who began the simplest of treatments—he looked on him as a human being, making it possible for him to live in the country and to engage in a limited but varied social life.

April 28
Every Day of His Life . . .

the man's head was so massive and heavy that he had to
sleep propped up on pillows. He finally died trying to sleep
like everyone else, the weight of his head strangling him in
the effort. But before he died he had come to terms with
himself and life; he had sensed his own almost hidden humanity and shared it with others; he reported to his doctor
friend that he was "happy every day of [his] life." The
memory of his courage and the affection and respect of his
physician friend have the power to move us still; we can
all dig deeper inside ourselves for the resources to scatter
self-pity and to find some kind of happiness every day of
our lives.

April 29
Breaking Bad News

Everybody says it should be done . . . by someone else, if
at all possible. None of us enjoys the idea of informing
other persons about death, illness, or the other failures
that touch their lives. Even husband and wife can avoid
painful truths, skirting around them, banking on presump-
tions of infused knowledge rather than difficult truths
honestly faced. How many statements of regrets have
begun like this: "Well, I thought you knew about it all the
time. . . ."

There are certain callings in life where confronting painful realities is commonplace. Doctors, clergy, even teachers
sometimes must tell others things that will change their
lives forever. Sometimes there are handoff plays between
these professions—"Let the priest tell her" . . . "I think it
would be better if the doctor did it" . . . or, as the buck

makes its final pass in our direction, somebody says "I think that *you* ought to do it. . . ."

What do we do when, sooner or later, we are called to break bad news to another person? Do we think mostly of our own feelings, trying to protect these as best we can while we forget the feelings of the other? Or do we attempt to come to terms with ourselves and then to enter the situation with as much of ourselves as we can? It is not an easy choice—and we may end up compromising these positions —but it is worth the try to put as much of ourselves in it as we can.

The reasons for this benefit both the other person and ourselves. As far as we are concerned, sharing a difficult truth with someone is one of the prime opportunities for the experience of meaning in life. We don't break bad news for this purpose, of course, but we cannot help but grow when we seriously try to be part of another individual's life. More of us comes to life when we take this seriously; it is the kind of growth that nobody can take away from us. Staying away from difficult events never deepened anybody's sense of self; it merely offers the illusion of escape while it springs a trap of its own.

More importantly, we do something rich and real for another person when we enter into his experience rather than treat it like a time bomb that may go off in our faces. We give people hope in difficult moments, not by false heartiness, but just by being with them in a genuine way. Hope can exist even when the news we break seems to be of a hopeless situation—a fatal disease, a lost loved one, a final examination failure. The hope comes because we refuse to give up on others, because we still care and do not write them off. That is what finally defeats people, being checked off as hopeless in the eyes of others. There is no event so desperate that we cannot give hope and life in it if we still believe in and stick with the other person. This has been demonstrated in work with terminally ill patients for whom medical hope has been abandoned. Human hope can still sustain them and see them home at last in peace and dignity. This is no less true in any other situation where bad news must be broken. We grow and enlarge life when we give ourselves along with the news, good or bad, that we must share with others.

April 30
Does Anything Go?

It is a dangerous overstatement to say, for any group of persons, that anything goes. This attitude, however, is certainly a staple of the new mythology of sex. As marriage counselor David Mace remarked on the subject recently, some people think that "as long as you break no bones, you have no cause for worry." Sexual relations are not just erotic gymnastics, however, and, while no one would want to return to Victorian prudery, it might be well to keep the whole situation in human perspective. The first thing to recall is that sexual innovation will not solve or make up for deeper difficulties that reside in the marital relationship. Secondly, despite the enthusiasm of certain advisers, it is still possible for people to get hurt in many ways when they emphasize athletic technique rather than tender sharing in their sexual behavior. Not the least of those things which can be hurt are the feelings of the couple involved; it is very difficult to heal this kind of hurt if it arises from carelessness, a self-absorption of the other partner, or a lack of tenderness which kills the essence of mutual sharing. Married couples have great freedom in marriage but that freedom only has value in terms of what they mean to each other.

May

May 1
Some Myths about Friendship

The **Friends-Are-People-Who-Tell-Each-Other-Off** myth is currently popular because of the distorted view one gets from looking at reality through the eyes of confrontation group enthusiasts; it is their version of the ill-tempered cry about the source of political power, only now it states that "all relationship comes from the barrel of a gun." To be close is equated with the freedom to fire on a friend at will, to tell him, in exquisitely detailed terms, everything that is wrong with him. He, of course, is supposed to remain your friend through this stormy weather; at least he is not allowed to flinch or he will be penalized for copping out on what is good for him. This myth generates a curious tension: it becomes a magnetic force pulling people toward it; once under its spell, they find it difficult to disengage themselves, as though they were irreversibly committed to hostile exchange as the only way of "opening up" to one another. A lot of grim-looking people seem to believe that this is the only mode through which friendship can be achieved and maintained; to them, freeflowing bile is somehow an anointing of the Spirit.

On close examination, the friend who insists on the right to tell you off may not be much of a friend at all; in fact, he may be quite lost in his own inner confusions, meeting needs that he has not learned to name by directing his anger outward. The friend who defines his relationship to you solely in terms of his own feelings ("You make me very upset;" "You are getting me irritated;" "You make me feel uncomfortable when you talk about that") is clearly an individual who has not emerged from his own

128

world of special self-concern. He isn't finished pecking away at the shell of his own narcissism; any friend who talks about his own reactions all the time is not yet mature enough to give or to receive friendship. This type, however, likes the myth about friendship coming from confrontation; it makes life a lot easier but not any more rewarding for him.

May 2
That Friends Are Always Together . . .

is a notion perpetuated by the emotionally needy, the persons so fearful that they may lose their friends that they never let them out of their sight. True friendship, however, is made to survive separation, even as, in the long run, it is meant to survive death itself. If you take a close look at the lives of people who are true friends to one another, you will discover that constant closeness is not an absolute requirement for their relationship. As a matter of fact, one of the best measures of friendship is how well it flourishes when persons are, for whatever reason, separated from one another. There is a deep mystery in this, to be sure; it is strange that a relationship in which people long to be together is so often characterized by their being apart. This is true in the most profound relationships of love; as life progresses, as children come and obligations accumulate, even the most devoted husbands and wives find that their moments of being quietly and completely together become fewer and fewer. Their friendship—and anyone who does not realize that lovers must also be friends has a great deal to learn—must be made of sturdier stuff than "togetherness." Friends who do not realize this—who are made restless and anxious about what their friend is doing out there somewhere without them—are really experiencing their own lack of maturity in the fact that they are not peaceful in the relationship. Friendship that is true is an almost indestructible commodity; it can stand the ravages of time and distance, it can take the minor and major separations that demand patience but build peace in the sharing that is sealed by the Spirit.

May 3
. . . Or Always Feel Deeply about Things

Closely related to the foregoing, this myth claims that every moment must be severely taxed for all the emotional content that it possesses, that friendship cannot be friendship without heavy breathing and soulful glances, that every meeting of friends requires a baring of the soul, a confession of the week's secret anguishes. Actually, friends are supposed to be able to *enjoy* each other in the very simple but deep meaning of that term: They must be able to be relaxed and at ease in each other's presence, able to be quiet or just to smile in common appreciation of some shared event. Friends are the people you have fun with, not the ones you must wrestle with in spiritual discomfort at every meeting. The friendship that generates tension, like a hum around high wires, is artificial and will quiver and snap under strain. Genuine friendship has a lot of give in it; it seldom needs to be drawn taut.

May 4
And Two More

The **Friends-Never-Let-You-Down** myth is the unrealistic kind of myth that leads us to make impossible demands on our friends—to expect them to be lesser gods or at least mind readers who always respond in exactly the right measure to our needs. As a matter of fact, in the human condition the best of friends are bound to disappoint each other at least once in a while. The marvel is that authentic friendship endures despite these cracks in its facade. Friends need not be perfect friends in order to be very good friends; lasting relationships, wherever they are found, bear the scars that go with the hazards of living.

The person who demands a perfect friend or lover is merely condemning himself and the relationship to a large dose of frustration. The miracle of grace that testifies that genuine friendship is the work of the Spirit resides in the way people who wound each other are also capable of healing each other, the way people who fail each other can also forgive each other. Friendship is not a smooth rink on which a marvelous and errorless brand of figure-skating goes on without even scratching the surface. Friendship is a broken turf, full of the promise of spring, but also marred by the ditches and holes in which friends may stumble as they try to stick together. Friendship is an imperfect work if it is anything, something we get better at if we make the effort every day, but never glossy smooth at any stage in life.

The **Friends-Have-To-Take-You-As-You-Are** myth. The operative word here is *have*, because if friends *have* to take you, then they are being friends on the terms you dictate, and that is the death of any genuine mutuality. Now it may well be that good friends do take us as we are, but they do so freely and without compulsion; their friendship is an act of love and not an act of duty. Many people, however, feel that there is no burden on them to modify themselves in order to make themselves more worthy of their good friends. It is, of course, very convenient to skip this self-examination and to place all the responsibility for patience and understanding on those around us. In reality, this myth is just an offshoot of the myth that makes our own reactions the complete measure of our willingness to relate to others. The sad thing about the individual, who believes that the burden for accepting him is on his friends, is that sooner or later, when there is no equal pulling of the weight in the relationship, friends begin to drop away one by one. The man who always wants others to accept him ends up alone with the great love of his life, himself, and he may always wonder why. The answer is simple: He never got far enough out of himself to be a friend to anyone.

May 5
Generativity

Generativity is a jargonish word for a dimension of maturity that we must all deal with whether we are parents or not; it is a part of our commitment to life that is important even if we are not married. This term, which unfortunately conjures up visions of kilowatt hours, refers to the stage of personal development during which an individual is challenged to look beyond his own interest and his own years and into the future with a sense of caring rather than just the passion of curiosity. In other words, the adult estate is reached when, having dealt with our own identity, we can concern ourselves with handing on and enlarging the life of the next generation. If you want a good sign of being grown up, don't look for sexual prowess, a massive limousine or a knowing way with headwaiters. Look for the person who has come to terms sufficiently with his own life to be able to give his energies to the lives of his children—whether these are his own children or those who are, for one reason or another, in his care or under his influence. The generative person—man or woman—gives away what cannot be purchased and cannot really be lost once it is given: the loving concern that opens life up to the growing generation.

Being generative, then, does not just mean being genital, although it includes this in a mature understanding and integration of sexuality into life. It is a funny thing that the movies that are marked "Adults Only" are hardly that at all; in their exploitation of all age groups these films often betray the destructive self-absorption of their producers and directors. A generative person is not—repeat *is not*—just the middle-aged individual whose love affair with his own lost youth leads him to wear beads and munch organic foods in order to fit into the ranks of young people. That person, like the teacher who plays favorites instead of playing fair, is a victim of his own needs to such an extent that he cannot enlarge the lives of those around him. He can only drain others for his own nourishment, trying to squeeze out of them a sense of himself that is always just beyond him. This is a terrible species of loneliness, self-inflicted and almost always fatal.

Being generative does not call for a superman or superwoman either. It is, in fact, just what ordinary persons have a marvelous talent for when they are themselves and have learned some of life's hard lessons of loving. Average people, unadorned and undefended, break out of themselves and the search for their own comfort when they continue to grow in their mature years. They have the human sense of direction that is strengthened by the Spirit; there is nothing sentimental about giving up yourself in order to bequeath life to others in the here and now. Generative love—the kind found in good parents, teachers, pastors, and even bachelor uncles—flows from an act of faith in the possibilities of today's children, not just from an expectation that they will like us for our concern or that we will be paid back for it here or hereafter. It is a commitment made for the sake of the young persons themselves, because, in and for themselves, they are worth caring about. This is the kind of love Jesus preached, the kind of love that allows people to discover their own lives out of the shadow of our own life. We remember our parents in a golden-rule kind of way—in order to do for others what they have done for us.

May 6
The Parent Trap

All America loves a godfather or at least Marlon Brando's version of him; Americans have, however, grown suspicious of parents, father figures, and the general run of adults. Perhaps it has always been so—the rising generation tests its strength against its elders in engagements that sometimes seem to tell the story of history itself. Mid-spring is a time for remembering parents and others who help us to grow, that is, if we can fit them into calendars that are already crowded with weddings, bar-mitzvahs, and other rites of passage. Both the book and the movie entitled *The Godfather* are terribly oversentimentalized narratives about men who are cutthroats by any other name; you really do not need an overemotional jag to think for a moment about parents. Too much emotion can be as indicative as too little, as we all know, and the things worth remembering do not necessarily call for tears.

May 7
I Remember My Father

My father died in May, and I have a rich store of memories to draw on when I think of him. If I had to choose one of my father's characteristics, I think it would be his gentleness, the gentleness of a strong man who was secure in his identity and his convictions. He had the kind of manly gentleness that modern-day commentators describe as difficult for many men to achieve because they are constrained to be hard or to seem uncaring in the face of life's strange tides. Being gentle never seemed to require much effort on my father's part; being strong did not either. He was himself—the kind of man in whose presence one could learn the lessons of manhood. It was not that he explicitly taught these to you out of fear that you might never learn them otherwise. It was more that you could not help but learn from a man who was so unself-consciously manly himself. He lived a long time, a good life, and his last blessing was that he died sitting in his own living room talking to my mother. He had just spoken a few gentle words to her in his marvelously deep voice about what good care she had taken of him. Death had to take him by surprise; it could never have beaten him in a fair fight.

May 8
Being a Parent Is Hazardous to Your Health

There are several reasons why being a parent may be hazardous to your health. Many of these reasons could be
found at the consulting-room door of Dr. Freud, who
helped make man so much more aware of himself. It is no
secret that man is sometimes too self-conscious about his
motives and that an endless and unforgiving searching of
himself may make it harder for him to be spontaneous in
the human condition.

Parents are well-known to be largely responsible for
most of their children's faults and few of their good points.
If this accusation isn't enough, parents are sometimes
charged with being responsible for what is wrong with
their grandchildren as well: "Mother, if you had raised me
differently, I would have raised him differently!" Don't
you hear those sentiments echoed around the neighborhood once in a while? In a reversal of the biblical
image, parents are visited with the sins of their children,
who, for their own part, sometimes affect the looks and in-
dicting style of Old Testament prophets. With the accuracy
and relish which Transylvanian vampires display for jugular veins, children find the flaws and sore spots in their
parents' character.

Parents are dumb, hopelessly naive, or at least vaguely
dreamy; that is the message of a great many television
series which, during the course of a week, manage to insult
adult intelligence, character, and good will. It would not be
bad if these programs could help us laugh at ourselves a
little more. Most situation comedies fail not because they
make fools of grownups; they fail as comedies to deliver
the grace notes of humor which lessen our burdens so
effectively. Most adults feel the tension of the double-bind
of trying to be generative toward their children and lovingly responsive to their parents at the same time. The le-

gions of the retired are also the legions of the lonely, despite the smiling ads from Sun City. It is a staggering emotional order for the retiree to respond to youth and old age while trying to save something for themselves—something of their own lives with each other.

May 9
Three Good Things

A Greek philosopher once wrote that a man's life is complete if he has accomplished three things: written a book, planted a tree, and sired a son. Most men, for one reason or another, don't get all these done in a lifetime. Planting trees is easy, but writing a book is much more difficult; after you are finished with either of these tasks, however, you must surrender the finished product to the winds and the water, to the critics and the readers. Siring a son is not a mammoth initial undertaking. Any number of people, fit and unfit, willingly and unwillingly, manage to do that every year. The hardest part merely begins with the birth of a son or daughter and is sustained through the long, demanding years of presence to the growing child as he or she moves toward a separate life.

May 10
And the Hardest One

It is, indeed, harder by far to sire a child than to plant a tree or write a book, because it means that a man and a woman must face that most delicate and testing of responsibilities—seeing a child through until he can take care of himself and then, loving him in a new way, permits him to do just that. The most important experiences of life are involved in these kinds of transactions; the fact that they are always composed of or comprise joy and pain merely validates them as firsthand evidence that we have truly been alive. One might wonder at the self-confidence with which some people decide to do without children. Will these people, at some time in their lives, wonder about this decision or about the depth of the lives they have led? Perhaps many will not, for there are trees to plant and books to write. Some, however, may sense an aching estrangement from their own possibilities, an estrangement which flows from decisions that can no longer be reviewed or revised. They may miss some of the harder parts of being a parent; they may feel more free and less alive as a result.

May 11
Facts and Fancies about American Parents

Fancy: Parents are materialistic, irreligious, and have lost the spirit of self-sacrifice that made America great. In sum, they are like the last generation to inhabit the declining Roman Empire.

Fact: Such accusations have been raised against every generation since the Roman Empire and they probably could have been made against most generations that preceded it. Modern American parents bear up fairly well under the burden of strain they feel every day. The remarkable thing is that they keep trying to do their best even though they have more than their share of mishaps and make more than their share of mistakes. Anybody who listens closely to average parents knows that they are more debt-bound than orgy-oriented, that they make steady personal and material sacrifices for their children and their country, that they still long for the stable virtues and the more enduring values, that they may not be perfect but that they are hardly a hard-hearted and perverse generation. There may not have been many generations in all of history that have acknowledged their faults and tried to mature themselves with as much seriousness of purpose and expenditure of energy as the present group of adults. Their inheritance, for all their humanly flawed good will, has been thunder and lightning on all sides. Such seems to be the natural heritage of adults—the bad weather that blows almost without letup across the lives of grownups. It surely does not help to wail and weep in the metaphors of Roman wreckage.

Fancy: Well, this adult generation is actually wrecking some of our most cherished institutions—marriage, for example. Doesn't that make them a little more Roman?

Fact: Actually, the facts show that marriage is one of the things that this generation of adults does take quite seriously. They want it to work as a successful personal relationship; they want friendship and trust together more than unbridled sexuality. Any institution shudders when people take it seriously, when people think it should be made to work effectively. As a matter of fact, despite the longing for the good old days, marriage is more popular now than ever. There is a higher percentage of Americans married now than there was in 1890.

Fancy: Well, parents don't seem to have much faith. They don't go to church like they used to.

Fact: This fancy is like the argument made to wisely nodding heads that they do not make cars the way they used to; it is a good thing, as anyone who can recall cranks and constant flats can tell you. The fact that Sunday church attendance has declined does not necessarily mean that people have less faith. There are those who argue, quite cogently I believe, that people are looking now for a deeper kind of faith, for a system of belief that will make sense out of and have application for the long and hectic weeks of their everyday lives.

May 12
Learning to Trust a Child

Trust is like the weather in that it gets more talk than action. Lots of the talk has to do with the demand for trust, a great contemporary battle cry that grabs the parental psyche at its sorest and guiltiest point. The story of trust, however, lies in learning to invest it in others rather than just collecting it for ourselves. Nothing grows that is not trusted, of course, and nothing kills living things like overprotection and smothering concern. Every parent who would be truly generative must trust his children or cripple them. The hard part is doing it, letting kids test their own powers in order to find their own paths and their true selves. Yes, but the children might hurt themselves, or somebody else might hurt them, or, during those long, lying-awake-at-night-agonies which parents know so well, they themselves might be hurt terribly by a betrayed trust or by the intervention of unpredictable fates or forces. It would be comforting if this element of risk could be factored out of the kind of loving which parents give when they trust their children. But then, of course, it would be an experience too shallow to give life or produce growth, too bound around with defenses and protective devices to count in the contest of life. The mystery of life itself is summed up in that finely shaded moment in which we are asked to trust another wholeheartedly. It should really be described as trusting *open*-heartedly, because this is precisely what trusting your children really demands day after day in generation after generation—a heart made vulnerable for the sake of the young who must be trusted if they are ever to grow up. It is enough to take your breath away, this business of meaning it when we trust others; it is one of the things we remember about the parents who instinctively knew our need for trust.

May 13
God Talk

It is not surprising that the symbols and analogies that are used in the Christian tradition to describe our understanding of God depend on our understanding of man and, specifically, on our appreciation of parenthood and the meaning of generativity. The mysteries in our understanding of God which gradually fall away a little bit at a

139

time do so as we penetrate more clearly the realities of sharing and deepening human life. There is a sacred business at the bottom of all this, this love of parents and children over which the Spirit broods and in which he is present. Life's painful beauty does not reside in waterfalls or in cloud racks shredding golden against the sunset; rather, it is in relationships, in the mystery of love's beginning and growth as we share ourselves and our lives with each other, in reaching out to each other, hurting and healing each other in the process—life lies in knowing these things firsthand. An understanding of God yields itself to lovers more than to dreamy mystics. We speak of God in the language we learn to speak and understand together, not in the beautiful thoughts we may have when we are alone.

May 14
A Final Word on Friendship

You cannot buy it or wheedle it out of others successfully. The truest path to friendship lies in the effort to make our best selves available to others, to strip ourselves of the obscuring dross of selfishness, and to give more than we demand. The man or woman who becomes even partially mature—who displays a real rather than a false and ensnaring self—will discover that friendship happens and that it does not need to be manufactured.

May 15
The Late Great Virtue

Faithfulness, of course, is not dead; it just doesn't get around much any more. It is not that people do not care about it. Deep down, by whatever name they recognize it, faithfulness is still important. But it is little emphasized and hardly discussed as a compelling part of life in an age that has adjusted its thinking and feeling to failures in faithfulness and clouds of unknowing surrounding belief.

Faithfulness is like a great actor who remains unemployed because there are no parts written for him any more; sometimes there just does not seem to be any place for faithfulness in the shooting script of contemporary life. Men fancy themselves more liberated when they do not believe and more sophisticated in avoiding the relationships that demand faithfulness—they prefer to swim playfully in the shallows rather than to take the risk of getting caught out in the deep waters of everyday life.

There is another aspect of this as well. We are all familiar with the old attitude—bite the bullet, make the best of the very worst of human relationships, and hold the whole thing together even when the marriage or pledge of service has fallen to pieces. And despite the fact that faithfulness —especially that connected with marriage and states of service in the church—was so rigidly and legally interpreted in the past, we have witnessed a modern-day rejection of that lifeless and distorted notion of it. In marriage courts and other procedures, church officials have come to shift the burden of their concerns in order to make it easier for persons to end marriages or other commitments that were once regarded as sacrosanct. Everyone realizes, of course that the new attitude is a step in the right direction, a human move that has Godliness in it, a welcome recognition that an unyielding application of the law sometimes caused more death than life and ultimately led to the disintegration of law itself.

The contemporary problem is similar to the situation of a small boat when all the passengers suddenly rush to one side; balance and stability are lost and the boat may go under as well. With all the new sensitivity to the fact that some marriages were never marriages at all, that some promises of service were never designed to last forever, the current emphasis has been on exploring those conditions of personality that diminish our capacity for binding choices or permanent promises. We have been trying to make it possible for some persons to get out of certain situations as gracefully and with as little emotional hurt as possible. That is all to the good, but it is this kind of rushing to one side of the boat that may pull the anchors of fidelity and commitment completely out of the water.

It is time to look again at faithfulness and all that it implies, if only to validate the experience of those many people who are still serious about their promises and who are beginning to wonder, under the pressures of so much contemporary psyche-searching, whether faithfulness means anything anymore or not. Life would be unbearable—it would be without meaning as well—if faithfulness were not one of the rich and indispensable experiences through which we find and enlarge our humanity.

May 16
Some Faces of Faithfulness

Faithful to Ourselves: this fundamental orientation toward the truth of our own personalities is basic to the understanding and development of any other kind of faith or belief in life. It is best nurtured by adults who are themselves faithful human beings rather than by grim and duty-conscious schoolmasters with birch rods in their hands. It suggests the voyage of discovery that every truly human life is and the fact that the man who reaches out toward his own destiny has a better feel for faithfulness than the timid man who hides behind uncomprehended duty and never knows who he is at all. A man cannot be faithful without becoming more of himself; the very act of faith—whether in God, in spouse, or in one's own possibilities—means we make ourselves more present in life. There is more of us there afterwards than there was before; it is inevitable because we never say *yes* in life without finding more of life. Unfaithfulness is a refusal to become, a rejection of life, a refusal to be oneself. The man who has no faith has little life to offer anyone else; small wonder, then, that his commitments are shallow or that his love is reserved for himself. He is just not present enough in life to make a lasting and enlarging difference to another person.

May 17
Faithful to Our Word

Promise them anything, they tell us, and sometimes we get
to believing that ourselves. What difference do our words
make in a world that already has too much in the way of
words, deceitful and otherwise? Modern men tend to forget that they are defined by their words, that in a very real
sense, they are not what they eat but what they say. This is
true only when men have remembered the sacred nature of
words and use them in making flesh of themselves to the
world around them. There is power in the word of a faithful man because what he says matches what he is, because
what he says is consistent with who he is, because his
speech and his person are integrated aspects of his presence to us. We have almost forgotten the significance of
this because we have heard too many political speeches
and unconvincing sermons. When a man speaks he tries to
get the truth of himself and his feelings out in the open;
when he realizes the importance of this, he chooses the
words that are true to himself and that say as finely and as
fully as possible what he believes. Life is a struggle to
speak the truth of ourselves before men; it has always been
easier to choose the babble of supposed gifts of tongues, or
the arcane phrases of the supposed mystics. The most important things in life about ourselves demand a fidelity to
clear words that is infinitely more demanding than
charisms and cabala; there is more prayer in a few honest
words about ourselves than in all the freaked-out and far-
out people and places in which faith is supposed to dwell.

May 18
Faithful to Those We Love

Ourselves, our words, the men and women we are: that is
all we have to give to each other, and it is the most that we

143

have to give to each other as well. Love means being with each other, not in the frightened clustering together of people who are afraid of the dark in the world around them, but in the richer and more abiding presence of people who are so present to each other that they can never really be apart. Friends know that they are present to each other in a special way which cannot be measured even though they may be a continent apart. Men and women who love know that their fidelity is not a sour and burdensome promise to behave when they are apart; it is rather the sense of themselves as belonging to each other that comforts, strengthens, and makes life mean something even when they must be away from each other. People who have loved can never be completely alone again in life, even though they may feel loneliness in a sharper way than others; that is the sign that they have made a difference, that they have been faithful, that they have, in other words, been alive.

These lessons are learned slowly—and, as a matter of fact, only by people who are willing to learn them slowly. They cannot be grabbed at, hammered down and secured in an afternoon or a weekend. Faithfulness is not a padlock or a burden on a free spirit; instead, it is the sign —and a great and glowing one indeed—of those persons who have tapped the deep wells of the world God made for us to make our own. The best lessons of faithfulness are read in the lives of those who have been brave enough to step toward each other in the truth of themselves and thereby discover the only way that men can find true love. It begins with a step in faith but it does not end there; it only asks persons for more of themselves in a lifelong working out of the meaning of genuine faith.

They have to think about staying with each other despite the stress or changes of life. They fall out of love only when they can no longer make their true selves present to each other, or when they have grown weary of it, or, in the rush of events, have let go of each other's hands. It is hard for lovers to be faithful because life is so unrelenting in its pressures, hard for lovers to keep each other in focus and to hear each other over the din of life's activities. That, however, is the way lovers are faithful to each other.

They must be sensitive to love as its seasons change, as it is now passionate and strong, or suddenly peaceful and calm. Lovers not only search for the words that sing of their faithful love, they must also strain to hear the words as yet unformed in the hearts of each other. They must learn to wait, remaining silent while something heals, or until they can look into each other's eyes again. They must be ready to comfort even when they would prefer comfort themselves: Love's faithfulness is told in a painfully beautiful tongue that is seldom a shout but often a whisper. This is the true gift of tongues which the world would like to learn to speak again.

May 19
Can We Keep Our Promises?

It is logical to ask, now that we are so much more aware of what is in man, whether he can believe in anything or in anyone for very long; after all, he drags the weight of history in his own unconscious, and he is as surprised as he is surprising in the why and how of his adventures and relationships. Does he really ever know enough about himself and his moods to choose a fixed course in love or in life?

These questions are fair because so many individuals now explain major changes in their lives by statements like the following: "I am a different person now than I was when I was . . ." (*married, ordained;* fill in the space to match the situation). And for many people this is a fair description of their life experience. Still quite immature and out of touch with their own identity, they entered into relationships or positions which were unrealistic or inappropriate for them. Later, after life had lined their faces a bit, they developed a better sense of themselves; indeed, it may be that they finally came to a genuine sense of themselves for the first time. They are right when they say that they are different now; it is the kind of melancholy truth that is underscored by the high rate of divorces among marriages entered into by teen-agers.

"I didn't know what I was doing. . . ." This is probably true for many people who, even though they might have had some understanding of their own personalities at the time, never really comprehended the nature or full dimensions of what they got themselves into. They may have persevered for a long time but not out of faithfulness; most were motivated by fear or shame or sometimes sheer necessity—motives which can now be recognized but no longer accepted as valid or sustaining.

Understanding these situations is vital to our understanding of man; they raise, however, a disturbing question: Is faithfulness a virtue reserved for the completely mature person? Is it something that has no meaning unless one is completely grown and in full possession of his or her own identity? To claim that this is true would be to price fidelity of any kind out of the market for the great mass of the human race. Few of us are completely grown up, but that does not mean that we cannot understand or commit ourselves faithfully to each other or to certain tasks in life.

May 20
Growing in Faithfulness

Indeed, faithfulness as a concept and as an experience grows like everything else associated with human beings. It may expand admirably, and deepen itself so that it is a remarkably sturdy phenomenon in the true adult, but it can be present in us even when we are young and faltering. As a matter of fact, it is in coming to terms with the meaning of faithfulness in our lives that we achieve our identity; the concepts are profoundly interrelated. It is no surprise that Erik Erikson, the distinguished psychoanalyst, in his famous scheme of life's developmental stages, matches the attainment of identity with the development of the virtue of fidelity. Knowing who we are so that we can give our true selves to life goes along with a sense of fidelity to the person we are still becoming.

May 21
How Do We Learn It?

Faithfulness, in other words, is related to maturity, but one need not have achieved absolute maturity in order to give a faithful response in life. Fidelity grows along with the rest of us; we get better at it but none of us ever gets perfect at it. In other words, faithfulness fits the nature of human persons. It responds to a deep and appropriate need in their patterns of development and it enables them to express their continued growth throughout life. The fact that we can make mistakes about ourselves should not discourage us in our own lives or in our judgment about the human race. The fact that we can change and develop, that we can become more subtly attuned to ourselves and to our life situations does not mean that faithfulness is impossible or even improbable. These realizations point to the human elements that go into building the personal fidelity that enables us to become more rather than less true to ourselves and to others as we grow through life. That is not to insist, as we did for too long, on the external coercions to fidelity that all too often failed to recognize the need for internal realities; it is rather to focus on the years and experiences that build authentic faithfulness in a person. Scaring children into doing what they are told lest they burn for an aeon; drumming Prussian rhythms of duty into their heads—these are not the avenues to fuller fidelity. Faithfulness needs care at the bud stage through human acceptance and inspiration, especially through providing growing children with models of adults who can display in their own lives the full growth of faithfulness.

May 22
When Is Worry Normal?

Worry, a word suggesting a mixture of striving and apprehension on our part, is normal in the sense that it is a common human reaction known and experienced by everybody. It is normal to feel worried, for example, when some danger threatens; we would be in bad shape if apprehensive fear could be bred out of us, as the Russians spoke of doing for their cosmonauts in order to prepare them better for their interstellar wanderings. That kind of move, never attempted in practice, would doom the fearless to an early death; edginess is a component in generating a healthy caution for responding to dangerous situations. Worry, in one form or another, is essential to survival, especially when it makes us inspect ourselves or our environment more carefully before making our response to a particular situation. Whether worry remains normal in the sense of being healthy depends on how we interpret its messages, on how, in other words, we feed it into our judgmental processes. A man may have good reasons to worry a little about his health because he notices some physical symptom; he goes to the doctor and does something about it. That is normal worry used in a sensible way. Another man may be worried about his health but, instead of doing something about it, continues to overeat or overdrink. He may get very anxious but, for complicated reasons, handles the worry in an abnormal and self-destructive way. You must listen carefully to the voices of anxiety, get them in perspective, and then make an intelligent decision on how to handle them.

May 23
Who, Me Worry?

Winters of discontent are not allowed to come until December, but the age of anxiety covers the whole calendar of the human spirit. There is almost always something to worry about—the hounds of care go on nibbling at the edges of sleep or sport even when a bland coolness is one of the most widely used defenses of the day. Indeed, were it not for anxiety in its many forms, there would be no need for the mask of coolness at all. So, what does a man do about worry, especially when the gospel tells him to be without care? The average man finds it hard to read that injunction with the kind of resigned surrender toward life that it seems to ask of him. It is just not easy to live without worries in a world that is so filled with deadlines and payment dates that birth certificates might well be printed on balance sheets.

May 24
Can You Stare It Down?

One logical step is to stare down anxiety—or at least to take a closer look at it—long enough to sort out its various forms. A man ought to know his enemy, especially when it lives so intimately with him. Just turning to meet anxiety is an improvement over the breathless effort to stay a step ahead of its unfolding shadows. Anxiety, for example, can refer to vague and unnamed fears, the ones we cannot quite get into focus although we daily feel the brush of their chill phantom surfaces. It is that cold and clammy grip on the heart that tells us that something—anything, for that matter—might happen to us, the "disturbing uneasiness" of which the dictionary writer so self-assuredly speaks. But the lexicographer is secure in the double protection of his books and well-ordered life. It is a different thing to have these feelings and to find what ruin they can visit in our own lives and work. Many times a man might say that he could handle a nervous situation better if only he could put a name to it, if only he could force it into the light to see it more clearly.

May 25
To Take the First Step in . . .

organizing ourselves for life in the too-often christened "age of anxiety," we sometimes need the assistance of someone else to do it properly. If we are going to search out the family tree of our worries, talking about it is a big help. Assistance of this sort need not always be professional; a friend who listens fairly well and does not interrupt too often can aid us greatly in getting at the origins of our uneasiness. However, we must be willing to talk, at least to ourselves, and to be biblically honest about it into the bargain. For example, the individual who has felt edgy all day—and who may have taken it out indirectly on family and friends around him—may discover, even beneath a glacial sheet of coolness, that there is something he cares about, something that is vaguely in danger. It may be as simple as jealousy of another that we do not want to admit to ourselves; jealousy, like a black and hungry mold, eats silently at the heart, turning a man prickly and uneasy when he refuses to accept what he is really experiencing. The live core of the anxiety is not altered by wallpapering the personality with affected indifference; nor is anxiety spooked out of the heart by denying that it is there in the first place. In facing this we are at the beginning of wisdom about our anxieties. We may worry a good deal about imaginary things, but we worry even more about things that are really true about us, the mottled verities of our shortcomings, the things about our temper or our tantrums that are too true to accept as part of our personal belongings. These truths cause anxiety because they drive a wedge between the image of what we like to think of ourselves and the image of what we truly are; it is through this fissure of inconsistency that the fumes of anxiety pour into our hearts. This is not the only kind of anxiety, of course, but it accounts for a fair portion of our sleepless nights and churning stomachs. The point is that this worry loses much of its force when we deal straightforwardly with it, when, in other words, we can find its real name in the truth about ourselves. The biblical injunction about not worrying may well refer to not letting ourselves be destroyed by worries that, with a little introspection, we can do battle with quite effectively ourselves.

May 26
The Basic Battle . . .

with this type of anxiety is waged with the weapon of self-knowledge; the surer we are of our identity, the less we have to manufacture one, and the less vulnerable we are to the uneasiness that flows over us when life, in one form or another, catches up with our inconsistency. The person, for example, who pictures himself as handsome and talented when he is really average in looks and abilities gets defensive about his illusions when others do not respond to him in the same way he does to himself. His assertion that others are against him is merely an effort to cover the cracks in his unrealistic self-portrait. Life is filled with anxious moment for the man who is bent on preserving or enhancing an image that does not square with the facts. Perhaps this is most clearly observable in public figures—celebrities of sorts—who communicate their own sense of inner strain to us as they strive to keep the right mask on for their audiences.

The scriptural urging to be without care brings us back to facing the truth about ourselves; it cannot refer to a mindless optimism about life. Nor does it mean that a man should never experience any anxiety, as we will observe shortly. This biblical attitude suggests that much unnecessary worry arises when we do not have ourselves properly in focus. The defensive man is so busy holding the pieces of himself together that he cannot be open in a healthy way to life. Excessive care for the heavily retouched self-image that is a contemporary form of idolatry is the enemy of the life of the Spirit about which the gospels warn us.

May 27
When Is Worry Neurotic?

Neurotic anxiety takes us beyond simple reluctance to sort out our worries reasonably and into the psychological territory where anxiety strongly controls an individual's reactions in major aspects of his life. There is a pattern to this, a stylized manner of dealing with life also associated with faulty self-understanding that becomes increasingly grotesque and painful. A classic example of neurotic anxiety is termed a phobia—a strong fear associated with certain behavior that comes to dominate a person's life and activity. In other words, the neurotically anxious person must avoid certain situations or objects or find himself overwhelmed by his fears. Phobias come in long lists—not all of them are as serious as others—and the reasons for their existence can be found only in the emotional lives of those suffering from them. The person has learned to stay away from certain things—flying, heights, elevators—as a way of keeping himself from experiencing the worry he would feel if forced into these situations. The problem is that the individual must build his life around his particular phobia; that is not always easy, especially in a world of high-rises and jet planes. When a deep neurotic anxiety is present, the person may find himself crippled in a major way from participating in life; he may, for example, never leave his home, or he may be forced to give up his work. Such anxiety needs psychological treatment more than prayers or hearty reassurances. One of the great tragedies of life is our sometime failure to read the signs of this kind of problem in the lives of those close to us; it is often accompanied by a subsequent failure to get them the help they really need.

May 28
You Can Tell . . .

neurotic anxiety in the compulsive behavior of some individuals. They develop stereotyped responses to life in an effort to keep the boiling pot of anxiety from spilling over inside them. The field of religion has always been a great area for compulsive neurotic behavior with all manner of people staving off their private terrors through repeated prayers and rituals. Sometimes persons would even get involved in the religious life of the church in a neurotic attempt to maintain control over their fears. "Scruples," these difficulties were called in earlier days when the difficulty was thought to be spiritual in origin and the pamphlet racks were filled with well-intentioned but misplaced wisdom about "spiritual" solutions for it. It was and is not a pleasant state, but it is clearly a compulsive psychological response to an anxiety-producing situation rather than a spiritual malady. It is a good thing not to let the setting for neurotic anxiety fool us into thinking it is something else and thereby causing us to fail to get persons the proper kind of help. Compulsive defenses are informative; they tell us that the person feels he can never get things right enough and so he must keep doing them over and over, perpetuating the response that keeps anxiety at bay without deepening self-knowledge. The worst part about neurotic defenses against anxiety is that they tend to prolong the person's fear rather than to lessen it.

May 29
The Advantages of Worry

At first inspection, there seem to be only liabilities connected with anxiety: lost sleep, uneven temper, facial tics and burgeoning ulcers. On the other hand, however, a little worry, even though it leaves its scars, beats apathy hands down. It is much better to feel the strain of caring about something or someone in life rather than to feel the dead calm of a passivity that can never be called peace. Worry is, after all, a sign of life, a pulsebeat of involvement, a hashmark that says we have been on active duty in the effort to be human. Worry is not something just to be wiped out by external noise or internal sedatives; in fact, it is compatible with some of our richest and best feelings, such as believing in, hoping for, and loving others. What would these commitments of the soul mean if they had no price tag on them? What would love matter if it never cost us at least the minor agonies of worry? It would never be worth joy or tears either; it would never show man, so utterly vulnerable at the heart, at his best in the human condition. Anxiety, when it is not vain, informs the heart of what it already knows—that we are called to be friends together and that this includes the special anxieties of closeness, the longings and the fears that always go along with love.

To deal with the problems of human experience that are truly important a man must have a certain measure of maturity and the kind of faith that allows him to put order into the sometimes jumbled and jarring world around him. The adult must be a believer, a man of faith, in order to take advantage of the headwinds which blow across most of our lives. The wonder for the Christian is the discovery that he does not have to be perfect at this, in other words, that he does not have to be able to drown out every worry with a draught of wisdom or grace. All he needs to do is deal with the challenges that come ridged with anxiety, face life and himself without expecting too much or demanding too little of himself. The latter strategy belongs to the underachiever, the one who protects himself against failure and the worry that goes along with a good effort by making his goals too easy or too difficult to achieve. He cannot be praised or blamed if anything goes wrong because there is no risk involved at all. Well, the Christian risk of living and loving is much spoken of these days; it is one that is seeded with potential anxiety, the kind of worry that goes with important things that can go wrong, the situations in which people can be hurt, especially by those they love the most. The man who knows that life does not cancel these debts of human concern for any of us believes in a God who draws us to himself through these experiences; his trust is in the Lord who understands our struggles and provides the power we need to heal and sustain each other along the journey. This man lives and confronts life with the confidence of God's help that goes to those who do not armor themselves against the inevitable pains of living and loving. This, ultimately, is the man of the gospel who is without care because his openness guarantees the peace that is the seal of the Spirit on a worthwhile life.

May 30
A Question about Worry

Don't some people have good reasons for their fears instead of just secret neurotic ones? Can't a person avoid a place or a mode of travel in which, for example, he may have been in a serious accident?

That, of course, is exactly what happens to many people; there is nothing secret about it because they can tell you exactly why they avoid a certain situation so carefully. The reason is nonetheless psychological rather than physical, and the fear or the uneasiness frequently tends to lessen as time passes. Even these situations can be helped —especially when the initial cause was some kind of physical trauma—by a graded reintroduction of the person to the activity in an atmosphere in which all factors that might cause anxiety are reduced as far as possible. That is exactly what goes on in the now popular kind of treatment called behavior therapy, although this is applied to emotional problems as well. For example, the person who has been in an automobile crash may be reluctant to get behind the wheel again. It would certainly not be sensible to have him start driving again in high speed metropolitan traffic; a series of lengthening trips on back country roads with a calm companion would be a much better way to start building the person's self-confidence again. There is, of course, no great psychological discovery here; that is just common sense, but, unfortunately, the kind many people neglect to use.

May 31
It Is Worth Worrying . . .

about important things, not only because this reassures us that we are alive, but also because our worries can be good guides to deepened self-knowledge. The size of a man's worry may well indicate the size of his soul; the man whose only worry is his appearance really has very little to be concerned about. Our anxieties tell us something about ourselves because they reveal what we consider important; even a brief inspection of the ones that cause the biggest twinges in our hearts helps us to see our psychological profile more clearly. Of course, anxiety is hard to look at sometimes, but it is also fruitful for the man who still cares about continuing his growth.

June

June 1
The Words We Speak

Words seem to preoccupy us almost as much as sex; we wait for a baby's first words and remember a man's last ones. The words in between actually tell our life-stories, and so a closer look at these words is a good approach to personal understanding. It is helpful to listen to ourselves occasionally; the kinds of words we use disclose something about us. And there is a variety of people whose words reveal them.

The man who always says no: Whenever another person proposes a project or a plan, this person's reaction is negative; and he is so accustomed to reacting this way that he does not even hear himself do it. He would, in fact, deny it, because he denies or downplays everything else. His words tell us who he is, and they limit him to a very narrow and cut-off space in life. Some of his favorite phrases are: "It'll never work." "We tried that once." And then there is the clergyman's special favorite: "The people aren't ready for it yet."

Job is alive and well in the man who speaks only words of woe. Sometimes these are about himself; occasionally he does not seem to be a human being as much as a collage of medical symptoms that would challenge any intensive care unit. This man needs attention, he keeps telling us in the same old words, because he has pains the world does not appreciate. He is not weighed down in body as much as in spirit; he can turn a fairly pleasant group gloomy in about twenty-five seconds. And he does this with his special assortment of words, most of them about tragedies that have just occurred or that are about to occur or that he is sure will occur. His words, like a cloud of vultures flapping across the sky, introduce a depressing note into an otherwise bright day.

The literalist, the man we thought had retired in the age of free spirits, was actually, as they say in the condolence cards, "just away." He is still hung up on squeezing joy out of life wherever possible. He likes the letter of the law and always has a hangman's noose ready for those who might try to think or live otherwise. The literalist would erase generations of biblical scholarship in order to preserve a blood-and-thunder judge of a God. He also remembers everything you have ever said, howsoever casually, and is ready to use it against you. Words, no matter what their meaning, are all that he needs to buoy up his heretic-hunter's heart. Naturally, he is not very good at words of comfort.

The man who says what he means is still around, thank God, despite the pressures and difficulties of the age. Without him we could not survive long, either as individuals or as a people. His words, you see, let us understand what it means to be human. There is no separation between who he is and what he says, even if he speaks bluntly on occasion. My father was such a man, and I can still hear the sounds of his words, the sounds of a man who was always himself and who could not abide false claims or phony words. I think he still speaks to me, especially when I am tempted to say what I do not feel or pretend to be, what, in fact, I am not.

June 2
The Need to Be Concrete

In some recent studies of effective psychotherapy an unsuspected yet valuable quality was *concreteness*. Simply stated, concreteness means that in today's world you can be effective only if you can clearly express your concerns and sensitivities to others. The therapist, for example, must frame his understandings in the right words; only these give life to another because they make understanding available in a potent symbolic form. This finding actually fits all relationships, including those of friendship and love. You cannot just gaze soulfully into your beloved's eyes; you cannot let your friend go without hearing from you. A man must not just stand there, even if his heart is filled with tender affection; somehow he has to express himself verbally—as clearly and directly as possible. In an age that has given up on *please* and *thank you,* in a time when the ceremonials that hold the membrane of civilization together are derided, it is striking to find research reasserting our need to put the best of our feelings into words. The experience of intimacy calls out for the right words to give it a form and a meaning that we can lean on for support. Sometimes we don't need much to pull ourselves together, or to get through the day; just the right word builds courage and hope in us. And this is a good thing for all friends and lovers to remember.

June 3
Whatever Happened to Pope John's Suggestion?

Pope John once suggested that the inflated language used to describe the activities of high-ranking churchmen be curtailed. Somehow, that suggestion got lost, and we are still awash in a soapy tide of "Eminences," "Most Reverends," and, God help us, "Lord Cardinals." Pope John was a man of few but simple words; that is why he found it so easy to tell the world that he loved it. This is also why the world loved him and still loves his memory. There is surely a lesson here about the way the wrong words destroy and disfigure the truths of faith. The gospels, however, were written for the average man in the language of his day; they are still best preached to him in the same way.

June 4
A Harder Thing by Far

It is extremely difficult, but humanly more appropriate, to
recommit ourselves to the quest for that rational vocabu-
lary which can help us verbalize our experience so that we
are its possessors and masters. The word still makes us
flesh to ourselves and to others; without the powerful understanding that only the right words convey, we lose hold
of our identities and blur the boundaries of our personalities. To match the correct word to our experience is no
easy thing; we must quarry deep within ourselves as we
strain to understand the meaning of our lives. It is well to
remember the old scriptural phrase—speak but the word
and we shall be healed. If we are denied those healing
words, we cannot be ourselves or understand our lives;
without words we are not made whole as human beings.

Perhaps lovers can explain this truth better than anyone
else. They may not understand the nature of the love
which they share, but they know that they must work at
saying it out loud as clearly as possible to each other.
When the words are right the love is complete; that is why
lovers never tire of hearing the living words of their love.
The biggest mistake lovers can make is to think that the
words may be taken for granted; even the strong silent
types must speak their love aloud. Love has a variety of
manifestations but none is more important than the simple
yet wondrous use of words. Actions and gestures may
speak volumes, but they never completely supersede the
right phrases. In the long run, each man must speak of his
love as clearly as he can, knowing that he will never say
it all; he must also realize that this knowledge does not
lessen the value of his effort to do so.

Therapists know that a patient's attempts to place his
emotional life in order require a steady search for the
words which allow him to recognize and make his life his

own. The words come slowly and painfully in real therapy; sometimes they emerge only after long silences. These are not the awkward quiet periods that mar a conversation between people who really have nothing to say to each other; rather, they are the fruitful and unself-conscious silences of persons who have learned to communicate on a deeply human level. Lovers know all about these as well; they do not signal the absence of words as much as the need to wait for the right words to form themselves in our awareness. A man who finds the right words for his inner experience speaks for himself the words that heal, the symbols that tell him in a new and more certain way who he is. A man can never lose the sense of himself that these words give to him.

June 5
A Teacher Spends a Lifetime . . .

trying to find the words which will give more than information to students; the master teacher seeks out wisdom just as energetically as the biblical writer did thousands of years ago. The teacher who knows how to help students grow does not recite or read from notes. Only the deadened teacher puts students to sleep; the living teacher, always seeking the right words, awakens them to meaning. And then one day a pupil responds by catching the message rather than just memorizing the lesson. In that instant the meaning of learning becomes clear as the student finds his own words for the first time; it is a moment of rebirth in which both the teacher and the pupil realize something new and profound about each other.

The person who struggles with prayer is a searcher for the right words; his dissatisfaction with prepared prayers comes directly from the fact that they do not resonate to his own pain or joy. Words so fashioned cannot speak to him and, consequently, cannot heal him or make him feel that he has made himself present to his God. The man who prays searches his life and his heart for himself, and he can describe this search only in his own words.

Sometimes we understand the subtle but sacred power of words best when a person misuses them, when he speaks from a region too shallow to be identified as his heart. You don't have to be a politician to do this, although at times it does seem to help. You can be a preacher reading the words written by someone else—a canned sermon that might as well be spoken to the wind; predigested words do not give life because they do not possess life. We have all said things we did not mean, of course, but I wonder if we realize what a failure of the self is always involved when we do. You see, we not only fail to reach each other; we also fail to reach ourselves. We speak, but our empty words lack flesh and they can neither instruct nor heal. These are the most truthless words of all because we are not in them.

Words are as precious as they are powerful. This is why God's words are described as keener than a two-edged sword. When they are properly understood, they cut through to the very heart of our experience as human beings, confronting us even as they light up the way for us. For this reason it is a sacrilege to fail to meditate on God's words or to neglect to let them speak to what is going on inside us. And that is why there is something very wrong in shouting them fundamentalistically so that the only message they convey is judgment and fear. Even the devil can quote scripture, we remember, and something like the devil is present in every use of the scriptures that estranges man from himself. The theologian who serves us best is the one who works patiently to find the right words for our Christian experience at this time in history; he illumines our way by speaking fresh words to us, enabling us to better understand our Christian identity and faith. Theologians must translate for us the living words that nourish and shape us, not parse long-dead verbs.

June 6
It Is Tempting "To Tell People Off"

There is no doubt that this kind of approach with its echoes of "no nonsense," let's-get-down-to-business masculinity is a tempting option, especially if we are frustrated or impatient ourselves. It is even more tempting if we have had to come to terms directly with some problem of our own without outside assistance and we are slightly irritated that others cannot be as seemingly strong as we are. Well, as a matter of fact, not everybody is as strong as everybody else, but it is a good thing to remember that the help of a lot of other people went into whatever strength any one of us may have. Beyond that, the direct, throw-them-to-the-lions approach also appeals because it responds to our own worndown toleration point; we feel better when we take this kind of stand. The only difficulty resides in the fact that it is the other person who needs our assistance, and the multiplication of their trauma has never proved very helpful. In fact, the individual forced into facing anxieties that are really deep may panic and end up far worse off than when he or she began. For example, pushing people into the deep water when they are genuinely afraid of it may not result in spontaneous swimming on their part; it can cause a kind of paralysis in the throes of which they may almost drown those who then attempt to rescue them. There is nothing more over-rated than the no nonsense approach in situations in which the anxiety is real rather than imaginary. The way of patient understanding is much better because it is more profoundly human; that makes it more religious as well.

June 7
Never Too Late

Very often people say that they did not know what they were doing at an earlier time in their life or that they are not now the persons they were then. These mostly painful discoveries indicate that certain people only begin to sense and respond faithfully to their true selves at a late and difficult time in life. There is little leisure time, then, for repenting their previous failures and perhaps not much time for them to practice a deeper and abiding kind of faithfulness. The emphasis with these people, in other words, should be that, howsoever late they came to deal with their real identity, this must be the focus for them now. If they have made mistakes before, every effort should now be made to help them avoid making others. Fidelity is still important even though these persons are only sensing its meaning long after they should have begun to appreciate it. A bad marriage, a wrong career—these are the kinds of devastating experiences which they can no longer afford. If they did not work enough on faithfulness before, then it is urgent to put this virtue into better focus now or they will re-create—as people have a way of doing—the same debacle for themselves all over again.

June 8
Trust Is the Tough One

Trust is like New York City: It is filled with what seems to be the heady essence of life and it is fun to talk about or even visit now and then. But, at the same time, it is hell to live in and with. Both the virtue and the city compel a response from us. You either enter into them, fighting them for ultimate rewards, or you stand on the opposite shore twisting your hat like a bashful exile who is safe but aware that he has missed something. Yes, we like to talk about trust; it is, after all, a word that can be used like a weapon by people who speak it easily but do not take it seriously. "Don't you trust me?" is a phrase that can mean any thing or nothing at all, a statement that can be made openly or used as a cover-up. Genuine trust is hard to give but easy to demand. It is either there or it is not; there is simply no such thing as a little bit of trust. Trusting and being trusted are two sides of a complex phenomenon. That is why trust, of all the virtues, is the tough one.

The truth, of course, is that trust is not in itself the hardest test we face. The hard test comes when people pass through the shallows of life and into some real depth. Trust is like turning off a daytime serial and walking out into the real world of pain and problems. It is filled with other persons, just as all of our most important experiences are. And wherever persons are, there one encounters the demands of trusting and being trusted. These are inseparable phenomena; there is no way, as the saying goes, that we can lead loving and happy lives if we leave trust out. Trust takes on its toughness—that is, we always feel the price of it—because it is so much a part of all the transactions through which we recognize and expand our humanity. According to many shrewd psychological observers, trust exists right from the beginning of our lives, and on the basis of what we experience of it in our first year we define our stance toward ourselves and other persons. It is in the first year, in the analysis provided by Erik Erikson, that the individual, especially in relationship to his mother, must develop a basic sense of trust. The mother is viewed as the important mediator of this experience because of the close and intimate contact she has with the child at this time; she is clearly the child's most important teacher. Through what she is and how she reacts the child comes to sense the world as trustworthy or not, as dependable or reliable even though he cannot put these experiences into words of any kind as yet. Healthy mothers, even without acquiring graduate degrees or reading Doctor Spock, have always had an intuitive knack for creating a trusting environment for their children. Psychologists, after all, merely explore the unself-conscious actions of ordinary people.

June 9
What Does It Take to Trust?

The act of trusting cannot be written down like a recipe, although sometimes psychological advice seems to come out that way. Trust begins, however, with two people who make some kind of personal difference to each other. Some persons talk about trusting to luck or to fate, but that is not the kind of human trusting with which we are concerned here. Real trust calls for something you can only do with human beings, and it enables us to make an important distinction between two common usages of the word *trust*.

Trusting another person—even in the case of the mother and the all but unknowing infant—requires a *commitment* of the self to the other. Trusting in fate, luck, or the guidance of the stars does not ask for a commitment but an *abandonment* of the self, and that is a very different thing altogether. Abandonment suggests a passive surrender of the self to the control of what one hopes will be benign forces; it is, nonetheless, a handing-over of the self, an abdication of personal authority that is as clear as the late Duke of Windsor's abdication. Much has been made of this kind of abandonment, not only in the irrational fancies of the day, but even in some forms of Christian asceticism. One must, however, wonder at it in view of the fuller meaning of active human trusting.

June 10
Active Trust

The act of trust that is defined as a *commitment* of the self is far more demanding than the abandonment of the self.

166

The latter approach, which makes pious-sounding noises about God's will and the cosmic forces that are ready to shape us, is fundamentally a refusal to be free and responsible. Trusting others in an active way demands that we be both of these, giving something of ourselves with full knowledge of what we are doing and of the possible consequences. When you abandon yourself, nothing can go wrong because what you do is dictated by an agency outside yourself; you always win, in other words, because you are merely passively carrying out what others have designed. When you commit yourself in trust, then everything can go wrong, and at any minute, because you have opened yourself to the painful realization of what it means to be free. Abandonment of the self—and it has many contemporary faces—is popular because it resonates with a sense of finality and the satisfying rhythms of the absolute. Actually, as far as the much harder business of giving ourselves to others in trust is concerned, abandonment is a cop-out because it semi-mystically removes us from the scene where people need us.

June 11
Committing Ourselves . . .

to others recalls two related elements that are essential in active trusting: First of all, we must be a *presence* in the life of the other and, secondly, we must be *creative* in our interaction with him. We cannot just stand there, in other words, with a blank expression on our faces, the way we get through boring wedding receptions, overlong sermons, and committee meetings. When we trust another person, we have to be there, even if, in haste, we are forced to come as we are, out of breath, slightly disheveled, and perhaps a little scared of the whole situation ourselves. Trusting others always disturbs us when we are not perfectly ready to trust, when we are prepared neither to be fully present nor to be very creative. It is a hazardous mission, and we make up for our shortcomings only by giving to a particular situation as much of ourselves as we can at the moments when we are needed. This means that we give of our attention, our time, and our concern; we make ourselves a reliable if imperfect presence to the other. The miracle is, that this flawed donation of the self is enough when we do it freely and fully, with no strings attached. In itself, the gift of ourselves to others is powerfully creative when it is done simply and straightforwardly without any effort to manipulate others or to hedge our bets. Being creative in the act of trusting does not mean doing a lot of things or shifting the scenery of another's life; standing with another in committed fashion is, of itself, powerfully creative because it releases those vital human forces of growth that we cannot see or measure but which remain the most real things we know.

The hard part of trusting comes from its demand that we actively involve ourselves in the lives of others for their sake. This involvement makes us vulnerable—to the pain that rages when something goes wrong in the process, and to the hurts that find our hearts faster than "smart" bombs find their targets but still do just as much damage. Trusting just does not work without this accepted vulnerability and there is no safeguard or early warning system against it. People we trust can hurt us by failing in their trust or because they themselves are hurt trying to manage the freedom which we give to them so they can find their own lives. It is certainly much easier on the emotions to take the route of abandonment, because that offers a shelter against caring so much. The nucleus of trust, however, resides in the caring for others that exposes our flanks at the same time; this is what makes trust work. The price, however, is always high, and a person can get tired or wary of the commitment of trust; perhaps that is why there is so little trust available these days.

June 12
The No Strings Attached Clause

If we look back into our own lives to locate the passages of growth, we may find them related to an individual or individuals who actively trusted us—those people who stood by us and with us as we found our own way or accomplished things in the fashion that was true for us. We may not remember how deeply we were trusted because, when it is done right, it seems free and does not impose burdens on those who receive trust. Some say that trust must be earned, but there is a further quality about trust which is equally true: Trust must be given away with no conditions or codicils written into the act. Trust is contaminated and rendered lifeless if it is only a subtle device to control the behavior of the supposedly trusted individual. In other words, trust cannot be part of a bargaining process; call that maneuver by another name because it is not the unadorned dynamic we understand as trust. The more strings attached, the less trust there is, and the less desirable are the results for everyone concerned. Trust is either wholehearted or it is nothing; and this is why it is extremely difficult to give ourselves to others, expecting nothing in return except their own further growth. We are great negotiators in human affairs, even in those which most deeply affect our hearts. That is why we are more familiar with the games people play than we are with the lively effects of freely given trust.

"No strings" is a phrase that is currently used to describe relationships in which individuals really do not make a commitment to each other; it describes those friendships or liaisons in which persons leave each other free to get out when they get bored, up-tight or restless. This kind of "no strings" arrangement is a modern example of avoiding the question of trust altogether; it is done, no matter how nobly it may be rationalized, in order to shield individuals against the vulnerability that goes along with real commitment to another person. It is better, as they see it, to block out as much as they can of the possibility of hurt right from the start; if there are no strings, there can be no broken promises, and, with luck, there won't be any scars on lovers' hearts either. You need not make an investment of trust with this arrangement. You do not have to pay its price, but neither do you get its reward. To bestow trust as freely and unconditionally as we can is something that we all spend a lifetime in learning. That, however, is the direction in which a person who wants to give growth and to grow himself must go.

June 13
Believing in Bad News

A strange but not often considered variant in the area of trust is the person who does not believe in anything unless it is bad news. He can hardly wait for messengers of ill tidings and seems to get a charge out of trusting their reports almost absolutely. Good news, stories of great striving or genuine integrity in human affairs are to be disbelieved and their announcers are to be considered untrustworthy. I am not sure that psychology has ever explained these people, but here are a few hints that will help you to recognize them.

Some people come to life when situations are at their worst; they positively relish the possibilities of disaster and are rather disappointed when the news takes a turn for the better. This may be called the "Fall of the Roman Empire" syndrome and it is very common today. This kind of people really gets to you after a while, depressing you with the bad news that elates them.

June 14
Not Believing Good News

Others are second cousins to the people who simply cannot believe in anything good at all. In their view, everything is fixed or phony, and there are just enough scandals to reward their appetites for the cynical defense against anything positive in human nature. Life is a great burden for persons who look on things and persons in this way; they get to you after a while, too.

Perhaps we should not close this section without commenting on the incredible power that even the wildest story or rumor gains once it has been set into print. For some reason or other, credibility is enhanced when you can reduce the spoken word to the written form. Researchers and dissertation writers have known this as long as journalists; it is what puts the magic in many otherwise unconvincing footnotes. And the pheonomenon is worth the reflection of serious people.

June 15
Learning Not to Trust

There is a balance involved in learning the lessons of trust. Many factors go into the judgment through which creative and committed trust is finally given to another. This is one of the reasons it is so powerful; it is a function of an integrated and self-aware personality. Moreover, trust is more than good wishes and/or some vague expression of concern. When a man trusts, he puts himself on the line; that kind of presence always makes a difference to others. Part of what does contribute to the judgment to trust is mastering a sense of when not to trust. Trusting and sensibly not trusting must be learned together or the action of trusting becomes mindless and insensitive to reality, a gullible performance that has no grounding in the world of men and events. Even psychologist Erik Erikson, who makes trust the keystone of human development, has emphasized our need to withhold trust if the situation or the person is inappropriate or ill-prepared for it. All this is part of what prudence looks like when it makes the leap from the philosopher's textbook to the exigencies of real life.

Giving our trust to someone else is a sacred action; it is not to be done lightly or it loses both its significance and its power to transform other persons. The man who says that he trusts everyone may never have come to terms with what the costs or realities of trust are. There must be some adequate communication between the parties who exchange trust. Trust is, after all, a two-way exchange: It is as solemn a moment for the person trusted as it is for the one who invests his trust. "Do not trust in princes," the psalmist sang, and we must be wise enough not to trust in a wide variety of things, from hawkers of patent medicines to fundamentalists who tell us that the Lord is a vengeful deity. There are things not trustworthy and persons not yet ready for trust in life; only the immature or those interested in self-punishment would think otherwise. But these are hard lessons to learn well, and one does not have to look far in order to discover some of the reasons.

June 16
Still Others . . .

trust everybody because they are really indifferent to what happens. These people simply withhold their emotional commitment in order to protect their own coolness. What looks like trust is merely their way of letting the world go its own way, of letting people do what they feel like as long as they do not bother them. This is the naive trust of the uncaring.

June 17
While Others . . .

make a show of trust because they are desperately afraid
to lose someone's favor—their children's or their students',
for example. Anything goes (and everything usually
does) as these persons work like movie stars at remaining
popular. They give away a pale semblance of trust, justifying freedoms in those not yet ready to exercise them, and
blaming everybody but themselves for the generally sorry
results. Such are the parents, for example, who give up on
being realistic mothers and fathers in order to be liked by
their children. Such is the naive trust of the immature.

There is, then, such a thing as healthy mistrust, the reaction of the person who cares about others enough to weigh
the factors and consequences of the situation at hand. It is
still just common sense not to trust your car keys with a
criminal or your matches with a pyromaniac.

June 18
To Trust Oneself

Trust, like charity, begins at home or it can never travel
very far. It is the unfortunate reverse power of those who
choose not to believe in others to be able to cripple their
own capacity for self-confidence. When a person is not
helped to be friendly toward himself he despises and
rejects his own strengths, locking himself in the chambered
darkness of self-doubt from which it is so difficult to escape. The world is already too filled with persons who
cower inside themselves because they do not much like
themselves and cannot forgive themselves for their human
state. But life and love are only possibilities for the man
who can look himself in the eye without flinching. This

173

man has made peace with himself and his limitations; he can, therefore, share his God-given trust with others. "Trust the authority of your own senses," Aquinas wrote in a sentence that draws us back to a healthy perspective on the world.

A few months ago a colleague and I were conducting the oral examination of a young nun who had completed all the other requirements for her graduate degree. "What," my colleague asked, trying to put her at ease, "What do you think you have learned in your years here?" She paused for a moment and answered, "I think I learned that I could be right." It was obvious that she had learned a good deal more than her lessons. She had a new attitude toward herself, a confident and positive one which enabled her to look at life and her future work in a new and constructive manner. She was leaving the university with new knowledge, but, more importantly, she was leaving with a new sense of herself, a new belief in her own reactions and judgments. She felt she was a worthwhile person whose life ultimately rested, for its direction, on her own shoulders. The capacity of human beings to recover a healthy sense of themselves, even after years of counterconditioning in not believing in themselves, is remarkable; it is a sign—one of the rumors of angels—that reveals the wonder of God's creation. Given a chance and a little encouragement the best that is in a person can still emerge. God made us to discover what is right about ourselves and to trust that discovery throughout our journey to a full life.

June 19
The Big Lesson

The experience which this young nun had in her years of training had enabled her to reclaim her birthright to her own life; I think she succeeded because she met many people who were willing to believe in her, to trust her in a new way. She responded, as persons always do when they are genuinely and deeply trusted, by growing toward the ideal that was right for her, toward the goals that matched her personality. She certainly looked happier and more confident as she left graduate school. And she took with her a deepened capacity to enlarge the lives of others through believing in them herself. Because she was stronger, many others will become stronger through her. Because others had believed in her, she had experienced the meaning of resurrection. What was deadened in her stirred to life once more; what was hidden was revealed; what was uneasy was shaped into wholeness. There was more of her, in other words, at the end of school than at the beginning because of the commitment of others and her rediscovered strength to respond to life. This kind of resurrection is a product of belief; it is the kind of experience that helps us to understand resurrection as an object of belief.

Indeed, it is impossible for us to understand important religious concepts unless we sense their fundamental meanings through the experiences of our own lives. We can believe in God in a rich and appropriately human way only after we have learned something of the substance of faith through the trust and belief others invest in us. Faith in God is not totally alien from what we sense deep in ourselves when we begin to learn the lessons of trusting others. Coming to life always follows on the gift of trust; rising to new life becomes understandable when we have grasped the essential elements of trusting and being trusted by each other.

June 20
A Case History of Trust

Parents as well as lovers know the inside of trust from repeated firsthand experience. They know the fiery grasp on their hearts when their trusted children are hurt in some way by the unpredictable forces that rage in the environment of a free life. Such was the case, related to me by a colleague who stood with a wondering father outside the doors of a hospital emergency room where the latter's son lay seriously injured from an automobile accident. The father was talking of the subject of trust and of what it had meant between him and his eighteen-year-old boy. "You know," he said, "I didn't give him the keys to the car lightly. I thought about it. I thought, well, maybe I could drive him to the prom . . . but I did that when he was fourteen and now he is eighteen. It was time for him to drive himself. And they all looked so nice going out. Who could have thought that they would be sideswiped by a drunken driver? . . ." He shifted his position and sighed: "But, if I had it to do all over again, I'd give him the keys . . . or I would have hurt him in another way worse than the way he's hurt right now. . . ."

June 21
A Test Not for Children

To trust, to believe—these are not just childish notions. They become, as a matter of fact, more difficult as we grow more mature and become more aware of ourselves and of our world. Trusting and believing are precisely what the man of mature faith is able to continue doing as he accumulates the scars of life. His faith and trust deepen because they are anchored in a personal response to Jesus which provides the strength to carry on. The road of faith leads only in one direction, and it is uphill all the way. The marvelous thing is that this is exactly where man belongs; it is the kind of passage each of us must make in order to achieve the fullest sense of our lives. Belief is what a developing person continues to exhibit in his life when he understands what Jesus really asks. It involves saying *yes*, not with the abandon of the fundamentalist, but with the confidence of one who will follow where his commitment leads him.

June 22
Myth Deprivation

In a recent interview, Dr. Jan Ehrenwald, a New York psychiatrist, suggested that modern men are suffering from myth deprivation. As a result, they turn to the occult and to other irrational behaviors in order to seek an explanation for life. Dr. Ehrenwald, of course, means that man needs myths in which to believe—not fairy stories but the kinds of legends through which we pass on basic truths about ourselves—just as he needs heroes to imitate and great visions to lead him on. When men make ruin of their myths, turning everything sour and making antiheroes to stand over the graves of the dead gods, when men, in other words, tangle the lines of their own belief systems they can only surrender themselves to the winds of fate. What we understand about man at this time in history confirms something we should never have forgotten: Men cannot survive without belief any more than they can survive without air and water. Man is not man unless he searches for what is trustworthy, unless he opens himself to some way of explaining the world and his life. It is a strange thing that this need keeps reasserting itself, no matter how often it is thought to have been eliminated for good.

Related to this is the research on dreams—something which man also seems to need at the unconscious level of his personality in order to integrate himself. Dreams are not random happenings; they are functional in human adjustment. If you prevent a person from dreaming—wake him up, for example, every time he starts to dream—he soon becomes irritable and disturbed. He can, in fact, if deprived of dreams for too long, begin to act in a psychotic manner. Man needs his dreams in the same way

177

that he needs the powerful myths that remind him of who he is and what his life is all about. Ehrenwald suggests that as various forces destroy man's myths—as these dreams or visions are denied him—he becomes psychotic in another way. He seeks for meaning in the pits of nonmeaning; he searches for a god in the devil. Something like this seems to be occurring in the world where the occult is common-place and tarot cards are almost as familiar as IBM cards.

Man's need to believe is obvious. Desperate things happen to him when he abandons the possibilities of faith and trust. He becomes more primitive and less a man, portraying his need for a saving faith even as he seems to reject it. What man needs again are persons who are willing to believe in him, to assist him to rediscover the dreams he needs in order to put himself together as a person. This is a religious business, not a humanistic sideline, and it is an effort to which we can all contribute as long as we preserve the capacity to trust and the will to make that practical in the lives of those with whom we live. Man needs to rediscover the richest of Christian myths—a man finds himself when he is willing to lose himself in loving and serving others. It is not an irrational or unbelievable proposition. Jesus taught us something that we can test very easily in our own lives and through our relationships with others. It is the myth that brings us back to life, that gives us back our vision of what God asks us to become; it is the step of faith that breathes hope into us and enables us once more to love.

June 23
Believe in Me

When you ask what did Jesus ask of us, the reply "Believe in me" is at once astounding and challenging. It is an invitation to trust with all that we possess of ourselves, a personal and profoundly human invitation to believe in Jesus rather than in a list of rules or even a set of dogmas. Belief in Jesus is just that; we cannot respond to him unless we do so with something more than our minds. And believing in Jesus is not just a matter of feelings either, despite the reassuring uplift that comes from "being saved." Jesus does not ask for sophisticated intellects or overflowing hearts; he asks for us, for all of us, with these elements of personality in proper relationship to each other. The response cannot be made except through the total personality; it is the kind of response that friends and lovers know, the commitment of oneself that begins with trust. Religious faith, then, is not an activity of part of our personality; it is the function of the whole man. We sentimentalize faith when we long, as some have, for the unlettered faith of the peasant woman. That is requesting a kind of faith that asks no questions, sees no problems, and satisfies itself by knowing less rather than more. Faith is not that static, nor is it that kind of magic force. Rather, it is an aspect of man which develops as he does, which opens him up to all the wonder and complexity of life instead of closing him off from it.

June 24
Believing in Belief

Francis Thompson once wrote of what it meant to be a child. He said that it "is to believe in love, to believe in loveliness, to believe in belief. . . ." It is the nature of a child to respond effortlessly in these poetic ways. Adult faith does not mean that we go on believing with the innocence of a child; it is far more exacting and quite appropriate for the person who has discovered the large servings of suffering that go into every life. It is a challenge to all that we are to believe and to love when we have been failed by some and hurt by others. That is the way it is when we believe in Jesus; the reward is not the untroubled faith of a child but the always-challenged faith of the grownup.

179

June 25
Small Losses

Life is seeded with small pleasures and small losses, and they both work on us in a similar way. The little pleasures of life—like the blessings of cool clear water on a hot summer day—keep us going; the small losses—like rain on a vacation day—keep us off balance just enough to remind us of our mortality. Sometimes these psychological debits are hardly noticeable when they occur; they accumulate daily so that, at times, we feel weighed down and depressed without being able to say exactly why. Small losses are the slow stranglers of the spirit and even acupuncture cannot find the secret places through which they invade our lives and do their damage. What are some of the familiar small losses of life?

Phone calls that are never returned, especially that one from the friend whose voice we really wanted to hear. This goes for letters too. A letter from a lover that is a day late has the awesome power to generate disappointment and frenzied wonder at its absence.

Birthdays that are not remembered by people who should remember them. Sometimes others do this to us and at times we do it to others; it hurts either way. A whole industry of greeting cards is based on this small loss in life, but it does not quite erase the situation.

Being embarrassed or put down by a correction or a sarcastic remark on the part of another person. Sometimes we learn from these things, but occasionally the pain is large enough to block the possibility of growing wiser because of it. Some small losses hurt more intensely and for a longer time than their size seems to warrant.

Lovers' quarrels are classic examples of life's small losses. Nothing is quite the same until things are set right again; wrongs between lovers cannot be righted without patience, time and understanding. In itself it is a small loss not to be able to provide these immediately. The old phrase, "Let's forget it," applies a bandage but it does not immediately heal the wound. The same goes for the vacuums that can occur in friendship or in marriage when people drift out of each other's focus for a while. It is nothing fatal or irreparable and yet it is a loss that has its deadening aspect.

There are the little lonelinesses that strike us at the oddest moments, at those in-between times, or when we wonder about each other and what we believe in, or whether we believe at all. These are momentary losses, it is true, but losses nonetheless.

There are slight illnesses that are just big enough to take the edge off enjoying something we have anticipated, like a holiday or an evening out. These illnesses need not be physical all the time; who has not felt blue during holidays?

There are literally hundreds of small losses that get charged against us when we are judged wrongly, misunderstood, or left out of other people's plans. Sometimes these losses seem too silly to talk about; but there they are, nameless and unnameable hurts—the everyday burdens of the human state. You can add to this list, perhaps by inspecting your own heart at the present moment. Small losses are no news to anyone who has ever loved enough to miss someone or to feel longing at the end of a beautiful day.

June 26
What Do You Do?

Small losses, like regrets, are hard to handle. There is simply no good place to put them, and so we often settle by pretending not to have them at all. Well, what does a man do if he is not to deny them altogether? Not even tears wash them away, and feeling sorry for ourselves is just another example of the small losses about which we are speaking. Actually we can learn a lot from these experiences if we are willing to face and to name them appropriately.

There is significance in small losses on at least two personal levels. First of all, they do tell us something important about ourselves. In a world where people clamor for the key to self-knowledge, a peek behind our small hurts lights up our inner-geography the way a lightning flash does a mountain range. What hurts us is not accidental; it reflects where we are tender, undeveloped, or sometimes too self-concerned. It is always difficult to learn about ourselves. Although we prefer the good news to the bad, it is in correctly reading their mixture (which makes up most of life) that we discover something of our real identity.

On a second level we can understand the small losses as an important part of our religious experience of life itself. At a time in which persons try to discover the mystical in the exotic and remote realms of life, it may be surprising to discover that mystical experience lies, not at the far end of things, but deep down inside ourselves. Small losses in life are the little deaths that keep our existence in proper perspective, the reminders of the cycle of life that are the normal and healthy signs of persons who are living the life of the Spirit. A man keeps in touch with himself and the direction of his life by acknowledging and working through the meaning of the things that hurt him, the things that challenge him to make a fresh start and to reach through his pain to the experience of resurrection.

But small setbacks in life also brace us for the large ones which no one can avoid. Even though we know they are out there waiting for us these can sometimes take us by surprise. A person who has made himself a stranger to loss or to pain may not be able to deal constructively with these larger difficulties when they do occur. The individual who faces the lesser reverses of life and integrates them into a vision of its larger meaning will not be overcome by big problems. Of course, this does not mean that a person should always anticipate bad news by carrying a stout shield across his heart in order to avoid disappointment. This is an awkward and uncomfortable way to live, an overcautious management of the self. It robs us finally of spontaneity and joy. The ability to understand and identify life's small losses allows us to see life and its disappointments with the available resources of wisdom and faith.

June 27
Some Questions to Raise

What about the overpowering urge to win? What is its true motivation? Is this drive a species of healthy self-confidence or a deeper neurotic need? The desire to win over all else may be related to one or the other of the following.

At times an individual is more interested in proving that he is right than he is in discovering the truth. There is a big difference between these two attitudes, and the neurotic winner cares far more about his own finishing position than he does about the nature of truth.

The emotionally needy winner envisions all the world as a contest in which others are persistently striving to get power over him. He responds to this situation by trying to expand his power over others. The trouble with his strategy is that he can never be at peace because others are always a threat to his exclusive possession of first place. Ironically, first place is not much of a prize for such an anxious person.

June 28
Winning as Losing

Sometimes a man must win in order to cover his own vulnerability, to act out again for us the ancient tale of the warrior who must hide his feelings lest his brotherhood with us be revealed. Winning, at whatever price, becomes a part of this individual's emotional adjustment, a grim

183

sort of satisfaction that isolates the winner in the moment of triumph.

The desperate need to win has led to a large number of dishonorable activities, such as lying, cheating, and stealing. When winning wrecks the rest of life then it is obviously an urge that is out of control. But winning—at whatever price—is dangerously important to the uneven and untempered personality.

June 29
The Death of Tenderness

Life's lesser losses teach us that wounds are unavoidable and that a sense of how to heal and be healed is essential for any kind of Christian life. Perhaps we must personally know the inside of hurt in order to be tender to other persons. The price of loving is partly paid for through the pains we get to know so intimately during the course of our lives. Ruthlessness may win promotions, raises, and an occasional gold medal, but its smoky breath turns every landscape ashen. Finishing first can mean coming out last in the only race that really counts.

When tenderness dies, love has no place to go. It can only dry up for lack of nourishment. It is fed by persons who know the human condition well and realize that small losses leave the scars that allow us to recognize each other as members of the same family. Everyone is looking for successful intimacy these days because human beings sense that this is our only response to the desolating loneliness that rages like an epidemic throughout the world. Some believe that intimacy can be grabbed at or that it is the object of conquest. Intimacy remains, however, a citadel which cannot be seized by force. It cannot be won; it can only be given freely by one person to another, and no individual can be close to another unless he knows the secret of facing the small losses of life.

Successful intimacy demands that we be ready to lose ourselves in the presence of another, to let ourselves be known—and sometimes hurt—in the close and quiet place of love. A man who cannot lose cannot be close enough to love. He never really understands life either. The secret is old but forever fresh; the experience of small losses deepens our appreciation of the Gospel truth that the man who gives up his life is also the man who finds it. Small losses bring a special victory, the experience of resurrection and fullness that belong like an unearned blessing to those who have not been frightened off by the constant small losses of life.

June 30
Life as Recreation

Many forces have been hammering the puritan ethic into splinters lately. Americans are trying to cure themselves of the notion that we are only permitted to enjoy life if we work very hard for a long time. Many readers will recognize their own persistent uneasiness about taking time off from the hard work they do. Others, however, are vigorously pursuing the new guilt-free lifestyle that prizes play as a greater value than work.

Life as leisure is a growth industry in the United States. However, relaxation and play have no meaning unless they flow from the context of a purposeful life. Leisure quickly cloys when it is the chief focus of a person's efforts. The person who overworks may have a hang-up that needs curing, but one should not hurriedly baptize the "play first" notion of life; hard work need not be neurotic. As we view our lives in perspective we understand the intimate relationship between work and play, between taking life seriously and being able to laugh at it too. The secret of unself-conscious play belongs to those who understand that life is more than recreation and less than obsessive drudgery.

July

July 1
Maybe It's the Way He Says It

On the wall that separates the counterculture from the expanding-awareness devotees of the middle class hang, like Monday's wash, acres of colorful posters. They represent one of the ways in which we talk to ourselves these days—they are a gaudy inventory of modern American beliefs, dreams, and even some defenses. This latter category seems to characterize one of the celebrated notions of the famous Gestalt therapist, Frederick Perls. Perls believes that . . .

> I do my thing and you do your thing; I am not in this world to live up to your expectations and you are not in this world to live up to mine. You are you and I am I and if by chance we find each other it's beautiful.

Perls has presented a philosophy of pseudointimacy that sounds good, especially if spoken in solemn tones; it also looks good outfitted with modern graphics against a lush green landscape on some poster. And it seems to be hanging everywhere these days. Why is this so? Why are these words so appealing right now?

Perls' statement has the advantage, like the famous ink blot test, of allowing a great deal to be read into it. In other words, people can bring more meaning to these words than the words themselves possess. We find what we want or need to find in this philosophy; few things are as convenient for longing and lonely persons. His idea sounds deep, not because it really is, but because it touches on something vitally important for all human beings—the mystery of meeting and responding to each other as friends. These words awaken our yearning for closeness and, in the next breath, dismiss it with a blessing. They have a bittersweet and self-contained ring to them, a private anointing for those who have been hurt by life.

Perhaps most importantly of all, these sentiments protect persons from further hurt in a world which seems bent on destroying people on the rack of broken friendship and unfulfilled love. If we do not have to hope for much from friendship—if it can come and go with as much glory and infrequency as a perfect spring—if we look at love as an occasional thing, then it cannot hurt us very much. Our failures cannot be charged to us but, like the weather, are the product of destinies outside our control. We need not concern ourselves with the meaning of fidelity or the other problems, each of which contains a little more potential for hurt. Instead, all we need do is grab at the ring, as the carousel turns; perhaps, with any amount of luck, it will be made of gold.

July 2
Is That All There Is?

This is the question a man or woman faces sooner or later if he or she attempts to live by the presumed wisdom of slogans. It is especially important for younger people who still have most of their lives and loving before them to examine this code carefully before adopting it as their own.

Such poster-words diminish rather than enlarge our views of human dignity. They are not deeply personalistic because they so sharply reduce our meaning and our possibilities with each other. According to this type of advice we are not far removed from protoplasm; we are, in fact, rather like one-celled creatures glancing off each other in the field of some giant microscope, our intimacy an accident of our juxtaposition on the same laboratory slide. This is not, however, how persons endowed with consciousness and will move through life. Healthy persons, when they meet someone to whom they respond, automatically want to know more about the other; when we discover a friend, it is instinctive to want to deepen the relationship rather than to run away to safety. Indeed this willingness to learn and share with others is one of the signs of good psychological health. Persons, even in their blundering attempts to get closer to each other, deserve more reverence and a better chance to succeed than they get from those who say that love is only a sometimes thing.

July 3
That Kind of Advice . . .

also denies one of the things for which we must have some feeling in order to lead a truly human and positively religious life. We can never escape from time, even though such posters offer us an invitation to make the attempt. They focus on the moment, excising it from its context in the lives of the persons concerned. This proffers involvement without engagement, a pinpoint of relationship that has no past and need not have a future. Human beings, however, have histories and their futures cannot easily be written off as though there were no consequences to their behavior with each other. The moments of a man's or a woman's life are not disconnected like the beads of a broken rosary; they fit together even if they occasionally get tangled in the course of events. We only relate to each other in and through the dimension of time; our love may make us young but we know that we must grow old together as well. It is not easy to come to terms with the passing of time, especially as it works changes in us or makes us aware of how swiftly it counts itself away before we have accomplished everything we had planned. Lovers have a keen and realistic sense of time which ultimately enables them to challenge and conquer it. Nobody can learn this by running away from time or by lightly discounting it in his life.

also deny one of our most powerful insights into the meaning of our lives. This tells us that events and persons must be seen whole; that, in fact, we grasp the meaning of our existence only as it fits into a pattern larger than our own concerns. The cool philosophy suggests that we are interchangeable pieces in a game whose meaning might disappear if we were ever to take it seriously. Such easy words fail to acknowledge that on the practical level we become something more when we are together than when we are separate, and that something new comes into being when we respond to each other with consideration and tenderness. We are absurd in the most desperate sense if all we can long for in life is an occasional glimmer in each other's presence as we move swiftly past each other.

A poster can lull us with magic but deceptive sounds. We do not hear the challenge—that pressing one through which we discover who we are—in facing the pain of the experiences that rack and discourage us as we try faithfully to love each other. Men and women will not live very long on the scant nourishment of such words; it is shallow poetry that may provide a way station for adolescent growing but does not serve for the long haul of adult life. The cruel outcome of attempting to live by this kind of advice is the terrible sense of frustration that people experience when they cannot break out of themselves.

Love, of course, is the great invitation to crack through the shell of our self-concern and to make our way toward the people in the world around us in order to share with them something of ourselves. We never do this if love comes like big-city mail—sometimes late and sometimes not at all. This keeps love, like the candy of childhood, always on the other side of the window. Some people, it is true, must adjust, for one reason or another, to a life without the kind of love they hoped they would have. They do

189

their best but they feel that something is missing even though they know they are spared some hurt through its absence. Lovers should be encouraged to look beyond the foreshortened view of love that is presented in popular posters. It is still better—it really is—to have loved and been hurt than never to have loved at all.

July 5
Obedience . . .

is being talked about quite a bit these days and largely by frustrated parents, teachers, and various authorities who cannot get other people to obey them. There is a proper way of understanding this difficulty, of course, but a preliminary exploration of the nature of obedience may be helpful. Obedience is not related to lock-step responses and, in its essence, it never has been. Obedience is a far more human commitment of ourselves to the actions in life that are right for us.

Talk about obedience frequently centers on rebelliousness—the refusal to obey. Most people, especially Americans, are not rebellious against authority, no matter what anybody says. This is true even in cases of religious obedience, despite dramatic talk to the contrary. Nostalgic talk about obedience always locates the test of obedience in whether we are willing to do something we do not want to do. The situation, however, does not often occur in life. Our common difficulties with obedience arise from other sources. Our deepest obedience is to our best selves, to the realization of the gifts which God gave us, to the enlarging of the lives of those around us. It is, in short, related to what we really want to do rather than to things we have no taste for.

The problem is that it is sometimes so difficult to be obedient to what we know is right both for ourselves and for others, to marshal the energies we need to make the gesture or say the forgiving word, or to do the work that will mean that we have taken ourselves and our vocations in life seriously. Obedience is tied up with living fully as the individuals we are meant to be. It has no relevance at all to cutting off our possibilities or forsaking our genius in the name of some mysterious religious decrees that are supposed to make us humble. We all remember the incident in *The Nun's Story* in which the young sister was told to fail her examination out of obedience in order the better to pursue humility. We have, thank God, gone beyond the days when people believed that this could possibly be so. Obedience asks us to be true to our nature, to do something during our lifetime with the equipment we are given, to be true to our ideals in good weather and bad, to be faithful to our promises and to our friends. It means triumphing over difficulties—not the imaginary ones in the old horror stories of obedience—but the very real ones that are intimately connected with genuine living. We sin against obedience not when we fail to do what somebody else tells us but when we back away from doing what we recognize as the right thing for us to do.

July 6
Improving Your Prayer

Many of us would like to find a book in the self-help library telling us how to improve our prayers. As a matter of fact, there have been innumerable books and tracts on the subject, most of them read eagerly by those interested in praying better and many of them put aside as having bestowed temporary relief at best. It may just be that prayer is one of those activities which is too important to be worked on directly, an experience that refuses to yield its secrets to those who, for whatever reason, push it out of its context by placing too much exclusive emphasis on it. The very titles of some of the writing done on prayer suggest that it has been placed into this category; you have heard, for example, about the *practice* of prayer, or about getting into the *habit* of prayer, words that fit into the general notion of spiritual *exercises*. Prayer may require concentration at times, but not the same kind that is needed to improve the swing of either a golfer or a baseball player; also, prayer may not profit from the kind of practice that supposedly gets you into Carnegie Hall. You may develop the habit, but that does not mean that it will be a living, human activity; prayers by rote, no matter how systematically or punctually recited, hardly seem like prayers even to the person trying to muster up the devotion needed to mutter them.

July 7
This Notion of Prayer . . .

puts too much emphasis on the polished performance of the one who is praying. Much of the stress connected with private prayer comes, according to theologian Gregory Baum in his book *Man Becoming,* from the old and inadequate definition of prayer as "lifting the mind and heart to God." According to Father Baum: "Prayer is always and every time initiated by God. God speaks first; man listens and responds. Listening always precedes response. Prayer must be defined as man's listening and responding to the divine Word." Prayer, I would suggest, becomes a by-product in the life of a person who has learned to open himself to God's Word in the whole experience of life; genuine prayer belongs to those who grow in awareness of their human responsibilities for life with and for others. Like most of the richest of man's experiences, it cannot be grasped directly, nor can its course be charted or predicted with the sure grace of a mathematical curve. Prayer falls more in the category of friendship and love than in that of athletic or social skills. You cannot practice it any more than you can practice life itself; you enter into it and respond with all that you are but you kill it when you get too mannered or self-conscious. Prayer multiplies itself as a problem for those who are too concerned about doing it well; the effort to preserve form almost always diminishes substance.

July 8
Praying Is Not Passive . . .

even though it begins with listening. To listen well demands
intense and active concentration; you must work at listening or you never really hear anything. That goes for all human relationships but it is just as true of our relationship
with God. The place you listen for his voice is not necessarily in the quiet cool of a cathedral carpeted in stained-
glass patterns by the afternoon sun. God is more likely to be
heard, as he has been before, in the whirlwind of human
affairs and relationships. He can only be heard by those
who are ready to open themselves to all the events in which
men struggle to discover and fulfill their human promise—
in those moments of tenderness and tragedy when man's
spirit and energy know their most agonizing tests. A man
cannot look compassionately on the world of men, at once
so noble and so foolish, and not pray as he does so. The
Word of God breaks across the ridges of our lives like the
sun rising on the desert; the Gospel is understood best by
those who listen to history at the same time. The man who
cares is the man who prays; the man who tries too hard to
make prayer an enterprise separate from the life of mankind will always have difficulties with prayer, and will always look in the wrong direction for a solution.

The man who does not flinch at the scarred beauty of
the world has learned not only to listen well but also to
give the responses which demonstrate that he is in contact
with the Spirit. Many people pray in this active and effective way but they do not realize it, or, because they have
been so conditioned to regard formal prayer as the only
real kind, they hesitate to give the name of prayer to their
activity. These people need encouragement to understand
that they are alive to the meaning of prayer in the
healthiest way we can imagine, with the unself-conscious
spontaneity that marks the lives of people who know how

to love. They need not look beyond themselves for a place to pray; they are there already. One is reminded of Chesterton's verses: "Step softly under snow or rain/ To find the place where men can pray;/ The way is all so very plain/ That we may lose the way" ("The Wise Men").

July 9
The People Who Pray Best . . .

indeed, the ones who come closest to fulfilling the Gospel instruction to "pray always," are those who fit together in life. These are the persons who are most sensitively in touch with themselves and with others as well as with the context of the culture in which they meet their obligations in life. Those moments are truly prayerful when we are not hiding anything from ourselves nor looking for ways to hold ourselves back from giving the best of ourselves to life. This special self-possession means that a person can tell his own pulse beat from the drumming of the crowd, that he lives and responds as he is. That is the kind of individual Irenaeus described long ago in his much-bannered saying, "The Glory of God is a Man Fully Alive."

July 10
How Can You Tell . . .

when a man is in possession of himself? That is not a very hard question to answer, although you may have to look carefully at the merchandise in this age of masterful image-making and dissembling. It is never really very hard to recognize the person who is in touch with his own personality; you feel it as soon as you meet him. I do not mean the strange experience of being overpowered that we sometimes have when we encounter a person who uses the smoothest tricks of manipulation on us. It is hard to breathe with people like that because, although they have a powerful presence, it is largely defensive and untempered by any naturalness.

The man in contact with his authentic personality will, first of all, be a growing person, constantly expanding his horizons of work and love. That does not mean that he will be a captain of industry or a famous hero; it does indicate that he is always opening himself to people, ideas, and the happenings around him. Secondly, he has the power to look at himself with some objectivity, to reflect, in other words, realistically on his life and behavior in a serious way. That does not make him a philosopher or a writer of books, but he will take time to think, to contemplate his movements and sense of direction in life. Thirdly, he continually works at keeping himself together; he integrates his beliefs and experiences, his thoughts and feelings, rather than permitting them to run on separate and distinct tracks from each other.

A person like this has control of himself; not some fearful or strenuous control in which he wrestles with his impulses the way Jacob did with the angel, but rather a peaceful wholeness that comes from things fitting pretty well together inside of him.

July 11
I'll Pray for You

What happens when we say that little phrase—something we find ourselves saying, writing into a letter, or otherwise promising many times in the circle of each moon? Do we really mean it? And, if we do, what do we mean when we say it? For some, it is a style of reflex sacramental, as easy to utter as it is to say grace before meals while thinking of something else, or as taking holy water at a church door. But now, people have come to ask if we can do each other any good by our promises of prayer. After all, God knows what is going to happen anyway, and, for many, praying to influence his decisions seems anti-theological and very self-concerned at best. It is a good line at sickbeds, wakes, or in other awkward moments during which we want to assure another of our Christian concern. But does it have any more meaning than, say, giving an oriental prayer wheel a few spins? Or did the prayer of petition go out with the bishops' silver-buckled shoes?

Petitionary prayer makes good contemporary theological sense; in a way it is a statement of faith about our understanding of the universe in which we live. I think that there is another level of profound significance here as well suggested by the reality of the exchange that occurs between two persons when one promises sincerely to pray for the other. The latter has actually placed himself into a new kind of relationship with the one to whom he has made the promise; he has committed himself to the other's world of personal concern; he has, in other words, made himself present to the one in need in a new and vital way. Promising a prayer is not the same as making a mental footnote to say an "Our Father" at a later date; neither is it some kind of imaginary benevolence comparable to a shouted "Good luck!" or "Bon Voyage!" It means that we have redefined ourselves in relationship to our friend or acquaintance, that we have enlarged the boundaries of our selves in order to stand closer to the other at a time when that is exactly what he needs.

A shift occurs when we cast the vote of our time, attention, and prayers for another human being; we are, through the power of the Spirit and the reality of our commitment, with them in a new and vitalizing way. In other words, the man who means it when he prays for another has given something of himself to that person; he communicates faith, hope and love in a truly living way. When we pledge our prayers we invest ourselves in a healing and enlarging way in our neighbor. Praying for our friends, or even for our enemies, is not some vague hope that everything will work out well. It includes a refashioning of our stance toward them, a new and concerned openness that means we are actually with them in a manner that makes a genuine difference to them as individual persons.

196

July 12
Not Asking for Much

There is an economy, even to happiness, that is understood only by the wise and the loving. Some of the principal laws run this way:

Pleasure does not equal happiness.
Only a small quantity of the right things in life is needed to produce happiness. Inversely, a large quantity of the wrong things (even when we mistakenly think they are the right things) cannot produce it at all.
Pain cancels out pleasure.
Pain cannot cancel out genuine happiness.
Large minuses in life can be borne on the foundation of small pluses in our human experience.

When you take a close look at man you realize that he neither needs nor asks for very much in order to achieve that relative and elusive state which we call happiness. Of life's delusions, none is greater than the idea that happiness is complicated, related to volume rather than value, and always far off or at least just around the corner. Man can be staggered by many blows and frustrated by many disappointments; life never looks very good when we are flat on our backs. The wonder—indeed, the very miracle—which we do not recognize often enough is how little it takes for man to pull himself together, stand up and once more head in the right direction.

One of our problems is that even though it doesn't take much to get us going again we sometimes do not know what the raw materials of contentment are nor how to ask for them. We continue to look in the wrong places or to believe that we can take the money and run toward the kind of security that does not necessarily go along with happiness. Maybe it is a rhetorical luxury to say that we do not need things. We are uneasy about proclaiming this until we really get the things we want; it is only then, after tugging and pulling at them as we do, that we can safely admit that they are not intrinsically satisfying. Attitudes are important whether we have possessions or not; attitudes arise from a complex of experiences that cannot easily be measured. A patient examination of our deepest attitudes and values alone reveals the nourishment that gives us life.

July 13
What Does Man Need?

Beneath the contemporary calls for the liberation of both women and men we find a craving for the simple staples of the good life which depend, in the long run, more on the way we look at each other than on anything else. There are plentiful signs of the times which tell of man's search for uncomplicated things and simple pleasures. On a weekend, even the city dweller dresses like a country gentleman while strolling in the sun and letting his imagination transform the high rises all around him into Marlboro country. He wants a more fundamental feel for things—the experience of fresh air, plain foods, and the tiredness that goes with honest exertion. A man might acquire many of these things and still discover a hollow feeling inside himself and that, in order to be happier, he needs the kinds of things that come only from other people. These things—qualities —come under very familiar headings: Belief, Faith and Hope.

Men are by nature believers; they seek something to invest their faith in, a plan or model that will make sense out of their experience. In Leonard Bernstein's famous *Mass*, the celebrant intones, in a voice that might belong to every man in this day and age, "I'd like to say I believe." When, for whatever reason, man claims not to believe in God, this does not mean that he gives up believing. He craves belief, turning to astrology, the arts, or some other course of meaning for his life; "I believe in music," the popular song recently told us. He needs to interpret what is happening to him and to put it in some frame of reference in order to justify his work and his relationships. Man never outgrows his need for belief, for the kind of faith that is at once expansive and sensitive enough to help him identify and live more deeply in his human experience.

July 14
Faith . . .

begins, of course, with simple human experiences, with believing in each other before we can believe in anything beyond us. The only thing we can know directly is each other; we can never imagine that we will ever find God by looking away from each other. Faiths wear out—they literally become unbelievable—when they are preached by men who speak about God's being near while they stay at a safe distance from people. I was reminded of this by a letter I recently received from a serviceman with a serious psychological difficulty. He wrote: "I went to the chaplain but all he did was tell me of how little faith the men seem to have and how little they seem to come to him for help. When I told him the nature of my difficulty, he seemed disturbed and said that he had never heard of anything so strange. I don't know any time when I felt so bad in all my life." For some reason people have resisted the simple truth that faith in God means nothing if we have not been able to express faith in somebody else.

Faith includes many elements, not the least of which is the ordinary virtue of trusting. There are two edges to trust and they are both quite sharp. But when we examine our lives, we realize that we do our best—that we have always done our best—in the presence of someone who believes in us, who thinks that we are able to do something our own way and succeed at it. We remember those people because of the simple but very profound investment they make of themselves in us. It is a living kind of experience that transforms and energizes us as nothing else possibly can. Only as we reflect on this do we come to see how much of the basic substance of life is involved in giving our trust to others. Trust, in addition to changing those to whom we give it, changes us as well.

July 15
And Hope

This quality is something else which, even in small amounts, enables man to go a long way. Hope is one of the most powerful aspects of human experience. Researchers are becoming increasingly aware of its vital role in many human transactions. It is not some vague well-wishing about the future. It is very closely related to the basic element of trust—the fact that we must open ourselves in an unguarded way when we commit ourselves through the special relationship of hope. Men need to look forward to the future; they need a future even if they have to break their way into it through dreams. We get some sense of the strength of hope when we see how much people depend on plans that will never be realized, notions that will never become realities. It is a fact, for example, that a very small percentage of people actually build anything on those wonderful lots that are sold to them for second homes or retirement places. They may pay a little on them for years; it is worth it to them just to feel the deed and to talk about what they intend to build some day. However, this is the fabled stuff of dreams and not real hope.

Genuine hope is far more realistic; it means that one person sticks with another through the struggles to grow, or to get well, or to write the great American novel. Hope means that there is actually someone who sees into the future with me, someone I can count on when my own hope begins to weaken, someone who can give me a transfusion of his or her own life energies in order to keep me afloat in heavy weather.

Hope is as many-dimensioned as trust. Important, for example, is the role of expectation in helping others to do their best in life. This is an underestimated role, however, and we have become estranged from the human magic that is involved when we believe enough in others to summon from them their best efforts. Perhaps it is more obvious when we look at the deadly absence of expectation in the lives of people. When we do not expect much from another person it is almost a certainty that he will not produce much. When we do not invest in someone, in other words, we cast a vote against his future. It is far better to make a person face the tension associated with reaching for ideals than to have him experience the kind of semidespair that falls upon people when we do not expect much from them. It is a part of leadership to expect one's colleagues to do more than they themselves think they are capable of. Leaders need not control, nor do all the work themselves; they must be wise enough and strong enough to hope for the best from others. Research has shown this to be true in settings as varied as army battalions and hospital wards. It is not a joke to observe the reality of hope translated into action when a teacher or a doctor or a priest expects the student, the sick person, or the penitent to be able to succeed in the future. Men really do not need much in order to do well; expecting them to succeed is one of the most important ingredients. That is why just a drop of water is enough when given in the name of the kind of life Jesus wants all of us to have. It explains why manipulation, no matter how stylized or seemingly effective, never produces lasting human growth or betterment; it is too contrived to give birth to any real life.

July 16
And Persons Need Love

We have known for centuries that a little of this goes a very long way indeed. It may be true that love, at its best, comes intermittently; but it also comes very intensely. Most of the time we live more alertly because we know that it is there, that someone cares, that there is someone who waits with the understanding that makes it safe for us to be ourselves with him.

And love lives on symbols which constantly sign its name to our lives. Man needs to celebrate his love, to remember it and to put it into words or gestures of tenderness whenever he can. Love means people can be close, that they are not alone, and that although they remain separate they can bridge the gulf that unsoftened individualism scours out between them. The first experience of love, or even its rediscovery, is enough to give a man heart against all the challenges of the world around him. Life only becomes drab and dull when we have forgotten love or given up on expressing it to others. We are not alive without it and, as we look at life, we know the marvelous effects of even the smallest amounts of it when it is genuine. Love comes best of all, of course, to those who give it away or at least try to forget themselves in their relationships with others. It becomes more elusive for those who disguise their interest in it, or pretend that they are beyond it, or self-consciously look for "meaningful relationships."

July 17
And We Need the Kind of Culture . . .

in which we can experience all these values. This is something in which we all must have an interest—the creation of a society where people have a better chance at the kinds of things that build their happiness. One of the tasks of organized religion is to alert man to the treasures which are on hand all the time, the small things that alone have the power to make us happy. It would be enough if the churches were able to be with us in our sadnesses and to remind us of the things that make us happy.

202

July 18
Man and Woman at Midsummer

There are thoughts you can have during the summer that you hardly have at any other time of the year. On the long days that trail slowly into nightfall, questions that stay buried in the snows of winter break into our consciousness to surprise us. There is a sort of ache that goes with these kinds of questions because they are so hard to put into words much less answer satisfactorily for oneself. The lull of summer lets us feel the pains we are too busy to contemplate at other times. Summer is a time for wondering whether we have come the right way in life, whether we have made the right decisions, and whether we are heading toward a future that will give us a sense of meaning we had always hoped for. Some of these questions touch men and women very profoundly, especially in a world where so much that is connected with marriage is being debated and discussed in a fashion that many married people never dreamed of when they were younger. Man and woman may not speak them aloud, but questions like these can trouble their sleep and distract them in their waking hours:

Does love really exist and is it possible for the ordinary man and woman in the contemporary world? So many commentators rank true love as a rare and temporary thing, a glistening treasure that, for too many couples, turns out to be made of paste and glass. They sound like the seventeenth-century observer Rochefoucauld who wrote that "true love is like ghosts, which everybody talks about and few have seen." Married people cannot help but wonder about their own love, at least for an instant, in the strange dry time out of time that the summer season brings.

Do I really know myself, a man or woman may ask, and have we ever fully met each other? Have I been as honest as possible and are there many things in my own development that I would have to mark as "unfinished business"? Are we in touch with each other or just with our ideas of each other?

July 19
More on Love at Midsummer

What is the meaning of the mixture of restlessness and longing, the unnamed yearning that I sometimes sense in quieter moments? If I listen to it, would it cause me to change my life from the way I am presently leading it? Or am I just afraid to think further because I do not like the idea of change?

Can people be in love too long? Can they grow tired of each other while hardly noticing it, drifting imperceptibly away from each other as the love they count on grows hollow because they have not nourished it properly? Do we take each other so much for granted that we only remember our love on bigger occasions like birthdays and anniversaries?

What is this pain, partly from my disappointments with myself and partly from the disappointments I have experienced with others? Does it mean that many of my decisions were wrong, or that I have just pursued them to a point where I can no longer turn back?

Do we spend time with each other in a way that enables us to break through our own confinement, or do we just tolerate life together, passing the time with smiles that mask the feelings we have never shared with each other?

The above are hard sayings and they come in many versions. They are normal questions, however, for living persons who are subject to the stresses and strains which come into every life and every relationship. These questions can be shattering for some people because they seem to tear at the very fabric of the only life these people have. They are dismaying for others who never thought that such wonders would work their way into personal consciousness. They are, nonetheless, typical of the underside of our souls which the vacation season gives us the leisure to inspect. They do harm only if we do not admit that the doubts and worries are there; they frequently disappear, once we can speak them aloud at least to ourselves, and recognize them as the signs, curious at times, that we are alive.

July 20
What Is the Worst Time of Summer?

There are several schools of thought on the issue of which part of the summertime makes people most vulnerable to the disquieting kind of questions we have already discussed. It is strange that we can feel the stress of life so acutely at vacation time. It is worthwhile to remember, however, that the insulation of our emotional lives always wears thin around the time of holidays. It is not surprising to find people sad rather than happy on occasions when one would expect them to be celebrating. The human heart turns to memories at the time of holidays and to thoughts of things done and undone, of words spoken and unspoken, of happier times and higher hopes. Sometimes a wide border, rather than just an edge of sadness, comes with such recollections.

As to summertime, the question becomes whether we are under more strain before, during, or after vacation. The answer, of course, is that there is a peculiar strain to each phase of a vacation. Vacation may provide some rest but there is a new kind of strain that goes with this. The miracle is that so many families manage to stick together throughout the vacation time with so little mayhem committed. Somehow it works and, despite the grimness of the trip, the rained-on picnics, or the outrageous prices, people have a way of making the best of things.

July 21
The Vacationer's Mistake . . .

is to imagine that, as a mother or a father, he or she could really be on vacation. Very few people have the luxury of getting away from it all. And most of those who have escaped do not look very happy in their expensive seclusion. Expect vacations to introduce a new and more challenging kind of strain, one that makes you wonder whether the whole thing has been worthwhile or not, and you will not be so upset when questions like these arise. These are the kinds of questions that are natural, a part of the mystery of man and woman and of family life in general. As a rule, expect to make more war than love on vacation and you will find that you come out at least even.

July 22
Sore Points

To be acquainted with the tender spots in the relationships between men and women prepares us to deal with them constructively if not perfectly. It also wards off disillusion, cynicism, immature escapes through fantasies, withdrawal, and other similar behaviors. The following are some of the constants in the tension that goes along with real love.

Man and woman are always capable of hurting each other, of betraying the trust that is at the very heart of their life. That's the damnable thing about lovers; they do hurt each other even when they really do not consciously wish to. This is part of the exchange of vulnerabilities that marks genuine marriage. The fear of hurt, however, can kill love and can cause persons to back off and remain a distance from each other. This may be the most destructive of all the strains that surround marriage.

The lack of self-understanding can project itself onto life and the world in general. Man and woman can generate confusion because of a failure to pursue their own identity. Constantly to be aware of oneself, of one's feelings and motivations, is a difficult task. It is a task, in fact, which demands that we die to ourselves many times in the course of each day. Furthermore, this awareness is essential if we want to understand ourselves and possess ourselves so that we can share life in an effective way with other people. Self-understanding is essential to the deepening of relationships which the course of love, howsoever true, demands. When an individual does not understand himself, or refuses to do so, then he not only fails in the pursuit of his own identity, he also strikes a death blow to any relationships in which he participates.

July 23
The Failure to Break . . .

cleanly the mother-dominating relationships in life can have a profound effect on how the man and woman who are husband and wife get along with each other. If husband or wife or both find themselves so dominated by their parents, seeking to please them more than each other, then they have not yet found a home in which they can live together. It is sometimes a long struggle for a man or a woman to grow out of the past in order to live in the present relationship with husband or wife in a fuller way. The healthy separation from one's parents need not be a harsh or destructive experience and it should be carried out with sensitivity—but it should be carried out. Psychological independence obviously does not demand physical separation; it does, however, demand a sense of independence and self-definition which frees the couple for a fuller relationship with each other. They will have troubles enough in building this life without having to face the ghosts of their own families.

July 24
Neurotic Needs . . .

can sometimes infect marriage relationships, imposing upon them a strain which sometimes seems to be invisible but which is nonetheless very real. The presence of neurotic need may be associated with some of the points which have already been discussed. The failure on the part of individuals to recognize the flaws in their own make-up or their own emotional difficulties, even when these are minor, can introduce a distortion into a marriage relationship which all the novenas or papal blessings in the world will never straighten out. It takes hard work, a willingness to develop insight into one's behavior, and a desire to modify oneself so that the traces of neurotic difficulties do not interfere with the marriage relationship. Now, as a lot of amateur psychologists like to remind us, to some degree we are all neurotics; it is not, by that very fact, a blessed state. If our ills demand compassion and understanding, they also demand hard work and a determination to grow up. This is true even when we are well past the years when our growing should have been finished.

July 25
Sexual Problems . . .

are also often related to the above points. The experience of sex in marriage frequently becomes the focus for many other needs or unconscious motivations. Men and women are very vulnerable in the sexual areas of their lives and they are not helped much by the prefabricated answers or over-enthusiastic advice that we find in many contemporary books. One principle, enunciated recently by Dr. William Masters, may be helpful in this regard. When people think that sex is something that they do *to* each other, they are probably in the grip of some neurotic difficulty or some immature state of development. When they think that sex is something they do *for* each other, they are in about the same situation. When they come to the point of understanding that sex is an experience which they have *with* each other, then men and women are on the right track, trying to grow and be sensitive and expressive of their true concern for each other.

Men and women can hurt each other because of the conflict of their expectations, because of their varying ideas about each other and what they can reasonably set as goals in life together. This touches on the champion sore points of all time—the use of money, the management of the house, and the manner in which the children are raised. The "Murphy Principle" applies here. Unless a man or woman can communicate on the basic elements of life, then most things that can go wrong will go wrong.

July 26
Renewing Your Marriage

Midsummer is as good a time as any, not only to confront some of the problems that plague men and women, but also to reflect on some of the ways in which they can respond more lovingly to each other. First of all, it is important for men and women to be able to realize that they are always going to live with the types of strains that have been discussed. Life consists largely of solving problems, not in reaching some plateau where difficulties no longer exist. This is as true for marriage as it is for anything else.

The question brings to mind the scriptural question, "How can a man be born again?" Each marriage exists in a religious environment. This environment, however, involves not merely going to church or receiving the sacraments; the couple must construct it in each other's presence. Living together and trying to love is a profoundly religious experience. Men and women must realize that their relationship to each other is not a preliminary bout on the card of life; it is the main event. What they are to each other, what they do with each other—these are essentially religious actions through which they actually give life to each other. Men and women live the life of the Spirit together, not separately, and when they realize that their struggles to reach each other (even when these struggles are stretched out over many years) are also their way of living in the mystery of Jesus, they can achieve a perspective on marriage which is very helpful as well as very realistic.

Religion and belief fit in with the struggle for wholeness which we encounter at every turn in life. The first step toward dealing with the stresses that sometimes become more apparent during the summer than at other seasons is the realization that life lies in facing and going to the heart of what these experiences mean. Life does not lie somewhere beyond them, or on a distant and better day, or after the time of retirement. Men and women must help each other to be born again on numberless occasions during their life together. They may find that the test of whether they are ready to love their enemy or not comes, surprisingly enough, not in their relationship with strangers but in their relationship with each other. People who stand close to each other are constantly discovering new things about each other. The richest discovery of all is that they make their journey of the Spirit in each other's company and that a love that is pursued sincerely has already introduced them to the meaning of eternal life. They already understand the answer to the question, How can a man be born again? They live it out each day of their lives.

July 27
The Spirit in the Summer

The notion will seem unlikely at first but, if you believe that the Spirit keeps revealing the truth of the world and ourselves to us, you may learn a lot during vacation time.

Take the beach, as a good example. Here we are revealed in many ways to each other although we sometimes do not look closely enough to truly understand the depth and the richness of what the Spirit tells us. The beach is as good a panorama of the human scene as we are likely to come across. Maybe that is why Jesus spent so much time at lakeshores and at picnics, why he preached to people from boats and seemed to have such a feeling for those gatherings of men, women and children who were hungrier than they knew. In the gospel we read that Jesus had "compassion on the crowd," that he had a feeling for these crowds of which we are so often a part.

Look around the next time you are on the shore. The people are not really very different, physically or spiritually, from those who crowded around Jesus. They come in all shapes and sizes, and few of them even come close to resembling the beautiful people who live in magazines and movies. Mankind unretouched roams the beaches of the land, out of shape, splotchy and sunburned. Look at him and you will see us all, showoffs and castoffs, young lovers and lonely old people with parasols, a great throng milling back and forth but somehow, miraculously, making room for each other on a hot Sunday afternoon. We all look splendidly vulnerable in our bathing suits, an image which demonstrates that we are at the mercy of everything that can go wrong and that, like all living things, we come out in response to basic things that are good for us, like sunshine and water and clean air.

July 28
You Cannot Gaze Long . . .

at the crowd on a beach without sensing it as a commonplace example of the living mystery of revelation; we are revealed in these moments in all our flawed grandeur, like peacocks who keep moving even though they have lost a lot of feathers to life. Look around at the crowd and think of the worries its members are trying to forget or the good time they are trying to find for themselves and their families. Think for a moment of the debts and mortgages, the sickness and the yearning that these people know and you cannot help but be taught by the Spirit of understanding. You learn to be more patient and respectful; you get a richer and more tolerant feeling for everyone who struggles against the odds to make a good life for his loved ones and his community. There are some mean people under those burdens, that is true; if, however, you could look deeply enough, you might find that you need not indict or be mad at them, that you might not, were you in their position, do half as well as they.

The longer you look, the more profound will be your compassion for the crowd and the better you will understand Jesus' desire to feed them generously. You will also come to believe that, knowing us as he does, God will never be too harsh on people like us—the sinners who can still find forgiveness and whose vulnerability and need for the Spirit are never more clear than when we gather on a summer's day on a sunny beach.

July 29
The Case for Anxiety

We have a way of transforming some of the most natural aspects of our human experience into estranged enemies who must be bested at all costs. There is, for example, our continuing cosmetic battle with aging, abetted by jellies, injections, and a friendly plastic surgeon. It sometimes seems that Sir Francis Crick, co-discoverer of the double helix, is correct in his estimation that Americans look on the human condition as a disease of which they must be cured. If this is true about our reluctance to grow old gracefully, it is even more correct about our attitudes toward anxiety.

The poet tells us that we live in an age of anxiety; we have, however, been doing our best to break out of it. Our dealing with anxiety is not always direct; we prefer, indeed, to try to look away from it, or to anesthetize it, or to lock it up in some unused jail cell of the psyche where, like the Count of Monte Cristo, it can only chip at our inner selves and wait for a good moment of escape. Worry, after all, is a far greater constant in our lives than either death or taxes, although these are related to our seasonal crops of anxiety. It is pervasive in our lives and it is related more to our personal relationships than to our technological surroundings. Instead of trying to get at the heart of our anxiety in order to deal with its causes, we play a game of psychological hide-and-seek with it. We would rather keep running than look it in the eye. Perhaps this is why the tranquilizer Librium is the most-used prescription drug in America.

It may also explain why, in giving advice to others or to ourselves, we employ a strange and impossible formula: "Now, just stop worrying! The thing you have to do is stop worrying!" We know that it is impossible to stop worrying but we keep telling people that it is a strategy of choice anyway. But is it? It may be helpful to look more closely at anxiety in our lives.

July 30
The Work of Worrying

The experience of worrying is not only acceptable but, properly understood, quite functional for all of us. Psychologist Irving Janis has used the phrase "the work of worrying" to explain this. This idea is patterned on Freud's insights into the meaning of grief and mourning in our lives. Mourning, as he saw it and as we can also understand it, serves a profound and positive need in human beings. We need to grieve. The loss of someone close to us, for example, is never something that we can just shrug off; it reverberates in our personalities on levels well below our conscious awareness of pain. The concept of mourning, far from being sentimental, as some inhuman observers would have us believe, is vital for the reintegration of the lives of those who are left behind.

July 31
Mourning Provides . . .

the time and the appropriate rituals through which we can "work through" the emotional loss we have sustained. There is, in other words, psychological work to be accomplished throughout the time of mourning—a set of experiences essential if the individual is to heal himself and feel whole again so that life can go on. Tears are not meaningless, nor are reminiscences about someone who has died; they are part of the work that we do in our times of grief. Persons who will not mourn or who feel that they cannot allow themselves the expressions of mourning only drive the problem under the surface of their souls; it reappears, as repressed matters often do, in disguised and desperately painful forms.

There is a native and intuitive wisdom in the sense people have about their need to mourn. They understand, for example, that it cannot be hurried and they will tell you, "I'm really still mourning; I'm not finished yet." The same wisdom tells people when they have completed the work of mourning. I recall a priest friend of mine speaking of his dead sister whom he had loved deeply. "One day," he said, "I realized that I had mourned long enough, that it was time to put away all the pictures and mementos I had kept out for so long."

214

August

August 1
A Time to Worry

Worrying is just as functional and purposeful as mourning and it can be denied or forced out of our lives only at our own peril. Janis observes that worrying enables us to "work through" our fears in much the way we handle our griefs in mourning. The difference, of course, is that worrying provides us with a way of dealing with our emotional reactions *before* rather than *after* we experience some blow in our lives. Worrying, by its very nature, anticipates something that is going to happen; it alerts us to some forthcoming danger by sensitizing us to its early-warning signals. Each of us has had this experience at some time or another; we sense what we might describe as a funny feeling about a situation, or we report some apprehension that we cannot fully explain. This is because at some level of our emotional functioning we are picking up clues that we cannot label accurately but which alert us to personally relevant developments. If we dismiss these signals out of hand we may miss something very important for our own safety or well-being.

The human person is made to notice things, even very small things—like a shift in the wind or a change in the tone of someone's voice—that translate into a healthy kind of worry response. Without this sensitive system—which is found in its highest form in artists and poets—we would not survive long and would soon be overwhelmed by sudden and unanticipated realities. This is why it would be extremely dangerous ever to try to breed or condition the capacity for fear out of a person; we desperately need it to stay alive both psychologically and physically.

Only the very dumb or insensitive experience no anxiety at all. That, of course, may lead them to do what may appear to be very courageous things. On the other hand, it may also suggest that they just do not understand what is happening inside themselves or in the world around them. The genuinely brave person is the individual who has some sense of the dangers ahead and who prepares adequately to deal with them. The courageous person understands what is going on both inside and outside his or her personality; in fact, his freedom to worry constitutes part of his armament against being destroyed by the dangers or difficulties around him.

August 2
How Does It Work

Research on the attitude of surgical patients is instructive about anxiety. Some people deny all concern and seem almost unflappable up until the moment of surgery; they are not going to worry no matter what happens and they make little inquiry into their own condition. A second group tends to worry about everything in an excessive manner, driving relatives and the hospital staff to distraction in the process. Their worry mechanism is set at high, an adjustment that is as dangerous as no worry at all. A third group, however, experiences moderate concern and seeks a reasonable amount of information about what is going to happen and what they can expect in the way of discomfort after the surgery.

August 3
The Ones Who Would Not Worry

The first group turn out to have a difficult time after their operations actually take place. Not having worried and not having anticipated the difficulties of recovery, they are frequently quite upset and tend to get mad at the doctors and the staff for not warning them about what they were getting into. The extreme worriers are not much better off because they are so flooded with worry that they cannot use the preoperation period intelligently as a time to prepare themselves for the experience. The patients who experience moderate worry and who have some idea of what will happen to them come out of the situation in the best shape. They require only half as much in the way of sedation and recover in a more self-possessed and peaceful state. They have, in other words, accomplished the work of worrying in advance of their operations; it has proved functional in preparing them for what they were getting into—and they get out of it better than the other groups of patients.

August 4
What Does It Mean?

Aside from the conclusion which we have already suggested about the functional nature of worry, this and similar studies suggest a crucial variable that is involved in the important and anxiety-producing situations of life. This is the role information plays in helping people anticipate what is about to happen to them so that they can rehearse the incident mentally and thereby prepare themselves more adequately to handle it. Information is the most important of all the variables in the hospital study mentioned above: it seems to make the difference in helping people to work through and complete the work of worrying before the surgery actually takes place. The most potent combination is the freedom to worry in a moderate fashion over facts that give a realistic appraisal of what the individual will actually experience. The persons who deny anxiety and who do not want to find out what is going to happen are far more vulnerable to bad reactions on both a physical and psychological level afterwards. This insight has application, not only for physicians, but for all of us who have responsibilities for other individuals in any manner.

Try to tell the truth: It is important that people know something about what they are to undergo, whether it is in connection with a family problem or a school exam. That gives them the raw material for healthy concern; the more it matches what actually happens the better they will get through it. Telling the truth does not, of course, mean telling horror stories that paralyze the reactive processes of others and make it impossible for them to do a little sensible worrying. We ought to tell as much of the truth as is necessary and do it as simply and unaffectedly as possible. Telling the truth does not include the "confrontation" techniques that are so popular among some psychological enthusiasts today; you are just trying to acquaint people with a realistic sense of what they are about to experience, not trying to rebuild their character.

Give people enough room to worry: The overprotective deny others the opportunity to face the truth of their own lives. This is a crippling thing to do to anyone and it is bound, in the long run, to have serious consequences for those deprived of the chance to experience constructive anxiety. Unfortunately, there is a great deal of overprotection in one form or another these days. Its common form is the "don't worry" approach but it shows up in many other guises as well. There is, for example, the "Keep cool, man" school of thought that cuts away a person's right to have upset and concerned feelings at all. A good way to wreck another's life is to convince him or her to deny his or her feelings in the name of a pseudo-adult stance of living above and beyond caring. This takes them out of the action altogether and makes them the prey of a life that can be very harsh and unforgiving when it finally catches up with them. The kids who live by coolness may one day react in the same way the unworried surgical patients did—with anger at those who failed to inform them about the nature of life.

August 5
Don't Offer Platitudes

Yet another way to prevent people from doing the worrying they need in order to survive and grow is the overpious and unrealistic appeal to religion. "God will provide," the preacher says as though the realities of the lives of people around him could be ignored altogether. That may be fine for the preacher but it is hell on his parishioners when they find that they cannot pay their bills because they have not taken the precautions that a little healthy worry might have inspired.

A variant of this approach, now currently enjoying a revival, is to face life by praying unrealistically about it. This does not just include the "deals" with God that we tend to make when we are sick or otherwise pressed against the wall. This new-style prayer has far greater implications because of the subtle and perennial pull it exerts in turning people away from the sensible and concrete things they can do in order to make the world a better place for everybody. Praying excuses us from the healthy anxiety we should feel about the enormous problems around us to which conscience bids us to respond. Praying all by itself has never been enough. Prayer works best when those who pray also let themselves worry about their contribution to the needs of mankind. That is why some courses of meditation to calm the soul may be depriving us, in the name of renewed piety, of the anxiety we should feel for all the work we have yet to accomplish. Here again, our anxiety should be moderate and informed so that we can reasonably take on those tasks which we can fulfill with our time and our talents. Faith never flies blind; it has a good sense of the world and it enables us to see it more clearly and to be concerned about it more appropriately. Mistaken prayer can lead many persons back to the exile from man in which prayer is just talking to ourselves so that we cannot hear the tremors of concern that should properly ripple

219

across our psyches because of the numberless challenges of what seems to be a wicked and uninviting world.

Vocalize things to worry about: Lovers can also kid themselves about the signs that should cause them concern in their relationships. They sometimes do not permit themselves to worry until it is too late to do anything constructive about their long-simmering problems. Have you ever heard a man or woman say "I never knew you felt this way about it!" or "Why didn't you tell me all this long ago?" When we do not want to give heed to the facts that should make us concerned enough to do something about them, we buy a little of what might well be termed "fool's time." Failing to read the signs, preferring not to experience the anxiety that is appropriate when something is out of phase in an intimate relationship—these give false and limited comfort to any man or woman; they are temporary and betraying strategies that may be regretted but not undone in the later wreckage of a marriage or a friendship. Worry, in appropriate amounts, tells us that something is wrong that only we can make right.

August 6
Signals in the Night

Sometimes the worries that we refuse to face during the day emerge at night to try to get their message across to us. They express themselves in dreams, but ordinarily these are difficult for us to analyze by ourselves. There are other moments, however, when worry nibbles at the edges of rest. We would be better off paying attention to these worries and trying to understand them rather than trying to drown them out. These worries include the battalions that march across our pillows, even when we are very tired, the moment we turn off the light. These thoughts and images may have been standing in formation and ready to proceed all day. When we have kept them out of awareness by keeping busy or distracted, they seize the first moment to make their entrance. Their parading makes us restless but counting sheep or multiplying nightcaps will not make them go away. They are telling us of the worries that are at work on the underside of our consciousness. We would do better to try to sort these out so that we can at least be concerned in a constructive way about them.

August 7
A Sure Sign

When we wake up early and cannot get back to sleep, it is frequently a sign of the same kind of worry. There may be no armies of worrisome images, no definite shape to this anxiety, and yet it is clearly there. Perhaps an exploration of our current activities or relationships will reveal the cause of this situation. Waking up early tells us that something is bothering us at a deep level. It is as clear a signal as we are likely to get; its message is that we should inspect the rest of our lives more carefully.

August 8
The Asceticism of Worry

We read in the gospels that Jesus told us not to fear; well, how do we square this with the idea that a little worry, like a little wine, is good for the human person? Jesus never asks us to do anything that is totally inhuman; he speaks always of those things which enable us to discover and realize a fullness of our real selves. He never means to rule out the work of worrying. Indeed, in the account of the agony in the garden, one can sense that, on the eve of his own death, Jesus anticipated and struggled through the reality of what lay before him. His was a realistic prayer, not that he be delivered from his anguish, but that he might face and accept the accusations, injustices, and sufferings that would mark the fullness of his work. Jesus did not fear excessively and run away or deny his experience; he looked straight at it, knowing a special loneliness that prepared him for the last lonely hours of his life. The tragedy is not that Jesus should have known fear in anticipation of his death but that he should have experienced it without the strength and support of his closest friends.

To face events realistically, to allow ourselves to know enough truth about them to become moderately and constructively concerned—these have never been easy human responses. They are, in fact, a part of the dying which we constantly experience when we are truly alive. The Christian senses a deeper mystery here, an understanding that even worry incorporates him somehow into the sufferings of Jesus. There is a profound asceticism involved in becoming aware of what is going on inside of ourselves and why. To do this a person must yield up preconceived notions, self-congratulatory stances, and the defenses that keep him from hearing the message of his own anxiety. He dies a little with each discovery of truth; what die, however, are those elements of self-encapsulation which keep us from knowing a fuller and richer life. Resurrection is an experience that may be incomprehensible to the person who has never suffered the small deaths of ordinary living that attune us to the presence of authentic religious mystery in our lives. Even worrying helps us to recognize something of the pattern of life, death, and resurrection which repeatedly recurs in our days as a sign of the ultimate meaning of everything we know and share together. Without anxiety, without the capacity to suffer and die and rise above it, we would never know who we are.

August 9
When Our Feelings Go the Wrong Way

"Say what you mean," the wise man tells us, but human beings find that in spite of all the good will they can muster this is sometimes the hardest thing for them to do. The reason is simple although it points to something about us that is complex: We find it difficult to say what we mean because we are often not sure just what we mean ourselves. Our words serve as the symbols for what is going on inside of us; they are meant to bear the weight of our feelings and so to communicate our identity and convictions to others. Problems arise because our feelings can be tangled within us, our motivations can be mixed, if not scrambled, and our conflicts can sometimes be too painful to face directly. The result? We say what we mean, but when any or all of the above conditions are present we say it so indirectly that we cannot understand it ourselves. Sometimes you can recognize this in others more quickly than you can in yourself but the same process works in all of us. We may be talking about the weather or ball game scores on the surface but, from the depths where we really live, we are saying "I am very angry!" or "I am very hurt!"

August 10
What Are We Waiting For?

We are, in fact, *waiting for someone to hear us,* that is, literally waiting for someone to hear *us* rather than just the words that we speak. We go about this indirectly for reasons we will presently discuss, but it is worth noting that we are all on a daily voyage in search of understanding. We want understanding from other persons far more than we want either arguments or advice. The problem is, of course, that when we express ourselves indirectly it is doubly difficult for others to sense the real message we are sending. This is why they end up giving so much advice, trying to talk us out of what we are really experiencing.

August 11
A Good Example . . .

occurs during one program of the public television series on the now famous Loud family of Santa Barbara, California, who permitted cameramen to trace their daily paths for several months. In one of the episodes, the attractive wife, Pat, goes to her brother's house to announce that she has decided to get a divorce, that after twenty years, five children, and the achievement of many middle-class goals, she is facing the fact that there was never much in her relationship with her husband, Bill. Her sister-in-law, in the classic manner of all novice helpers, either does not want to hear or cannot hear what Mrs. Loud is actually saying; she keeps telling her that what she is actually saying about the wreckage of her marriage cannot be true. Mrs. Loud cannot get through the barrage of counterarguments and so it becomes increasingly difficult for her to say what she means. Underneath all her accusations of Bill's infidelity, absences, and broken promises, she attempts to tell her relatives something like this: "It hurts too much to pretend anymore. There has never been as much in our relationship as there seemed. Everything has turned sour and I am just beginning to realize how empty and painful life will be when the distractions that have kept me from looking at this—a household of growing children—won't be there anymore. I'm angry about all this and I want out while I still feel strong enough to get out."

We may not approve of this kind of statement but that is not a good reason for failing to be able to hear it in all its heart-wrenching truth. Each of us, in some way or other, is like Pat Loud, sending out sounds about ourselves as a ham radio operator might click out messages into the darkness, hoping only that someone, somewhere, someday, may hear and respond. Understanding alone enables us to hear the whole message and to find our true selves and the true personalities of others in their deeper layers of meaning. Our largest troubles come when we fail to listen carefully to what we are communicating in this indirect mode; that goes for listening to ourselves as well as to others. To explore another contemporary example, let us turn to:

August 12
The Generation Gap

We want to consider the generation gap especially in regard to religious obligations. *"I'm not going to church any more,"* the young man or the young woman announces to parents who could not be hurt more by a blow with a two-by-four. The tug of war then begins with the parents getting more exasperated even though they come to settle for a little apostasy in the name of keeping the family together. There is no more frequent question after lectures these days than "How do you get the college-age kids to go to church?" This all has a familiar ring, doesn't it? Well, it is a classic example of symbolic communication, of emotions being shifted into the wrong gear, of messages that come in a package marked "religious faith" that have nothing to do with religious faith at all. The real message —the one from the feelings that, on the surface, go the wrong way—usually involves something more fundamental in the relationship of parents and children. It is one of the ways in which young people test and express their own inner longing for some independence even while they are, by circumstances, quite dependent still. The struggle to separate oneself from one's own parents is not unhealthy or inherently disrespectful; it is an aspect of the way in which we develop a sense of our own identity and work out a more adult relationship with authority. The issues beneath many religious discussions spring from this level of reality but they come out as disputes that are quite different. The message of the young is "I must move away from being a totally dependent child if I am ever going to be an adult." The parents, taking the tempting bait of the religious discussion, may offer any number of rational arguments to persuade their children of the desirability of going to church. Sometimes they even resort to authority —obviously employing a device that is part of the problem —in hopes that this will have the desired effect. They bring in the priest or the minister, or they quote the reasoned discourse of some distinguished ecclesiastic, in what is usually a vain hope that this will get the children back to the Sunday services. And the parent is symbolically saying, "It is hard for us to let you be independent when we are convinced that this is the best thing for you."

No rational arguments ever healed a situation that is dependent on a sensitivity to the nonrational elements that are at the heart of it. And nonrational does not mean irrational; it suggests rather that what is going on outside is confusing to all of us and that we must listen with a talent for translating emotional symbols if we are to understand what is happening to us. Americans have classic difficulties with displaying strong feelings—for example, with the expression of their aggressive feelings in a clear and human form. That is why so much emotion comes out so twisted, why so many angry messages are sent in disguised form across the networks of the human condition.

August 13
The Name of the Game

Frequently we play the game of *displacement,* a psychological strategy through which we handle our feelings without letting ourselves know quite what we are doing. Through this mechanism we take the aggression generated by a certain frustrating person or situation and express it not at him but at somebody else. Many innocent dogs have been kicked in the name of the displacement of aggression. Why do we do this sort of thing?

Our anger gets out indirectly when we would be ashamed or would feel guilty if we expressed it more appropriately. A person may feel, for example, that he cannot get mad at somebody he is supposed to love—so he gets mad at somebody else instead. We also displace anger when we are afraid that a direct attack would lead to retaliation; this is how bullies are born—by picking on people who cannot effectively fight back. It also helps if there is some similarity between the object of our indirect aggression and the one who is the real target. If the substitute is too similar we will find it just as uncomfortable to express the ill feelings; if the substitute is too dissimilar we will not be satisfied enough by striking out at him.

Scapegoats are individuals who meet all the requirements for the roundabout expression of aggression. They must also be easily identifiable and incapable of mounting effective resistance to any attack. This is why minority groups frequently suffer during periods of war or of economic distress. It is much easier to shift our corporate frustration onto these people than it is to direct it toward the actual sources of our dissatisfaction. This is precisely why the Jewish people of Germany, in the aftermath of World War I, came into such sharp focus for defeat-stoked hostility of the nation at large. The failure to deal with the real causes of our anger can lead to massive and otherwise unaccountable events like the killing of many innocent people.

August 14
We Can Also . . .

be just as guilty of scapegoating as the Germans were. Look around the school, social organization, or office where you work and you will be able to observe this process. You can even find it in the church these days; haven't you heard the following phrases uttered from time to time?

The church's troubles are caused by women leaving their convents . . .
The church's troubles are all caused by those know-it-all theologians . . .
The church's troubles are caused by young priests who don't pray anymore . . .
The church's troubles are caused by psychologists and sociologists . . .

227

The church's problems are caused by the Catholic press . . .
The church's problems are all caused by these old-/new-fashioned bishops . . .

You can extend the list indefinitely, but note that each of these groups is relatively small, easily identifiable, and that they cannot comfortably or easily retaliate to any of the accusations. It may make us feel good to assign blame so freely but it does not further the work of the church nor the discovery of the deeper causes of our frustrations. Indirect aggression offers unconstructive relief for conflicting feelings; it almost always makes things worse instead of better.

August 15
What Would You Say?

Giving advice is a traditional pastime that is more blessed for the givers than for the receivers. Advice is something that only seems easy, as we ourselves may have thought in reading the punchy advice columns in our local paper. "Why," we say, "I could do that just as well myself!" Maybe so, but at the same time we may be underestimating our responsibility and overestimating our talents as occasional givers of advice. When we are asked for advice we are invited, for the moment at least, into the sacred territory of another's personality. It is a place in which we could easily trample on feelings and meanings, especially if we are absolutely sure that we know what the other should do. This is something for all advice-givers—from parents to preachers—to think about. Test yourself right now with these excerpts from real letters.

What would you say to this military man? "So it's not the sickness that bothers me so much, but rather taking those first few steps, finding my way out of the desert. Confession is one of those steps, yet I resist. I'm afraid. I'm afraid because I don't know how to handle it, how to straighten things out. (The harder I try to disentangle myself the more tangled I become, like Brer Rabbit and the Tar Baby.) The prospect of confession looms as an incredible ordeal. Maybe I could do it once, but I shrink from the very real possibility that I will have to endure it over again—because of the very real possibility that I will fall again. I can tell you in writing and from a distance about my sickness—even in detail, if necessary—because I don't have to face you in the light of an office or even in the darkness of the confessional. I can recount my sins because the prospect of eternal damnation for inaccuracy does not hang over me (though I know how childish and foolish a notion that is). What do I do? . . . How do I grow up?"

And what would you say to this elderly lady? "My husband and I were married over a quarter of a century ago. During the early days of our marriage, he informed me that while I was not unattractive to him, marital relations were. Months elapsed without physical contact except very occasionally . . . . There were no hugs or kisses, except a peck when he got home from work. All our married life has been devoid of any marital closeness. I did suggest that we see a marital counselor but to no avail. I feel guilty because the love which motivated our marriage is missing in my feeling toward him. The doctors I consulted suggest that he is lacking in an attraction toward the opposite sex. My friend has also been deeply hurt by her husband who has taken sides with his family against her. He claims that his former alcoholism has been her fault, and that he agrees with verbal castigations his family have given her on many other scores. We have tried to rationalize our mutual difficulties in order to give one another some support. My friend and her husband have grandchildren. While God has not sent us any children, many years of teaching have provided the company of children for me. My friend's suffering would be changed to joy if her husband could tell her that he was wrong in attacking her and deserting her while she was under fire. Do you have any suggestions for two marriages which are being lived out in a kind of deep freeze? We are both supplementing our frustrations by occupying ourselves in volunteer work for the church, etc. But what torments us is that we feel that it could be different."

August 16
Or to This Lady?

"Although my letter may appear to you rather blunt or even disgusting, let me please point out that I am no religious crank. My views on sex differ greatly from those of the church. My views however, unlike yours, are based on sound, undistorted reality. I have not only read and studied about sexual feelings—I have also experienced them. I had a very strict Catholic upbringing both at home and at the convent where I was educated. As far back as I can remember every word, movement, or thought was either 'dirty' or 'immoral' if in any way it had even the remotest connection with the human body. My teachers seemed to be obsessed by sex and were forever warning us of 'carnal evil.' My mother would blush if a pregnant woman would enter our home. To say that the modern world was sex-conscious seems to me a ridiculous fallacy when the generation who are responsible for my upbringing seem to think of little else but *sex*. . . . I look back and detest my teachers and the doctrine that conditioned me to my present state of mind. I am constantly attracted to other men and overjoyed when I realize that they feel the same way about me. I have been 'on the verge' of infidelity with four or five men and have afterwards hated myself for not going ahead. Yet at the same time I hate myself for the fact that only a deep-rooted 'pseudo' morality stops me every time. I have a desperately unhappy marriage although no one knows of it. Everyone we know envies what appears to be an idyllic relationship . . . . Please spread the word around to your religious colleagues that you've all done your stuff remarkably well and have succeeded in ruining the sexual lives of millions of Catholics. You have done this by making us aware of it and by informing us that we cannot have it. Have you ever tried swimming without going near the water?"

August 17
Or to an Older Lady Remembering?

"There are two things you did not say in your book: Who is boss in the animal world? Also, the devastating effect of too much sex on women of all ages. There is nothing that will usurp the beauty of a young girl's face so fast. Now for a story: About sixty years ago I was an independent, only child of wealthy parents. My lovely dad used to call me princess. Of course I had never heard the word sex. Such words were not used in those days. Okay. I was fifteen years old sitting in the kitchen listening to our housekeeper sing. My very old lovely granny 'enjoyed poor health' and usually stayed in bed but she was my best friend. While I was listening to the singing I watched an old cow in the barnyard stretching far out across the rail fence to reach a sweet green branch of a peach tree. She was very intent on grabbing that lovely spring sprig and *seemed* not to notice a big black bull, Tom, approach her. So Tom came along behind her and instantly she let both hind legs strike him violently broadside on his poor head. You could hear the blow a half a block away. He shook his poor head and departed up the lane still shaking it. She did not even look back at any time! I went in to see Granny and asked her about that brutal kind of treatment. She started to laugh, much to my astonishment, and kept right on for several seconds. Then she wiped the tears from her eyes and said, 'Now I'll tell you something about the animal world and always remember it. The female is absolute boss, always was and always will be, that is the way our Heavenly Father made them and if silly women would go by that law, they would not need to run to a hospital all of their lives.' Well it took me several years to enjoy that joke and poor Tom did not enjoy it at all. I wish more people would remember this. What do you think?"

231

August 18
Some Simple Guidelines

Perhaps you have good answers for all of these people. But, after some years of experience in this, I would be very careful about trying to refashion their lives in a hurry. There are two principles that I try to apply to letters like these or other requests for information or advice.

What are the people really saying? Frequently this has little to do with the words they use. They are telling you one story in the narrative of their letter but what they want to say to you is inscribed between the lines. They may seem to be attacking you, for example, when they are really expressing pent-up frustration that gets directed toward you because, for the moment at least, you are the most available target. In counseling, one must be attuned to the meanings that lie beneath the content of the expressions which the individual uses. The real messages of people's lives are contained in these rather than in the stories they tell. Most of the stories are there for illustrative purposes in order to make their main message clearer to you. This is why we must, while reading letters, be alert to the hints of feeling that come from underlinings, exclamation points, and the general tone that at times almost leaps off the page. At one moment it may be rebellion and at another moment sadness; yet in another letter, as in the one immediately above, you sense that a person just wants to share something of a secret that she has long thought to be quite delightful.

What are they really asking for? Here again we must learn to sift the words which the individual uses from the motives for their directing questions to you in the first place. Ordinarily we presume that people are asking our opinion, that they really do want our advice on a particular point. Very often, however, and especially in the kind of letters that I get, people merely want to express some deep and anguished feeling and, for some reason, they feel they can do it to me. This may happen to you as well, for example, while you are traveling. The person sitting next to you suddenly invites you into the story of his or her life. There is something profoundly human in this urge to be heard even when that, in itself, does not take away the difficulty or solve the problem which is described. This urge to tell somebody else is a fundamental and important part of our human nature. We are all like ham radio operators of our emotions, waiting for an acknowledgement of our signals. We want to be recognized, to have the attention and presence of another human being; we want others to validate our existence by at least saying that they hear us. It is something like the feeling expressed by the mother of actress Julie Harris who was recently widowed after a marriage of almost fifty years: "Now I don't have anybody to tell anything to." There is something simple and healthy in people's trying to say out loud, as clearly as they can, what their life means to them. People need this as much as they need food and fresh air. We should not be ready to give them advice when all they really need is a hearing.

Eager advice-givers should also remember that sometimes people only want you to agree with them. They really don't want your opinion or your suggestions; they just want you to stamp "approved" on their feelings or intentions. Things can get quite sticky if we are not sensitive enough to hear this demand in the inquiries of others. The issue becomes, of course, why do they need our approval; why don't they trust their own judgment; why do they seem overly dependent? But don't think that they really want your opinion. You will only be confused and disappointed when they do not seem to hear, much less follow, your advice.

August 19
What Can You Do for Others?

This is a fair inquiry, especially to self-confident advisers who always have a suggestion as to how other persons

233

should lead their lives. Often enough, these bits of advice are given even when they are not requested. You can also observe this in the individuals who set out to save other persons from a fate that they are pursuing quite clearly by their own choice. I am not for eliminating do-gooders, although they have inflicted an enormous amount of discomfort on the world. I am, however, prepared to suggest that before we involve ourselves in the lives of others with homespun free counsel, we might stop and ask just what we think we can accomplish.

One outcome, of course, is that we can feel better. This is especially true if we are plagued with a need to be helpful. I have often thought of starting an organization called "Helpers Anonymous." Every time an individual has an urge to be helpful, he calls up a comrade who comes in and sits with him until the feeling passes. You would be surprised how many disasters and broken hearts would be avoided if such an organization could be called together. The problem is that the people with an incurable need to help often relentlessly pursue those they intend to help. They give no quarter in their determination to find helpees. These enthusiastic helpers act as if others were incapable of running their own lives or of choosing and pursuing their own goals. The ardent helper helps himself far more than others, making a career out of rescuing people from situations from which, in the long run, they may not wish to be rescued at all. "Helpers Anonymous" would be a great advance for civilization; it would temper the enthusiasm of those individuals who feel infallible about prescribing life-plans for others. These helpaholics might redirect their zeal to their own inner emotional states, with which they should come to terms before they begin sorting out the lifestyles of those around them.

A related question asks simply how can we be helpful? Not all the good advice in the world ever prevents people from ending up doing what they want to do anyway. What gift can we actually give to others with some sense that it might be helpful? It is hardly ever advice, especially in this world of the discredited expert. It is, as we have always recognized, something of ourselves. That is what I believe most of those people want in the letters quoted just previously in this book. I do not think these people want advice as much as they want a validation of their own existence that comes from feeling they have been heard by another person. You would be surprised how well people can sort out their own affairs once they have this sense of being heard.

August 20
En Garde

Unfortunately we live in an era in which many helping people feel that the intervention of choice is always to confront the other as abrasively as possible. This confrontation will supposedly cause the other person to abandon defenses and start to reform his or her life. Confronting others may possibly help in certain situations; I never encourage people to do this unless they are very sure of their motives and of the possible rewards which may be accruing in their own emotional bank accounts as a result of this style of therapy. It is a presumptuous thing to do, something laden with far more danger than the amateur psychotherapist even imagines. Perhaps the most we can give to other persons is that understanding presence that acknowledges them as individuals, does not try to run their lives, and respects the choices and decisions which they arrive at honestly and openly. That is what we do give to each other in our best moments. This is, in fact, one of the ways in which we operationally define the meaning of loving our neighbor. God has never meant that we were merely to think beautiful thoughts about others; loving our neighbors means making room for them in life so that they can find their own way; it means giving them the blessings of freedom and trust that allow them to set out on the journey of life with the confidence that they will find their way successfully.

August 21
And for Yourself?

Most people are reluctant to do much for themselves, feeling that they should stay in the penalty box, or work off their guilt or shame rather than even forgive themselves for the smallest infractions of life's rules. They are kind and understanding to others but sometimes they are very harsh on themselves. Perhaps they should realize just how wide human experience is, how differentiated and twisted it can become, and how true it is that we all struggle with problems and difficulties in the human situation. Perhaps we can confront ourselves rather than someone else, not to challenge our faults, but to try to find out why we can be so unforgiving.

August 22
The Worst Advice of All

Next to the old standby, "Offer it up," the least helpful piece of advice connected with the experience of anxiety reads like this: "Stop worrying!" Of course, this is ordinarily just what most people cannot do or they would long ago have followed this hoary suggestion on their own. The man or woman who blurts out fears and concerns—even when they seem small or insignificant—is communicating the raw material of their worry, the strands and coils of human experience which they cannot get together in a smooth manner. Because they cannot do this they are particularly vulnerable to the overriding fears of not knowing what will happen or what they will do in response. The individual will be much better helped by no advice at all than by the injunction to cease and desist from the very activity that cannot be blindly or successfully stopped merely by an act of the will. Even a few minutes' worth of trying to understand the worrying person will do more to calm the inner storms for him.

It is useful to remember that you do not have to solve other people's problems completely in order to be a great help to them. Indeed, to communicate the understanding which enables them to take a less hurried and less frenzied inventory of their own emotions may be as much as we can do for anybody in such a situation. The next time you have the urge to tell somebody to stop worrying, ask yourself why you are so sure that, at your bidding, he will be able to do so. Then try to look with him into his own life, not as a spectator demanding order, but as a fellow human being who can understand because you have had your own share of grief. You will be surprised at what a difference this attitude will make in both of you.

August 23
Are You Enjoying the Trip?

Despite the fact that men and women know that the shortest distance between two points is a straight line, they seldom take this route in the course of life. We are all on a trip, of course, and the style in which we make it tells us as much about ourselves as any psychological test we are likely to take. Not one of us walks toward his ultimate destination in an unbroken and direct manner. Oh, but there are people who do, you will say, remembering those compulsive people who scoot along through the years looking neither to the right nor to the left, so consumed by the tiny steps of their journey that they do not even have time to glance up at the scenery or to appreciate the changing seasons. And, sadly enough, compulsive people often bump into things precisely because it is the swiftness of the trip rather than its meaning that possesses their attention. Sometimes these people complete an arrow-like journey in record time—like the old-church priest who finished his breviary before breakfast—only to discover that they have headed in the wrong direction. This is the fate of compulsive individuals, to be so worn out from their strong-willed concentration that they cannot even enjoy their achievements.

August 24
Some More of Life's Voyagers

There are people who stagger through life in an amiable sort of way, pausing to enjoy something here and then rolling away like an errant billiard ball until another bounce gives new shape to their journey. These trippers burn a lot of fuel—alcohol, tobacco, or drugs—as they go. They seldom have long-range goals for their travels in mind so they wouldn't even recognize the destination if they got there.

Then there are those persons who really never get started, or who lose their passport or their courage and decide finally never to poke their noses out of their comfortable nests. Sometimes it is too late in life when they finally realize that there is a journey to be made.

You could lengthen this list indefinitely to include, for example, the person who thinks that life is one long coffee break or an indeterminate extension of the senior year of college. But it is time to turn to the rest of us, the great mass of ordinary persons who are, interestingly enough, known in the Christian tradition as "wayfarers." We understand that we are to complete a purposeful journey through the years that are given to us and we must learn to trust that, by God's grace and some good human instincts, we will find our way successfully. There are many aspects of being fellow-pilgrims that are important for us to reflect upon. The willingness to set out on our own passage through life is profoundly significant. It is the beginning of meaning for most persons. Our first steps on our own affirm something of our own identities; in the long run only we can take those steps. The temptation to hang back, to avoid the loneliness and possible hurt of moving out on our own, is always very great. The first challenge is one of our biggest but through it we come to terms with our responsibility for ourselves.

August 25
In the Age-Old Stories . . .

of the human race you hear the echoes of this truth. All the great myths, which constitute the storehouse of the truths that we want to preserve in a special poetic language, present this setting out as a recurrent theme. It is not surprising to find that in the Gospels men are forever beginning journeys to distant countries along uncertain trails. Even in the legends of King Arthur we discover a reflection of this. The knights are in pursuit of the Grail; it is clear, however, that the effort to find the Grail is more important than the actual discovery. The stories tell us that each knight had to leave the round table and "enter the forest at its darkest part." This is the point each of us comes to finally in his own life; each individual must enter life at a place where no one has gone before. Each person comes with certain graces and gifts; these cannot be tested nor can the person even grasp their meaning unless he is willing to cut his own path. The unique meaning of life is revealed to the men and women who are not afraid to find their own way. The great myths of history are the stories which we eventually live out in our own lives. So, in a true sense, we are all standing by that darkest part of the forest, that place which we must enter by ourselves if we are to know ourselves and find each other.

Jesus spoke often of journeys, telling us even that he is "the Way," that something about his life on this earth reveals something to us about our own. The point is, of course, that the journey to holiness is not made by looking away from our true selves or by making a potlatch offering of our own talents; rather, it is by actively accepting our individual journeys to personhood that we are enabled to make our way safely. If Jesus is the way, then becoming men and women is the way for us as well.

The journey demands a recognition and acceptance of our own specific identity but it is not a trip that we are forced to make alone. Some corruptions of Christian asceticism have made it seem that heaven could only be approached single file by those who stayed at a safe and respectful distance from one another. The truth is closer to Thornton Wilder's famous observation that we are supposed to "go through life two by two." The Christian life is one of friendship rather than stoic isolation. We may have to begin the trip with a clear sense of our own identity but we are also called to share the identity with others along the way. This is the great secret of the Christian pilgrimage; living by the power of Jesus, we are the ones who make the yoke sweet and the burdens light for each other.

August 26
Losing Ground

Average people are at once caught up in a journey that is mysterious and ordinary, one that commits them to the richest experiences of life while it asks them to confront the most common experiences of living. There is a part of the trip that each of us should expect but which usually catches us by surprise. Yet this is as much a part of the Gospel language of journeying as anything else. It is true, of course, that we can lose our way or, worse still, lose heart at times and be tempted, due to discouragement, to curse the fact that we ever set out in the first place. Men and women sometimes even discover that they are retracing parts of the trip which they thought they had completed long ago. Thunderstruck and guilty, they realize that instead of making progress they have actually fallen back. This happens, for example, when a person is shocked to find that a fire inside, long thought to have been extinguished, can suddenly be fanned to life again by some new situation. The problem, whether it is anger, envy, or lust, lay sleeping in the embers, sometimes for years, and it is hard to say just why, after this long time, it should stir to brightness once more. This, however, is the human situation and such homely truths cannot be argued or wished away. There are some angry names for people who find themselves back in the middle of difficulties they thought they had left behind; some of the self-righteous call them "backsliders" and other moralizers call them worse than that. These terms are unduly harsh to describe something which is so common and so forgiveable. Besides, yelling at people who already know that they are in trouble has never helped them at all. They feel bad enough at discovering themselves in such a fix and, more than the judgmental observers, they want to extricate themselves.

August 27
A Man off Guard

This man loved his wife dearly. He had survived a thousand business trips without ever feeling tempted, even in his lonelier moments, by other women. All he had to do was to think of his home and family and he was at peace. Then, as things will happen in real life as well as in the movies, he accidentally met a woman he had not seen in years. She played up to him and, to his own surprise, he found that he was responding; it all ran counter to reason, as he told it, but he could not deny that the very thing he was sure would never be a problem had suddenly blossomed without warning in his own life. He did not dance his last tango on this trip but he did not emerge entirely unscathed. He was shaken by the experience and newly ashamed of what he described as a weakness that had come up out of the blackness of the past to plague him anew.

This man's story is not unusual. Who is to say what combination of fatigue, unconscious need, or something else might have contributed to his reaction? It is not easy to say but the situation, in itself, should not be difficult to understand. This does not mean that we approve of it or think it a good idea that it occurred. It simply means that

241

we know that ghosts can appear out of the night for any one of us and that if we are not startled by their appearance, we have a much better chance of handling them without hurting ourselves through self-destructive shame or an inability to forgive ourselves.

August 28
Count It a Fact . . .

that our past is not dead and that, in times of stress, we may find ourselves in its company again. The psyche is the only true time machine that we know and we can, long after we have presumed that we were mature, find ourselves transformed into selfish little children or self-absorbed adolescents. The best of quarterbacks gets thrown for a loss occasionally and that is what can happen to us if we are groggy or have our signals mixed up. The important thing is not to believe that we have come to the end of the world; these are the occasions for which forgiveness is made. It is in facing up to the personal complexities that are revealed at these times that we gain the wisdom to live more calmly and compassionately with ourselves and others.

August 29
Losing Ground Only Seems Easy . . .

when we are young and strong enough to get up right away, brush ourselves off, and start again. It is far more difficult when the best of our youth is behind us, when we are scarred enough by living to become the prey of discouragement. Losing ground gives us a few moments to learn more about ourselves and what our lives mean. It is searing to face the residual selfishness that we can carry into our adult lives, but it is strengthening to realize that, in the Christian view of things, losing ground does not mean losing hope. Confronting the deadness inside of us would be totally discouraging if we were incapable of beginning afresh and finding redemption in a renewed commitment to forgiveness and love.

Losing ground helps us to accept our identity as sinners, not out of some vengeful self-hatred but out of the realization that of such is the kingdom of God. For this reason, the Gospels are filled with stories of journeys, and of people who lose their way on them; our belief assures us that Christ calls us just as we are to come home with him. He came, he tells us, to preach to sinners, to offer healing to those who need a physician, to help us to stand again after we have fallen back into the behavior of our self-centered childhood. The real problem arises when we are afraid or ashamed to admit our faults, when we hurry by them, or pass them off as caused by others or generated by the hard luck of life. Sin closes its grasp on us only when we cannot call it by its rightful name. Whether we are forgiven or not depends on whether we can admit and forgive ourselves in the presence of an everfaithful and understanding God. We need to come to terms with the forces within us that work against our doing that.

August 30
That Is Why . . .

the married man previously spoken of needs to talk truthfully about his unexpected throwback to problems he thought he had left behind on the trail of his life. Instead of reassurance he requires someone to listen to what he is trying to understand about the ground he seemed to lose. He needs to hear the truth about his adolescent possibilities from his own lips; he needs to admit this as still a part of himself and to accept it rather than to run away screaming and searching for sackcloth and ashes. His best repentance lies in being better acquainted with the truth within himself, something which is far more complex than he realizes. Only as he sees more deeply into his own motivation and patterns of action can he regain the lost ground. He will live more comfortably—and with less danger of future setbacks—as he lives more truly with the man he actually is.

August 31
Pseudo-Innocence . . .

is dangerous, psychologist Rollo May tells us, because it avoids dealing with the shadowed side of our personalities. Neglecting to sense the strength of our potential selfishness we can only be overwhelmed by it when we least expect it. This is a part of us that does not die easily, that cannot very effectively be stifled just by force. Growing people are not estranged from their capacity to be small and prejudiced but they do not smash themselves in order to destroy the infection. People must learn to hear these alien voices inside themselves, to recognize them, and to take away their strength by facing them honestly. Only through this openness can we bring peace and wholeness to ourselves. The more we understand rather than panic in the face of deeper knowledge of our personalities, the more we possess ourselves and the less we will betray our own growth by reverting to infantile modes of adjustment; the more compassionate we will be toward our fellow pilgrims who may be having some kind of personal difficulty; the more surely we will experience the joy that can only be known by those who are comfortable with the human situation.

September

September 1
Autumn Syndrome

Kenneth Grahame, author of *The Wind in The Willows*, could look at September and write, "The year was in its yellowing time," as indeed it is when cooler winds begin to blow through the crack that Labor Day makes in the calendar. Things are never quite the same after the Labor Day holiday even though it is technically still summer and the days are as warm and appealing as freshly buttered toast. The wind has a sigh in it which says that the days are changing . . . and so are we, right along with them. Autumn tells us, in a way that no other season can, that time is passing; perhaps because of the days' deepening mellowness which somehow says that the year is spending itself all too quickly, we realize that we have not quite caught up with the changing seasons, or with many of those important things that are always just beyond our grasp in life. The winter may try a man's soul but the fall can break his heart; it is too full of things just ending and others yet to be done, too rich in memory and promise not to turn a person inward for a while.

The first trouble with autumn is not, however, very poetic. In fact, its reality quickly drains the lyricism from a man's spirit. You have to get back to work in the fall and the remainder of the year, with the storms of winter crackling already in its lungs, stands like a black-cowled judge waiting for all of us. There are a thousand worse things in every man's life but few are as desolating as getting back to work after a vacation; the challenge of this re-entry has never been licked satisfactorily for the individual whose spirits fade with his suntan. In a very real way, the man getting back into the routine of his work—no matter how much he enjoys it—experiences a sense of alienation at the reality of it all. Then, if ever, a person may muse on other choices he might have made, and different dreams he might have dreamed; but there is his work before him and how strange and repugnant it can look as he struggles to get into it again.

A man seldom speaks of these feelings, momentary as they usually are. For one thing, he does not know how or with whom to talk about these feelings. What is this strange voice within me, singing a song of discontent? The average man hardly takes the time to ask himself that as he turns to the roster of autumn distractions—football, a new television season, the first long weekend; but these are trifling compared to what he might learn if he listened more carefully to his own longings. For there is something deeply human beneath his difficult readjustment to even his favorite labors; it breathes a smoky mixture of hope and sorrow that fills the air of life like a fall bonfire; it tells of the molten and restless core of a man's soul and of his perennial ache for something beyond himself.

September 2
Few People . . .

who recognize this experience think that the painful readjustment to work can be remedied by going back on vacation. It is a hint, if ever we had one in our noisy lives, that our fulfillment in this world is never quite final, that we are made for other things and richer experiences. It is a longing for redemption which we feel in those flashes of disenchantment with getting back to our routine, a flame curling at the edge of consciousness which, if we do not dampen it with a sodden mass of distractions, will light our journey toward a deeper sense of meaning. The passing of the seasons catches us off guard for an instant and reveals a religious longing that we may easily misidentify or neglect to explore. Every human heart knows these yearnings and they are not just some neurotic evolutionary residue; they tell us, in fact, that anyone who is truly alive feels the tether of the Spirit. At such moments we understand again Augustine's words about hearts that are restless until they rest in God. At such moments we know, in a way altogether different from the way we know the creed, that we live in a sacred rather than just a secular city.

September 3
But Men Do Not Like Such Thoughts

There is, after all, so much to be done, and the restlessness will soon be submerged in a thousand other cares. What does a man lose when he fails to listen more carefully to the groans of his spirit as the wheel of the year turns? He misses the chance for the long thoughts that are essential to a seasoning of character, the kind of thoughts that make a man look more closely at life and death and the thousand questions in between. He loses the opportunity to sense the rhythm of existence with its seasons of gathering and scattering, planting and harvesting, without which his own roots are dry and unnourished. One of the high prices for the new era of leisure that has opened so grandly for the western world is that it substitutes energetic behavior for the kind of playfulness of spirit that enables a man to contemplate the heavens and the earth. The ache of readjusting to work gives a man a chance to think long thoughts, to face the pain that he does not like to feel at the puzzling, scarred beauty of being alive. The man who tracks the vein of his discontent back to its source has, whether he gives it the name or not, become religious again as he searches for that explanation which holds the world and the seasons together.

September 4
When Friends Fight

One thing you really should know by September is something about the imperfect way in which human beings get on with each other. No man should reach the fall of his life or of his friendships without learning how to get out of the way when two of his friends are fixing for a fight with each other. This need not be a major engagement; a good disagreement over football or some forgotten episode will suffice when two people have, for whatever reason, been rubbing each other the wrong way. The man who has achieved a small measure of autumnal wisdom will not hurriedly step between them when they start exchanging hostility. Why not, you ask; after all, the peacemakers are supposed to be blessed and nobody likes to see friends quarrel. All of this is true but there are times when it is best to let people fight their own fights and get their venom drained off directly rather than indirectly.

Many a would-be peacemaker, watching the storm clouds gather around the heads of his colleagues, has intervened with peaceable intentions only to become the object of his friends' mutual wrath. When presumably good friends start flying emotional storm warnings, you can bet that the difficulty lies deeper than the content of their current discussion; the real reasons for their abrasiveness may not be easy to get at, but it is not helpful to step between them in an incident which is more a symptom than a problem. In fact, it may be better if they can at least get some of their bad feeling out in the presence of someone who does not actively intervene; this serves as a certain constraint on them and, if the third party listens carefully, he may pick up the clues that tell what the real difficulties are between the two. That information may be much more helpfully employed after the tempers have died down. For example, two friends who are very competitive may accumulate grievances arising from their unverbalized contests with each other; they may not recognize nor wish to admit that they experience jealousy or some other petty feeling. Instead, their tension expresses itself in small ways, in disagreements that enable them to express their uneasiness without really getting to the bottom of it. A good example of this was the friendship of writers F. Scott Fitzgerald and Ernest Hemingway; they were never able to admit their hidden fears about their contesting talents, and when they actually fell out, it was a sad and final thing; a number of their friends got splattered by their bad blood. A good piece of Christian wisdom, one that will serve you well into the winter, suggests that when your friends are determined to have a duel it is better to hold their coats than get in their line of fire. You will be much more helpful to them when their tempers die down a bit; that is when the peacemaker both gives and receives blessings.

September 5
Mid-life Crisis

September can be as stormy as spring. According to psychiatrist Herbert L. Klemme of the industrial mental health division of the Menninger Foundation, the transition from young adulthood to middle age is as difficult as the shifts of adolescence. A failure to resolve this crisis of growth leads, according to Dr. Klemme, to the high rates of alcoholism, depression, suicide, divorce and other problems characteristic during this period. The long-recognized "mid-life crisis" explains why many highly creative and productive persons burn out in their mid-30s while others only begin to come into their own at that time. Following the work of psychologist David L. Gutmann of the University of Michigan, Dr. Klemme speaks of three phases in the stage of adulthood.

Alloplastic mastery: the period roughly from 21 through 35, during which the young adult attempts to gain mastery over the world outside of himself, with an emphasis on material gain and the approval of others. *Autoplastic mastery:* the true middle of life from 35 to 60 when a man turns inward to achieve self-mastery; there is an emphasis on personally satisfying tasks at this time. *Omniplastic mastery:* the period from 60 on, during which the man who has passed the earlier tests of life successfully, turns to broader issues of an altruistic and social nature.

According to Dr. Klemme, some men do not pass through all of these phases successfully; they get "hung up" and "may spend the rest of their life making futile attempts to work it through." It is possible, for example, for the person who has thought of himself as quite successful during young adulthood to become disenchanted with his work, his wife, or his entire lifestyle, as he heads into middle age. It is common for him to believe that his job is no longer important or very fulfilling. The individual with this September problem in his life may try to use a solution that worked for him when he was in his April years. He draws on earlier behavior patterns, perhaps to avoid the pain of advancing to another developmental level. It is the middle-aged dog who dislikes learning new tricks. The person may try an extra-marital affair, or involve himself in risky behavior—such as vigorous physical activity or a dangerous stock market venture—in an effort to restore excitement to life. At this stage alcohol can seem the solution to the challenge of mid-life. The woman whose children are grown may find herself depressed because she is no longer needed; she may decide to have another baby. In any case, the transition to the autumn of life is not automatic or easy; for current preoccupation with the young partially blinds us to this human challenge of the mature years. Also, being able to recognize the possibilities of this "mid-life crisis" in our own lives may enable us to understand it in others and help them through it.

September 6
Autumn Is a Good Time

The time of changing leaves is perhaps the best time to think about our feelings because it enables us to meditate forgivingly on the intricacies of the human condition. It is not a simple thing to be a man or a woman, nor to stand in relationship to others throughout a lifetime of stress and difficulty. It is hard because so many of the feelings that river through us come from almost inaccessible headwaters in our personalities. It takes a long time—and a lot of patience—to understand the complications of our own reactions, especially those which involve strong feelings.

This is a time to become acquainted with our feelings rather than just to renew some stern resolution to control or repress them further. It is not easy to admit how small or mean we can be, especially when we are expressing indirect aggression toward some innocent bystander. Perhaps the death autumn asks of us is the one we must undergo if we are ever to accept ourselves in our complicated yet fascinating state. The wonderful promise of the fall season is that joy awaits the man and woman who are not afraid of such deaths, that a deeper happiness comes to those persons who are unafraid of the depths within them, and that peace is the final possession of those who can give up unnecessary wars on themselves or others.

September 7
A Virtue for the Season: Hope

Faith starts us off but it is hope that keeps us going in almost any undertaking in life. A man needs hope in September not only because he knows that the summer is gone but also because the engines of life that have turned sluggishly under the sun now begin to churn in earnest again. He must get back into gear knowing full well that the trees will soon be bursting with fire and that, if autumn comes, winter cannot be far behind. We speak more about hope in the springtime and autumn is the real season for this. Hope is much easier in the spring; the soul cannot help but feel better when everything is turning green. Hope, however, meets the needs of our tightening insides in the season when things show signs that they are dying. Hope beats resignation hands down as man heads back to hard work and hard weather. Hope breathes life into us as the weather changes in our hearts as well as in the landscape around us.

September 8
What Is Hope, Anyway?

It is strange that at a time when man is so concerned about the future he seems to have run low on hope. Hope seems a shadowy virtue to many, hard to define or even to talk about very clearly. It gets mixed up with wishful thinking and other projections of the yearning soul. Diogenes called hope the dream of a waking man. If this is true and if the concerns of the future are as urgent as they are pictured, then modern man must sort out his dreams in order to separate whimsy from vision. The escapes which fantasy provide allow us to kill time in the present but they open no true doors on the future; we arrive in the present only if we see what is truly happening in the world around us. Hope is more durable than a pipe dream; it is not an attempt to talk to ourselves in the same way that we might whistle our way through a darkened alley. Hope is both more substantial and more realistic than this.

Some people think of hope as a force that is somehow independent from us, speaking of it as we might speak of "nature," as though it were a rainbow of energy quite distinct from our lives, something we get a free ride on now and then. Sometimes the rainbow is given supernatural hues, the better to attract the religious-minded who are told by some preachers that the good times are always just over the horizon. Of course, this kind of hope is not hope at all. Hope is a vague assurance to others—a huckster's guarantee that everything will come out right in the end if we sign on the dotted line and accept his interpretation of things. Hope is hard to see clearly in these circumstances, because we can fool ourselves so easily in matters that are personally important to us. It is, even for the best of us, difficult to distinguish what we desperately want from what we truly need.

Others view hope as a form of elegant despair, something you take with a quick draft of cognac and a pithy quote from Camus. Life is easier, the saying goes, if you give up hoping in hope and dig in unblinkingly before the indiscriminate wheel of fortune that decides our lives. That vision sounds brave and it is quite popular; in the long run, however, it is as unrealistic and inhuman as the pipe dream variety of hope. Man is too helpless in this view— and real hope never comes to the helpless.

September 9
A Further Clarification

Hope is a human function, something you only find where persons strive together to discover and realize the fullness of themselves. The big chore in life is rooting our hope in what is real about ourselves. It can, after all, be as unrealistic as the vain expectations of clergymen who wait for the honor of being made a bishop. They think they are hoping but in reality they are merely longing, because of inadequate self-knowledge, for an office which they look on as a reward more than as a responsibility. Hope can be unrealistic in the lives of the husband and wife who have some vague desire for things to get better between them but never do anything to deepen their relationships; things generally get worse, especially when the man and woman have no insight into themselves and no will to change their

253

way of getting on with each other. You cannot speak of hope in such situations. It just does not come out of thin air or as a gift unrelated to what we are like as persons.

Hope, perhaps more clearly than any other virtue, depends on what we are truly like. There is no measure of fancy in the real substance of hope. It completely changes the experience of people who work patiently at understanding and transforming themselves; hope goes along, in other words, with men and women who take their own growth seriously and who understand that individual growth is always intimately linked with the growth of others. Hope is not grandiose nor does it promise the fulfillment of wild-eyed dreams. The truly hopeful are those who are not self-conscious about it: They are too engaged with their present commitments in life to become anxious about what they will be like tomorrow. These people build their tomorrows in the love they share today. This is hard work, much more difficult than dreaming, and far more demanding than turning down an empty glass after toasting a hopeless world.

September 10
Hope Is Never Separate . . .

from the persons we are and the way in which we move through life together. Each step we take strengthens the meaning of hope both for ourselves and for others. When we speak of people we can count on, we are referring to the solid persons who are there when we really need them, the individuals with some depth who do not scatter at the first sign of pain or danger. They generate hope by the fact that they are alive and always prepared to share themselves. Hope, like many other precious realities, is learned only through experiencing it. In the same way, we teach it by committing ourselves to the lives of others. Hope is the vision we possess of what we can be and what we can realistically build in the world in which we understand that all we really have is each other.

September 11
What Does Hope Tell Us?

Hope tells us that despair and indifference are defensive options for the person who believes in God and in the purposes of his creation. Hope tells us that the script of history was not written a billion years ago by a self-amused deity who mischievously allows it to unwind in our prearranged lives. Hope, in other words, tells us that we are not victims and that what we do to and with each other makes a difference in the course of events. Hope tells us that tomorrow can be different from today, that the universe is not a closed and self-devouring system. Future-oriented hope tells us that truth reveals itself as honest men commit themselves to the long slow task of discovering it. Hope reassures us that those who give themselves fully to life will find their way successfully through its snares and difficulties. Hope gives us the confidence that we will find our true selves if we allow our old selves to die. Hope is not a subtle whisper of stage directions to those who are uncertain about life. Although they may not realize it, hope is the virtue that is possessed by people who try to believe in and love each other. God does not deny hope to anyone who faces life and its many discouragements straightforwardly.

Distance lends enchantment but it also permits us to see hope in better perspective. We can, for example, look back and see the ways in which we have changed during our lifetime, the goals we have achieved, the ideals we have reached or revised more realistically. That we have changed reassures us that we can still change. Hope is the ingredient that enables us to achieve the modest miracles (the best ones we have) of being faithful to our word, our friends, and ourselves. Hope, in other words, has a familiar face, to anyone who has tried to do his best in life. Hope is a vital sign about the way we believe and try to love. It is in the very breath of a man who takes other people seriously and who tries to see all of life in the perspective of the truths which Jesus taught. Faith in Jesus allows us to put the world and ourselves together, giving us the sense of direction that is the pulse of living hope.

Furthermore, hope tells us that we need not fear, that we can move into the future calmly if we take our commitments seriously. Hope reassures us that there is no necessity to repent drastically if we are sincere in trying to give life to others through our work and through our love. Hope tells us that religion is not built on threats of what might happen to us if we do not behave; hope illumines religion as a function of the person who is trying to be alive. Hope, in other words, says we do not have to hide in the mountains waiting for judgment day. Instead, hope invites us to come down into the valley where men live because that too is its dwelling place.

September 12
Security vs. Hope

There is a big difference between being secure and being hopeful, although many people do not understand or even take the time to think about it. When a person emphasizes security, he may be avoiding the risks that are involved in being truly hopeful. He may skirt around the edges of life, hoping to forestall its dangers at the risk of not tasting life very fully. That is why there are so many financially secure people who smile ruefully, if at all; and there are many financially insecure people whose lives sing of the meaning of joy. Security is a good thing; it is crazy to live on overextended credit with some notion that this is the same thing as being hopeful.

Living with the kind of emotional security that keeps us armored against life itself is a very different business. That kind of uneasy security kills hope. Here's how to tell one from the other. The person who invests everything in security wants the guarantee that nothing can ever go wrong in his life, that no one will ever double-cross him or say an unkind word or be false to him. You can be this secure but the price is withdrawal and defensiveness. The hopeful person, on the other hand, lives always on that perilous rim of life where everything can go wrong, where openness exposes him to this possibility at almost every moment. It also frees him for an experience of the fullness of hope.

The man who wants to be secure aims at getting everything down perfectly, with no margins for error. He is very anxious unless he has a bond or a double lock against the thieves who can break in and steal. The man who lives by hope is not so obsessed with security and perfectionism that he is afraid to try something again. He knows that, when you live by hope, you also live by vision. You know that life is never over and done with and that, despite the risks involved, the freshness of a new experience in friendship, love or work gives a meaning to life that those who can only think of security never understand.

September 13
The Seeker of Security . . .

buys the mechanical marriage manuals so that his lovemaking will be perfect and this becomes more important than his relationship with his beloved. The man who lives on hope, and does not want to perform like a machine, can live with the varying quality of his lovemaking, knowing that the love in which it is set generates the hope that makes life worthwhile. The man who values security wants to know the way the story ends before he begins it. He likes to be sure of the outcome of things. This is admirable in some forms of human experience but it is almost impossible to live this way. The man who lives on hope can never be sure of how things are going to turn out; he can never plot the future for others or be sure of how they should live or what they should achieve. He has to live with the doubt and agony of trusting others; he also leads a life that is filled with the surprises and delight which accompany the experience of genuine growth.

September 14
A Person Who Emphasizes Security . . .

does not want to be hurt, so he builds his life in a way that will mimimize this possibility. The man who lives by hope, however, can be hurt at any moment. It is a fragile thing, the loving heart that believes in and opens itself to others. But the man who will not be hurt will never know real love while the man who is not afraid to be hurt will drink deeply of the waters of life itself. The man who emphasizes security is prey to discouragement when, despite all his plans, life overwhelms him and he finds that he does not have the inner resources to respond. The man who lives by hope faces the difficulties and hurts of life realistically and is ready to move forward once again. He is like the courageous lady in Rapid City, South Dakota who, viewing her flood-wrecked home, looked up at a TV reporter and said, "Well, let's get on with it." There was an echo of Christian joy and abiding hope in that little lady. It is little people like that who fill up the supply of hope that the world needs badly in order to face the future.

September 15
In Every Reaching Out

It is important to remember that hope does not just come through stirring words; you would think that campaign oratory would have convinced us of this long ago. In fact, it is difficult to believe much campaign oratory precisely because so little of it is founded in reality. The finely honed words and the dramatic pauses take our hope away when they are spoken by someone attempting to manipulate rather than communicate genuinely with us. You feel uneasy when people do this but you cannot quite say why. In a very existential manner, you have experienced the defilement of hope. Hope dies on empty words; and this is precisely what kills us too.

Hope resides essentially in any sincere human gesture of reaching out to another person. This movement, wearing words or gestures, must reveal a measure of concern or commitment to another. Hope demands only these conditions—that we make ourselves both present and available to others. In that moment, hope, like an electric flash, leaps across the gaps between us.

Even the beginnings of hope—the initial sign that it is in the wings—awaken new life in the other. Our understanding of life depends upon our appreciation of the fact that imperfect people can and do help other imperfect people to face and overcome life, to understand themselves, and to redeem each other. Hope depends on the faith that says we are more than passively concerned about each other. The strange and hard-to-kill heresy of religious perfectionism has obscured this central truth for a long time. People have been so concerned about making a perfect act of hope or love or even contrition that they have forgotten the potent quality of imperfect acts. As a matter of fact, hope, love and contrition are hardly seen except in unfinished forms; their perfection comes from the fullness of the hearts that offer them. Whenever people reach out they give hope. This truth is one of the liveliest sources of hope; hope is for humans and its existence depends on beginning, somehow, to reach out. Hope works even if we do not complete the gesture.

September 16
The World Wants Hard Facts . . .

exact numbers, and cold cash, but what it really needs comes from a different order of experience altogether. Men and women respond, as they would to fresh air, to the things that cannot be measured or calculated like quarterly interest, to the elements that are mined not out of the earth but out of our relationships with each other. Hope is one of the most significant of these spiritual realities that tell us that for the Christian hope is more than a beautiful thought. Our hope springs from the risen Lord but only as we strive to create the conditions which make it possible for hope to live. There are some things we should remember, however, lest our alleluias ring like cracked bells across the land.

September 17
Never Just Ourselves

Sometimes, in our desperate or lonely moments, it may indeed seem that way, especially if we have focused exclusively on our own fate or on our chances for success or salvation. There may be a place for self-referent hope but it is not likely that such hope will be very effective if it has not first discovered its identity in relationship to others. Hope grows in the midst of persons who are trying to grow in relationship to each other. We must dig into ourselves for the energies of hope when we are challenged to invest it in others, for their sake. Hope has a difficult birth—and sometimes a short life—precisely because it forces us to break the bowl in which we hoard our self-concerns. That is one of the basic lessons of the Gospel of Jesus and it is small wonder that some people in every age have turned aside from such hard sayings. I learn to hope when I can see another separate from me and can reach out and spend some of my strength for that person's needs rather than for my own. The Spirit is the source of that response, of course, but the Spirit only comes to us in the moment in which we allow some portion of our self-concern to die for the sake of another person. Hope abhors a vacuum; it is not something we are likely to understand if we pull away from the hurting community of mankind in order to lead an isolated spiritual life of our own.

September 18
Hope Has a Homely Face

Hope never looks spectacular and we might easily miss it altogether if we search for it in shining and transcendent moments. The problem of the human situation is that even though we might like to have them, most of us must survive without incandescent experiences of the Spirit. Hope is more readily found in the commonplace of every day— where friends touch and separate after an embrace or a handshake that says, in effect, "I am with you whatever you do today." Hope sometimes has a face filled with wrinkles that remains young because it can still turn toward other persons. Hope is in glances, in letters we remember to write, in promises we take the trouble to keep, and in every simple being close to another—even in silence —at a time of need.

Hope does not have retrospective showings. We may recall times when we have hoped in the past, as, indeed, the disciples did on the road to Emmaus. "We had hoped," they said in the very presence of the Lord who called them back to the immediate nature of the experience. Hope has been in the present tense for Christians ever since. It is not something connected with the past; it comes alive here and now, in this time and place, as soon as we are strong enough to give it away. The idea of hope orients us to somebody else's future but with the instruction that our caring must begin now. It is, in a sense, a moment to moment commitment of ourselves that falls apart if we look too much to the past or too far into the future. Hope simply asks us to look at each other just as we are right now, before we have a chance to pull ourselves together or hide our emotions because we are afraid that nobody will be around to hope in us. Through hope we look into tears and pain, at big mistakes and little embarrassments, and say that none of it makes a difference as far as we are concerned, we are sticking with our friends as long as they need us.

September 19
Hope Works Even in Small Amounts

Hope is fundamentally a small miracle of life and it has its effect even when it is not completely developed; a little bit of the right kind of hope, in other words, does more good than a great deal of bland reassurance. Hope, after all, does not merely say, "Everything will be all right." Rather, it says, "I'm sticking with you whether things are all right or not." The latter is harder to say and to mean and this is why even a good effort in that direction gets across to another person. The essential ingredient is that we transmit a regard that is more *for the other* than for ourselves. Hope is strong enough to communicate itself even in an imperfect state. Research on students in school, for example, has demonstrated that the teacher's expectation that they will do well has a positive effect on student performances. The problem in life is to make even this minimal investment of ourselves in the possibilities of others; the trick is to do it freely and without any effort to manipulate. Even uncut or unprocessed hope lifts others up when they are discouraged or unsure about whether they can go on.

Hope makes us examine our beliefs in others. So intimately calibrated to our own attitudes is the development of hope that we must carefully inspect what is in our hearts toward the innocent bystanders in our lives. Just a quick check may reveal, for example, that we do not, in fact, trust other persons very much and, as a result, we do not hope for much from them. With the peculiar circularity of such things, this leads to a deadly outcome: When we don't hope for much from others they usually won't deliver much of their own promises. Perhaps the worst killers at large today are the individuals who withhold hope out of cynicism or some private sense of self-defeat. Hope has always been built on faith and, far from being something connected totally with an unseen world, our faith has its first roots in what we believe about or for each other.

September 20
Getting Ourselves Together

Maybe, if we can get some perspective on it, life can be seen more clearly for what it is—a succession of good recoveries from our inevitable mistakes. The art of living well—and certainly of living well as a Christian—lies in mastering that part where we have to get up after a hard fall or a bad misplay. The trouble is that it is very hard for us to admit that we have made mistakes in the first place. It is better, we think, to gloss them over or to tell the story in such a way that it is all somebody else's fault. This covers up our uneasiness or our shame, but it does not get us very far along the road to recovery.

September 21
Never Again?

The trouble with most people, when they think about trying to pull themselves back together, is the grandiosity with which they apply themselves to the task. If they have somehow tripped, then the immediate resolution is that they will never—never, ever—let themselves stumble, even gracefully, in the future. The more absolute we make our resolutions, the less staying power we have to keep them. There is, however, something about the unconditional resolution that helps us forget about the mistakes we have made. The first step in a good recovery is to avoid making any resolutions at all; what we really need is a little distance between ourselves and our errors, a little time in which both the mistake and our own selves can settle back into life-size proportions again. After a time lapse we will be better able to make a sensible evaluation about the meaning of what we did, whether it was in losing our temper, drinking too much, or failing to come through in a difficult situation. The least helpful move is to plunge into some absolving promise never to do this or that again: We may feel better temporarily but we will not be better in the long run.

The perspective that we gain through some patient waiting allows us to see our action in relationship to the rest of our life. Often the sudden outburst that shames us is merely the tail end of a long connected line of behaviors that we must understand in their totality if we are going to make a sensible recovery. If we do not hurry into a resolution we may discern a pattern in our lives that will help us to understand ourselves and avoid mistakes in the future. The fall, if we may so style it, may just be the symptom of some way we have adjusted ourselves, or learned to present ourselves to others.

September 22
Things That Happen by Themselves

Despite our American ingenuity and pragmatism, there are certain things which cannot be coaxed or forced ahead of their time. The seasons, as unpredictable as movable feasts, come and go as they will, despite the Farmers' Almanac, rainmakers and our vacation plans; they happen at their own pace if they are going to happen at all. Many other things occur in accord with inner rhythms of their own— for example, pulses which we can feel but which we cannot deliberately alter. However, problems arise when we forget our feelings for the way things are, when we forget the lessons of waiting that are connected with many of the important experiences of life. You cannot work at these the way one might at an external goal to be achieved or a skill to be mastered. These things yield neither to frontal attack nor to the style of incessant practice which we might try with a piano or a guitar.

There are few nobler resolutions to be forged in life

than the one through which we determine to act more naturally and spontaneously. It is obvious, of course, that being ourselves freely cannot be willed without the whole concept self-destructing in our faces. Nonetheless, some persons put an extraordinary amount of effort into being natural. Why else would we find so much make-up and clothing designed to give us a "natural" look? There must be something amiss when the appearance of being natural is cultivated through artifice, no matter how understated the greasepaint or the tailoring. Becoming and being ourselves just happen; they are the fruits of a proper investment of the self in life rather than a cautious limitation of it; being oneself is the easy part for those who do not back away from the hard parts of life.

Securing a reasonably good sense of our identity requires a healthy inwardness on our part, a willingness to listen and follow out the messages that arise from within our own personalities. We must also learn to tell the difference between what is really struggling to come alive in us and the phoniness or lack of development we are sometimes tempted to settle for. How can we tell the difference? Honesty with ourselves is a great help and that, of course, includes an openness to what takes place in our emotional lives. If, for example, we find that we are striking poses in order to impress others, then we are on a track that leads away from rather than toward our true selves. Similar signals give us the clues we need to sort out the complexities of our inner lives. The discovery that we are imposing a burden on other persons just by "being ourselves" is a major sign that we misunderstand our own potentiality. "Take me as I am," can have a good meaning, but it never needs to be spoken by the individual who is freely and genuinely himself or herself. Often enough such declarations have the faint odor of hostility about them; they are battle cries that say we would rather not listen to or believe in what we can truly become. The burden to seek out our true selves is ours; it does not belong to those around us. A person who is in touch with himself never stops developing; it is constitutionally impossible for such an individual not to grow. The fakery of settling for anything less than our genuine self is, therefore, easy to spot; it is a symptom of the individual who has given up on growing altogether.

September 23
Being a Friend

Friendship is a mystery, isn't it? We know that it cannot be pushed, pulled, or imaginatively pretended. You either are or you are not a friend and all the quoted poetry of Gibran cannot transform a nonrelationship into something alive and life-giving. Friends, therefore, do not play games with each other or with the most important elements of their lives. Being a friend may entail work and sacrifice; one cannot doubt that, but work and sacrifice follow from the friendship; they do not—and can never—produce it. Friendships happen and nobody quite understands why. There are, in fact, social science researchers presently engaged in trying to write equations which will allot the factors that seem to make for mutual attractiveness. However, as soon as you begin calling friendship "the study of dyadic units" you may have manhandled it so much that little that is recognizable will ever survive. Friends *respond to each other*. They do not draw maps or design strenuous and self-conscious resolutions about doing good to or for each other. Friendship may demand work but friendship is not work in itself. Perhaps no persons are lonelier than the individuals who approach friendship and love as tasks that one can engineer or master by reading a book.

September 24
Don't Tear It Apart

Friendship is in the order of the things of the spirit to which we give ourselves without much planning or analysis. It works if we don't inspect it too scrupulously and if we feel free of having to explain it away; since it is the same kind of miracle that spring is, it deserves more wonder than rationalization. Being a good friend to somebody naturally leads us to think of and enjoy the presence of the other; this relationship, however, is not hysterical and friends are strong enough to survive separation and distance as well as misunderstandings and random spells of being out of tune with each other. Friendship just happens when persons are open and undefended in each other's presence; it grows when two persons can see each other as separate and can respect and live with this truth. Friends may do things *for* each other, but they are very careful not to do insensitive things *to* each other.

September 25
The Curse of Productivity

Large bands of people who are otherwise among the most charming and good-hearted individuals in the world suffer from the semineurosis of *productivity*. This is not unconnected with some of the issues discussed earlier in this book. It is not easy to describe the productivity neurosis; it is so widespread that many people believe it to be normal. Its main feature involves the individual's feeling that he or she is good only insofar as he or she is productive. This smacks of the image of economic man rather than that of the pure-hearted who easily inherit the earth.

The predominant difficulty of the productivity hang-up is the conviction, frequently unverbalized, that a man or woman's worth is dependent on his or her achievements. Such people do not, in other words, feel worthwhile just in themselves; they have learned a style of relationship through which they barter for everybody's affection by hard work. "Look what I've done," they seem to say, "and you will like me." This places a high mortgage on their own individuality and estranges them from any sense of their own God-given goodness. It is no accident that the book entitled, *I'm O.K.—You're O.K.* is important to contemporary America; these are ultimately soothing thoughts for people who do not think they are O.K. unless they can prove it by pointing to some accomplishment outside themselves.

These persons can never take a day off without feeling so guilty that they work twice as hard or twice as long the next day to make up for it. The same type of person is forever making a deal with his or her psyche: "I'll work all afternoon so that I can feel free to go to the movies tonight." Never trusting that there is something of inherent worth in themselves, they do not get to know themselves or let themselves out to others very easily. They find it hard to love themselves but they love to be hard on themselves. To work is to be productive and for them this is to be lovable as well. There is something desperately isolating about this lifestyle. Those cursed with the productivity ethic cannot enjoy themselves or others very easily; it is even hard for them to take the time to watch the seasons change.

The wonderful thing about what Jesus teaches us is that he loves us just as we are, faults, foibles, and mistakes notwithstanding. His kingdom is a kind of come-as-you-are gathering. Jesus does not invent reasons for justifying his faithful affection and concern for us; he understands and accepts us and bids us to do the same thing for ourselves and our neighbors. Perhaps the beginning of appreciating the great mysteries of those things which happen by themselves lies in letting some things about ourselves happen without forcing them or feeling that we have to explain them or justify them by excessive and self-punishing dutifulness.

September 26
The Sounds of Shallowness

These are unfortunately more familiar than the sound of music in contemporary culture and they may be heard in many places besides uncomfortable cocktail parties. Special sounds exist, as a matter of fact, in the lives of persons who have never understood that the best things in life just happen and cannot be manipulated into existence ahead of schedule or out of due time. Being successful at intimacy is practically a national problem; more people are interested in learning something about friendship and love than they are about wife-swapping and weekend orgies. People want to get to the lasting values in life—the ones that really count; the greatest handicap to this is the shallowness that goes along with the underdeveloped personality. One feels deeply for the individual who yearns for closeness but who does not know how to make the journey there. In America today we may be rapidly multiplying the situations—in high mobility, broken homes, and a general orientation for undeferred pleasure—in which we mass-produce individuals who are handicapped in being able to respond with reasonable emotional freedom to the deeper experiences of life. Nothing is worse than a person with the ache to be close who is without the capacity to be close. Such a person's life is made more poignant when it is filled with the sounds of shallowness.

What are some of these? Perhaps the most familiar are the words and phrases that fill such persons' vocabularies. When you hear an individual describe everybody as "beautiful" you can be fairly sure you are tuned in to the sounds of shallowness. "Beautiful" is a wonderful, contemporary word; it can mean everything and yet it may mean nothing in particular. That it is a popular word does not make it a profound one; a frequent user may be telling more about his or her longing than about a sense of fulfillment. Lots of hugging and kissing sometimes accompany this style of self-presentation; sometimes, however, lots of shallow hugging and kissing may be a substitute for a little of it that has real meaning. Further sounds of shallowness are found in the grandiose resolutions about "building community" or "more meaningful interpersonal relationships" that seem to abound these days, even from dedicated religious groups. People who like each other seldom clothe their feelings in abstract and jargonish language; such language, indeed, mocks the true depths of love and friendship.

September 27
It Is Difficult . . .

to imagine a loving family that would counterpoint its life with the sounds of shallowness. A healthy family never assembles to frame resolutions about building their community; they simply respond to each other in a thousand symbolic ways instead. A mother does not plan her response to a sick child; a husband and wife who have hurt each other have an inner and unself-conscious sense of how to bring healing to each other. Real closeness does not have to work hard at touching the meaning of life; it lives in and with it all the time.

September 28
"Into" This, "Into" That

Another contemporary sound of shallowness filters through the conversations of those who are forever embarked on finding themselves and have successively been "into" yoga, meditation, natural foods, and God knows what. To be up in the air about one's identity has become a large-scale problem and there are those who mistake such fogginess for a mystical state. Roots and goals are difficult for the persons who float from the moorings of one fad to another; they do not often grow old either gracefully or comfortably. Before it is too late I think it might be helpful for persons who find themselves living in this metaphysical twilight to focus on just one relationship and gently attempt to deepen it by calmly sorting out the problems and facing the truths connected to it. The results may be the beginning of a far richer life, one lived in the depths where joy is finally found.

September 29
Creativity: Letting Things Happen

There are lessons for us in the things research tells us about the creative process—that much misunderstood phenomenon which, like the idea of the sacred, is all too often thought of as a distant, undeserved and quite rare experience. You need not, however, live or even look at the world like Picasso to be a creative individual; in fact, you don't even have to know how to paint or read music. Nor do you have to be a temperamental genius, for that matter. People can be creative in many areas of life and many are quite unconsciously this way in things as profound and common as being good parents or friends. This means you don't have to move to Greenwich Village or set yourself up as a nonconformist in society in order to draw water from your own creative wells. The only thing you must do is listen to yourself and to your own inner experience.

Creativity is one of the things which you must allow to happen; it requires a willingness to let yourself become a little disorganized in view of achieving a richer and more integrated personal response to life. In other words, creativity demands a certain letting go of ourselves and our habitual ways of doing things, a surrender of what is staid about us in order to discover what is free and real. In friendship or love one may have to throw away a former style of relating in order to reach across a chasm that has suddenly opened up between oneself and another. Healing never comes from reasserting old attitudes any more than it comes from an effort, however strenuous, to prove who is right or wrong. Our creative power is engaged when we can allow ourselves to become different, when we can permit the old mold to be smashed, even though this leaves us temporarily uncertain about how we should be.

The creative friend—much like the artist—listens to himself in relationship to the challenge and, without combating this challenge directly, surrenders to the process of self-disorganization which necessarily precedes a better reformulation of the personality. For example, the man who has always insisted on at least some of the trappings of the old he-man dominance in relationship to his wife may be very threatened by her sudden fem-lib challenge. It is a scene acted out a thousand times every day and, sadly enough, often not very creatively. There is usually what passes for a rational argument, then some withdrawal on both sides, some pouting or self-pity, and perhaps a new coming together after things have cooled down. This happens over and over with nothing really changing in either party. The hostility is merely impacted by the lack of a more creative response; then it all comes up again at a later date.

September 30
Far Different . . .

are the individuals who listen to themselves and hear something of the dissonance of their excessive insistence on particular views of life; this is the point at which each of us must be willing to let go of at least part of the shell of our characteristic adjustment (which, of course, tells us that we must never do that). Now, the slightly overmasculinized person will not know exactly how to act for a while because he has, in effect, thrown away the script from which he has been reading his lines. Although it is painful, this is the kind of dying that makes it possible for new, rather than just restyled, life to emerge. The only condition is that the person permit this creative response to take its own form within himself. Something that was always there—something his defensiveness would not permit him to recognize—will come into being and he will actually be different in the way he presents himself to his wife. More of what he is truly like will be present and this makes it possible for more of what she is truly like to come alive as well. This is genuine creativity in human relationships and it happens, without people giving it a name, every day. It also incorporates all of us into the Gospel's death-resurrection theme with a greater awareness of how this dominates and gives shape and religious meaning to our lives. The creative Christian dies and rises to the good purpose of greater life for himself and others. He also knows that he cannot awkwardly force these things to occur, he can only assent to the invitation of the Spirit within him that speaks of the promise of recreating the face of the earth.

October

October 1
Inside Depression

There are few things worse than feeling bad on a good day. When we feel down, of course, even the bluest of skies can be ruined with a gray blackness that we pump up out of our own hearts. Our moods change the landscape far more than the landscape changes our moods. A bad mood can strike us suddenly, enveloping us before we know quite what has happened. So we dread these emotional lows but, as with the weather in general, we may still not know how to predict or prepare for them. What is going on here anyway? And what can average persons learn to help them understand and deal more effectively with the sometime emotional guest of depression?

First of all, there is almost always a recognizable reason for depression; it is not a mysterious force sweeping across our psyches like an ill wind. There are causes to this effect and, with a little reflection, we can begin to trace them down. Sometimes the thing that depresses us is absolutely clear; at other times, however, we find it hard to look at its roots. So we get depressed. The textbooks tell us that feeling down is usually associated with some form of loss. When someone we love dies, this very real loss may trigger a depressed reaction. The same thing can occur when a good friend moves away or when some other longstanding association is broken off. The loss of our possessions through a natural disaster, a theft, or some other circumstance will cause us to be depressed. We feel depressed by the loss of status, something which can be obvious, as when an individual gets fired or indicted after a lifetime of presumed probity. It can also be subtle—an internal loss of self-esteem whose meaning can only be appreciated by the individual concerned. This occurs, for example, when we fall short of some ideal we have set for ourselves or when some project with a highly personal meaning collapses on us. There are hurts that cannot be seen by the naked eye, invisible losses that can be added up only by ourselves; yet these are all powerful sources of distress nonetheless.

October 2
An Added Feature

Why should we not be able to point to the cause, admit the effect of depression, and thereby rob the whole situation of its strength over us? The answer lies in the fact that, although feeling depressed can be associated rather clearly with certain events, the emotions that live beneath the blues are not easy to see nor to admit to.

October 3
Anger Down Below

The experience of depression is related to the anger which we feel because of the loss we have sustained. The anger is not handled on a conscious level; it is too threatening to allow this anger manifestation outside so it turns inside instead. Depression, in an approximate image, may be thought of as anger inside out. The man who feels, for example, that he has been undercut by his business associates —with a consequent loss of status and self-esteem—may not be able to do anything about this directly without risking further loss. He consequently feels depressed; this is the wound of anger festering almost literally in his breast. It is no accident, you see, that we speak informally but accurately of "swallowing" our anger on occasion. Not all the Alka-Seltzer in the world will take away the resulting heartburn. When we turn our inadmissible anger toward ourselves it has the bitter taste of the blues.

October 4
What Not To Do

Most of the homemade solutions concerning depression are not very good; they compound the problem, if anything, or at least delay a more constructive handling of it. It is not always helpful to use the old "buck up" routine on ourselves or others. Shocking people out of depression is a delicate and imprecise art that is tricky even for experts. The old jovial "cheer up" is almost as bad because such false heartiness, no matter how determined it sounds, does not touch the hot inner coils of the problem. This is equivalent to saying, "You shouldn't feel that way; there's something wrong with you if you feel that way!" Yes, exactly, there is something wrong and *that* is what needs attention if the person is to make any progress in lifting the depression.

Don't delude yourself into thinking that a night on the town or some other escapade will offer a long-range solution either. It is not at all unusual for persons to turn to certain powerful pleasures, like sex, at times of mild depression but the effect is temporary at best. When trips, parties, sexual experience, or filling your life with enough noise to drown out the depression fail, you will probably feel worse and a little more estranged from yourself. Drinks and drugs are closely related to these escapist solutions except that they add chemical effects which may prove to be quite complicating in other ways. Addiction never helps the sagging soul and despite all the mythic nonsense about merry drinkers, the people who try to drink away a depression only drink themselves more deeply into it. You are not doing a depressed friend a big favor by suggesting that he have a few drinks and try to forget the whole thing. His depression is telling him that he has not yet remembered well enough to bring his conflict into the open. His job is to remember properly, not to forget sloppily.

October 5
Talking about It

Everybody knows that it helps to be able to talk about the things that bother us. The problem is to whom do we talk and where do we find them when we need them? Think about your own experience for a moment. Have you ever felt lonely or mildly depressed and turned to your best friends—including your husband or your wife—only to find that, at the very time you need them most, they are temporarily out of the listening mood? It can happen: They reassure you, change the topic of conversation, or drift off into some subject they are themselves interested in.

There is another variant of this as well: You look around for someone else to talk to—maybe it is the only time all year that you do—and you find that everybody else is in greater need than you are. Before you can say anything, everybody overwhelms you with problems of their own. Maybe after a while you are comforted by the fact that they seem worse off than you but that does not lessen your burden at all. Maybe that is why some people turn to running, jumping, or hitting golf balls when they are depressed. The vigor with which they do these things may reflect some of their repressed anger and get it out even if it blasts off without insight. The difficulty in finding someone to talk to explains the popularity of dogs and other pets; they at least seem to listen loyally even when they have no glimmer of what we are talking about. And they don't borrow money either.

When we are frustrated in finding somebody to listen to us we may well resort to humor, to the soul-releasing laugh that can redeem us when we are caught in one of the homely binds which the human condition provides so abundantly. And there is some support in recognizing that these things happen to all of us, that we are better related to each other because of the small betrayals fate arranges for us each day. They trip up all of us regularly—and being able to laugh together may be as good a medicine as we can find.

October 6
Follow the Anger

The everyday depression, the analog of the common cold for our emotional lives, can best be handled by tracing the sparking fuse of our anger until we can find and identify the situation or person we are really mad at. Until we do this we will just go on being mad at ourselves and feeling depressed. And that impacted anger takes us out of relationship with others and almost out of human circulation. For the average, otherwise healthy person the best response is found in facing the anger which, for some reason or another, is just what we don't want to do. Being able to do this has, however, saved lots of friendships and marriages in which unacknowledged angers have separated people into detached and poisoned spheres. Until they confront their anger they can only stay at a distance from each other.

October 7
Signs of Bigger Problems

I am not talking about severe emotional problems in which depression is such a common ingredient, although it is clear that the amateur remedies are to be avoided there. When a person has a long-standing depression marked by other symptoms of withdrawal, indifference, appetite loss, sleeplessness, etc., then help from a professional counselor should be sought. This is also appropriate for the individual with major and regular fluctuations of mood; these can be signs that cannot be ignored nor treated with home cures. The ordinary person who gets depressed can, however, do himself or herself a great favor by looking into the situations from which hard-to-face anger seeps like a deadly fume. Depressions vanish swiftly when the real causes can be inspected.

October 8
Faith and Depression

We have often been given the idea that the eyes of faith enable us to see another and invisible world beyond us. Actually, faith enables us to see this world and ourselves more clearly than we otherwise could. It does not bid us to look into the hazy distance but into the close-up present to deal responsibly with ourselves and others. The eyes of faith allow us to understand that the deaths that are involved in finding the truths about ourselves are neither random nor meaningless. We all die daily, as St. Paul, that man of many moods, did. The life of the Spirit does not light up remote and unfamiliar tracks in the soul; it throws into better relief the places where we live all the time. The eyes of faith allow us to recognize and affirm ourselves, to come more fully to life in the steady struggles in which we are joined almost every day. These include the death to ourselves that comes from facing the anger we can turn destructively inward. Faith challenges us to redeem ourselves by an honest look at the complexities of our own reactions and an effort to slowly make ourselves whole despite them. It helps us deal with the depressions not by bland reassurances, such as those uttered by rosy-cheeked clergymen on television, but by supplying hard truths about what it means to be human and alive. Our faith helps us to see and deal not only with the blues but with all the other flawed products of our personality—the little evils of jealousy and spite and the small murders we commit out of carelessness and self-concern. All of that, plus the promise of forgiveness and growth, are revealed by the vision of faith. Faith is full of light and it enables us to see where we stand in relationship to ourselves, our neighbor, and the loving God who gives life to all of us. Belief does not invite us to look away from our pains but to see them in a realistic context and to take as much responsibility as we can for resolving them.

October 9
A Sense of Loss

So goes the title of a movie about the suffering in Northern Ireland; it is a theme that can be applied to many experiences in other parts of the world as well. Take the contemporary church, for example, in which people have known so much scene shifting of late. Depression is frequently the reaction that follows an unrecognized or unadmitted sense of loss, especially about familiar religious practices or institutions. I have occasionally marveled at the "hate mail" that I receive from some avowedly religious persons, including priests and nuns. They write things you might not find on a New York subway wall. I realized one day that I was receiving a lot of the anger they feel at the losses they have suffered in being routed out of seminaries, monasteries, and motherhouses or just out of cherished routines.

October 10
What Does Hate Mail Say?

Instead of just being depressed, many of these people are getting their anger out in another way, displacing it onto me and other available contemporary targets. It is the kind of unreasoning thing that happens when people feel betrayed or estranged, when, at some level, they know that a whole way of life is ending around them. That is why there is no point in answering hate mail; it doesn't look for an answer because it is meant only to be a statement, an expression of unprocessed emotion. It does not begin a dialogue; it tries to end one. And it does not do much good just to provide for the physical future of these upset people through retirement homes and the availability of social security. Their needs are emotional as well and, across Christianity, we need a greater sensitivity to the complexities of this very common situation.

October 11
Is Displacement All Bad?

Displacement of deep anger is obviously a serious matter because it can blind us to our true selves and may work harm to others. The mechanism can be found in less treacherous forms, however, and in certain circumstances it is extremely functional. Take a family or a group of close friends or co-workers for example.

It is almost impossible for any of us to live and work closely with each other for very long without rubbing some of the insulation off each other's nerves. No way, as the saying goes. Displacement of a mild sort becomes an important way of handling the hostilities that arise inside any vital gathering of people. It is ordinarily expressed in the kind of "needling" that is found in close groups; this sharp-edged kidding is not just the fruit of good fellowship. This is the kind of thing people do in order to remain friends and lovers as well as co-workers. No great venture could come to pass without some safe passageway through which the inevitable tensions of close living could make a more or less harmless escape. Friends stay friends by kidding each other about their shortcomings; they get a message across in a joking way. Families can criticize each other, sometimes making fun in a way that puzzles outsiders but which is very important for the family members themselves. The interesting part—and the proof that displacement is at work—springs from the fact that outsiders cannot enter into the needling or the witticism; they cannot precisely because they are not sharers in the group's intimacy that makes it all right for its members, but not strangers, to mock each other's foibles.

People setting out to find friendship or to build community should possess some understanding of the secret languages which people learn to speak to each other at close quarters. Men and women need to express their irritations; to try to build a relationship without making room for the playful displacement of harsh feelings is to undertake an impossible task. Communities, families and friendships only work when they are imperfect enough to allow us to externalize our tensions in an eminently human way. That is why it is good advice not to get into the middle of some other family's minor battles; families need a little fighting to be able to stay close and they are just as likely to turn on you if you try to prevent it.

October 12
Looking Good

Despite Narcissus' fabled difficulty with his reflection and all our homespun wisdom about appearances not counting, we still set great store in looking good. We are, in fact, always sneaking glances at ourselves to make sure we don't lose our trial membership in the "beautiful people." Watch people inspecting store windows and you will get the idea; they are checking themselves out every bit as much as the merchandise on display. Even the wild-haired youth and the matron whose rear view is mercifully hidden from her eyes do the same thing—and to themselves they look like Peter Fonda and Bess Meyerson. By such small vanities we manage to survive; I doubt that God has ever condemned anyone for these all too human actions.

Looking good can, however, go way beyond straightening our ties or renewing our lipstick. It can become a way of life that at first only reassures us, then gradually distorts us, and finally destroys us altogether. The temptation of the age is to settle for looking good, for holding everything together on the surface while everything is falling apart underneath. After a long season of accepting appearances for reality, a person forgets what truth even looks or sounds like. You can get by with that for a long while—it seems as harmless as those quick glances into store windows—until finally the whole thing falls in on itself like a collapsing star which, in its last moments of life, has only a glimmer of its own light left.

Enough words have spilled out about various American scandals—and enough righteous indignation has been pumped up—so that there is hardly room for more. Except perhaps to wonder why, as a culture that has sold out so much to looking good, we should be surprised at inheriting the monstrous children of this attitude. Maybe there is something fitting in this stifling problem. If those who live by the sword appropriately perish thereby, it may be right and just that a country that has set so much on looking good should be smothered by false faces. It is the American original sin and it goes right along with fake antiques, deceptive advertising, sawdust hotdogs, fixed athletics, ghost-written great statements, the surface glow of the sensuous man and woman, and the phony stained glass that peels off White House worship services like skin off a sunburned back.

October 13
"What Oily Unguents Still Can Win Us . . ."

wrote poet William Rose Benet, "How little truth we perish by." Now everyone wants the truth, an admirable notion, but a hard trip back when we have bought its image rather than its substance for such a long time. Strange that truth is treated as a last resort; if all else fails, tell what really happened. This is a problem for each of us to confront in our own lives and work. We may not all have been guilty of the assassination of great leaders in the sixties, as some would have had us believe. But, as surely as an audience is an ingredient in a magician's illusions, we have been a part of the stylish fakery that has made us look good or at least look away from our inner problems in the seventies.

October 14
A Big American Temptation . . .

centers on thinking about lying in the cause of looking
good as something that other people are guilty of. "They"
is a strategy of projection that permits us to be wrathful toward others for the inclinations we can find in ourselves.
The big fight for wholeness in any area of life always involves us in the battle against hypocrisy. This was the
quality Jesus attacked most vigorously with images of white-
washed tombs that still rivet our attention. It is not that
we are all phonies ourselves. We may, in fact, have only
contributed a little bit to building the atmosphere in which
looking good gradually passes for being good all the way
through. We may do this every time we let somebody give
a nice name to a rotten deed or fail to wince when a
prayer arises from a heart that is more gross than godly.

Hypocrisy is the kind of thing we contribute to when we
give up on seeking our own truth or fail to speak it fully to
those we say we love. We contribute to it when we settle
for prelates or politicians who look good even when they
don't do good. It took a long time to create the atmosphere
in which our current scandals finally blossomed. "They"
didn't do it; we did. And finding the truth about Watergate
is just the beginning—not just of greater revelations but of
the smaller victories we must all win in laying hold of the
truths beneath our surfaces. This is a situation in which we
can do something besides being horrified or indignant. It is
finally the truth about ourselves that will make us free.

October 15
How Much Truth Is Enough?

What about being truthful? After all, we do not live our
lives in a courtroom in which we are bound to tell the

truth, the whole truth, and nothing but the truth. Nobody is going to arrest us for perjury for a little white lie or we would all be in jail by nightfall. And there are those who say that even people who love each other very much need not tell each other *everything*. I had a wise old professor once who, in confidential and earnest tones, would say to us, "Tell the truth . . . but not too much!" Well, how much truth is enough?

We must face and share the truth that defines us in what we really mean to ourselves and to others. That leaves plenty of room for not hurting others' feelings needlessly and it also makes a clearing in the soul where fidelity to ourselves can take root and grow. There is a living and invisible force that is generated by faithfulness within ourselves that weathers and strengthens us like a warming sun. This is the heart of stable truth about ourselves which others can touch and sense as reliable and trustworthy. It is the rock on which our identity rests and its outlines can be seen even through the light mist of exaggeration or the heavier weather of an occasional self-administered snow job. We have to hold on to that fundamental truth that springs from a good sense of ourselves or we cannot even recognize much less share who we are with anybody else.

There is a tension connected with keeping up with the truth about ourselves; this is because we are constantly having new experiences which we must face and name accurately in order to incorporate them into ourselves. Of course, this is simple enough with relatively easy things like disappointment when our favorite team loses or excitement at the arrival of good news. It is more complicated when we must keep up with the subtle and hard-to-name emotions that can arise in the course of friendship or love. It is difficult for a person to mark down jealousy as a feeling of his own, or to accept and label a hurt unwittingly inflicted by another. These are the very truths, however, which must be met head on rather than denied. Each of them has a meaning that we must uncover if we are to keep our relationships loving and true.

October 16
Love Can Face Hard Truths . . .

and survive quite well; it has a terrible time, however, when it is denied the truth or is misled in some way or other. This is the "not enough truth" that kills friendship and love the way a boa constrictor does its victims—by a long, steady suffocating pressure. People who are caught in this never can quite remember where things started going wrong; they can only look back after they know that things are, in fact, very wrong and they do not know how to put them right again.

October 17
Truth and Fidelity

Enough truth means that we know what is happening to us in our relationship with another and that we are willing to communicate that as clearly and sensitively as possible. Enough truth means that faithfulness to ourselves is functional and central in our experiences. Enough truth means that we are not afraid of what is real about ourselves and that we can face it without distorting it too much in order to make it more attractive. Enough truth means that we meet each other with our own voices and our own words and that we never give up trying to express, even a little at a time, our own truths to each other.

October 18
Letting Go

It may be that the hardest thing to face about love is the fact that it never stops asking something from us. Love, in other words, does not repose like a trophy in the chambers of the heart; it is more like blood, nourishing us but demanding nourishment at the same time. Love gains strength from truths that don't seem to fit together at first glance. Item: People who long to possess each other must also learn to let each other go. This takes a lot of love and it incorporates us powerfully into the living mysteries of incarnation, death, and resurrection. I am not sure that it ever gets any easier for people, even for those who understand it quite clearly. It may be the great, deep secret of lasting love, the very thing people are clamoring to discover, the kind of willingness to give up our claims on each other that makes us free and full as human persons. But some people don't find it because they are looking for something more complex and majestic.

Letting go is the opposite of another strategy that many persons use to protect their ravaged hearts—the noninvolvement syndrome by which friends stay clear enough of each other never to get snagged on each other's emotions. That works but it does not make love deeper; it only builds a higher wall around each one of us. Real lovers head right for each other's hearts, getting tangled in each other's feelings all along the way. This is why it is so difficult—so downright painful—to face the deaths of self that necessarily follow on coming alive to each other.

Love is seeded with this Christian paradox all along its path; the more we want each other, the more we must be willing to respect each other's separateness. The more we would be sensitive to each other's needs, the more we must be willing to let each other go. Love means that we keep making room for the other to live in and that we surrender some of our space in order to do that. The biggest miracle of love is not that two persons dissolve into one but that, remaining distinct and contrasting as human beings, they can freely and gently share the treasures of their persons with each other.

287

October 19
We All Like to Think . . .

of things in the possessive case but that attitude can destroy friendship and love more quickly than arguments about finances or in-laws. The person who honestly wants to love another does not sacrifice his or her natural liking or respect for the other. He must surrender something of a different order altogether, something whose roots go back down deep inside himself, his almost instinctive tendency to take and make others a part of himself. This only seems natural, you will undoubtedly say, something that is very much a part of ourselves, as much as wanting to stake a claim on one's own land or home.

That is why a genuine death to ourselves is involved in yielding up the things that make us want to close our hands possessively on persons around us. At a certain stage of love this is exactly what people want to do. They must, however, grow through this if they are to attain a deeper and more lasting kind of love. Ultimately, lovers free each other by acknowledging each other's individuality and giving each other the strength and the room to fulfill it. We cannot free another person unless we are willing to cut through the chains by which we would make them fast to ourselves. Persons who love each other ride freely through life at each other's side; the public promises they make are not meant to shackle them together as much as to witness to the mystery of trusting freedom through which they remain alive to each other.

Letting go through putting to death our own urges to dominate the attention of another actually deepens the relationship instead of destroying it. When we can make a clean and unconditioned gift of life to each other we enter together into the mystery of resurrection, a realm we may only enter when our selfishness begins to die. Lovers empty themselves on each other's behalf, letting the other be separate and yet finding greater union within the other at the same time. Through such profound exchanges we make the Gospel journey with Jesus; it has never been a sentimental trip but always one that asks us to give of ourselves each step of the way.

October 20
How Does It Work Out in Ordinary Life?

You do not need to look very far. Take the husband whose wife wants to return to school, for example, and all of the small deaths he must be willing to accept in order to free her for this further opportunity. The deaths involved in letting another person go are not dramatic; they have as much to do with washing dishes and surrendering a comfortable routine as with anything else. Those freely accepted small deaths, however, enlarge life greatly.

A husband and wife must free each other—literally let each other go—when their work or other circumstances place them in contact with other men and women, the very situation in which jealousy can breathe withering dragonfire all around. A measure of dying, in other words, goes into that special trusting through which man and woman share each other with the world around them, and those neighbors, friends or associates who may need to draw on their strength for a while. This is the kind of expanded love that is not afraid of losing anything by giving itself away.

This latter kind of gift of man and woman to others begins at home because exactly the same redemptive dynamic applies to the way love must enlarge itself to make room for children. When children are considered an intrusion on a married couple's relationship with each other, they will be treated that way. They can die of the emotional malnutrition caused by husbands and wives who have not learned to give each other away.

October 21
Letting Another Person Go . . .

is the lesson that must be learned by a wide variety of loving persons: A teacher must die to his or her own self-interest, for example, in letting his or her pupils find their own way toward learning; a clergyman or a counselor must let his own wishes die in order to make sure that the freedom to move away on their own is available to those he helps.

Resurrection has a simple and familiar face; we glimpse it wherever we respect others enough to allow them to be separate from us even though they are surrounded still by our love. New and richer life always comes when we can loosen our hold on what we desperately want to make ours alone. Poverty of spirit comes down to this far more than it does to living in a hovel or giving away your shoes. Lady Poverty asks for hearts, for letting go of others not because we want to be detached (a fairly selfish motive) but because we need to be free. The wonderful part is that once we have learned to let go we discover that we can never again lose anything.

October 22
Where Does the Spirit Speak?

Everybody knows by now that becoming a good listener is important for a wide variety of occupations, from counseling to being a loving spouse. It seems hard enough to hear each other, what with our own preoccupations and the world filled with prophets, false and true. How then can we possibly hear the Spirit? There is increased talk about the Spirit in our lives but you need not be a Pentecostal to be eligible for his messages. The Spirit, an equalizer rather than a maker of elites, is given to each of us, and our only task is to open ourselves to what the Spirit has to say to us. But it seems to be getting harder to hear him or to be sure that he is guiding our religious and moral bearings. Never did we need the Spirit of truth and wisdom, individually or collectively, more than at the present time. But how can you be sure of the difference between the wind of the Spirit and the hot air of the destructive volcano or the quickly spent fury of the tornado? Here are some perennial ground rules that may be helpful.

The Spirit speaks to us as persons, that is, to the fullness of our human identity rather than just to one or the other aspect of it. Just as we are extraordinary compounds of intellect, emotion, and imagination, so the Spirit understands and addresses us. The Spirit does not excite only the intelligence or fire the imagination, nor does he merely stir up the embers of the heart. The Spirit is concerned with us as persons and does not manipulate us like a clever orator or a fundamentalist preacher. Just as we recognize that it cannot be the Spirit if our only reaction is fear, so we can identify alien spirits if they speak to or mobilize only one part of our personalities.

In everyday life we often resent or at least feel diminished when somebody fails to treat us with the respect due to a person. This works the same way with the Spirit who always reaches us in a way that touches our deepest sense of self. We become more ourselves because of the integrated manner in which the Spirit regards and prizes us as individual persons. A clear example of this wholeness of the Spirit's presence to us is found in a good liturgy where the ritual, the symbols, the music and the reflections of the speaker blend together in a way that enables us to respond with all the levels of our personality, including the unconscious. The sacraments have traditionally captured elements of teaching and human symbolism that speak to all our layers of spiritual need. We can, in other words, be sure we are listening to the Spirit when we feel we are being elevated and transformed in the completeness of our persons. The breath of the Spirit always enlarges rather than lessens our humanity.

291

October 23
A Standing Invitation . . .

is that which the Spirit gives us to get outside of ourselves.
This is the hardest part of becoming more human and the
most important part of being a Christian. The messages of
the Spirit are not to be relished in the dark but to be
preached from the housetops. The Spirit tells us basically
good news and, in the same way that we want to share
good news of any kind whenever we hear it, we cannot
keep the Spirit's message all to ourselves. The Spirit does
not close groups or individuals on themselves but breaks
them open to life and to the service of others. Pain cannot
be factored out of this part of the process, but neither can
the kind of joy that goes with getting out of the jail of our
own self-absorption.

October 24
The Spirit of Responsibility . . .

makes us more aware of our judgments and decisions. This
is one of the often overlooked signals that the Spirit is
speaking to us. That it is forgotten is especially unfortunate at a time when a renewed interest in the Spirit can
generate the kind of enthusiasm that lets persons get
carried away with the crowd around them, their own identity diffused like sugar in a cup of tea. The Spirit of unity
builds a community, not by obliterating the individuality
of each of its members but by developing it so that it can
be shared honestly and freely. The Spirit does not call
forth mobs nor flatly docile regiments but works a far
more remarkable miracle in which distinct and differing
persons are able to meet and enter into life together. The
Spirit, in other words, builds friends and lovers instead of
allies and zealots.

October 25
Is This the Place?

Anybody who has ever lived, visited, or made a retreat in an old-time seminary or religious house can remember the kinds of signs that dotted the long, sun-filled hallways, the admonitions from the holy men and women of the past that were as revered as their bones and clothing. In the seminary I attended, one passed, on the way upstairs, an old print of a venerable saint who, although he was apparently being stabbed in the back, held his finger to his pursed lips to bid us to be silent. The placards reminded us that the Spirit speaks in whispers and that the Lord is not to be found in noise. You remember those days, I am sure, with the quiet of great cathedrals that was hardly broken by the subdued voice of the priest reading the Latin Mass. Undoubtedly the Spirit spoke in the roomy old silence of our recollection just as the Spirit speaks to us still when and if we can find quiet places in our own lives.

Finding these quiet places is, however, about as likely as coming upon a quiet night in Belfast. We cannot very well address the Spirit and say, "You know we can't hear you when the world is running." Perhaps the Spirit also speaks in the hurly-burly and agony of the crowded world, in surprising places and at unusual times. It may be that we just have not looked or listened closely enough. But we can find the Spirit. Bad days are as unlikely a location for the Spirit as we are apt to find but He is there, sometimes more clearly than at a prayer meeting. Bad days are, of course, those times when everything is wrong; short of going back to bed, there seems to be nothing else to do but to wait them out the way one does a tropical storm. However, if we have the courage to look, the Spirit may teach us many things about ourselves that we would never learn in better emotional weather.

293

like a jagged streak of lightning that illuminates a darkened countryside, can help us to learn some hard but true things about ourselves. And this is all part of the mystery of continuing revelation in which our lives are set. A faulted day may permit us a good look at things about ourselves that we would otherwise disguise or never bother to inspect. We can find out about things that gradually need to be changed, or we can come to terms with realities that seem to resist change. The Spirit even gives us the strength in these moments to forgive and heal ourselves, something we cannot do if we don't even know that we are wounded.

These revelations can center on quirks as diverse as bad tempers or the regressive behaviors we give in to when we are disappointed or frustrated. At the headwaters of the river of self-pity we may find a new and more modest version of ourselves and our talents. Even being treated unfairly or meanly by others may turn us back to fundamentals, to strengths we forgot that we possessed. The Spirit speaks in all this pain and confusion, even in the embarrassment and guilt we feel when we have to face our sins and shortcomings. The truth hurts but it always redeems us if we can face even a small portion of it without flinching. Whenever we give up being defensive we make room for the Spirit in our lives, and, if we can put aside excuses, rationalizations, or countercharges, we make ourselves available for his healing and strengthening.

The Spirit also speaks through the painful moments of love, at those times when lovers may hurt each other or, for reasons they cannot quite fathom, when they get blurred in each other's focus. Christians are taught that they must be prepared to forgive their enemies but few expect to meet them at the breakfast table. The Spirit is never very far away from a genuine test of love, from the effort that is needed to start again at a relationship or to piece it gently back together when it has been shattered. The Spirit of love breathes on us far more in moments of meeting during which we forgive each other for our faults, than in heady and deceptive stretches of romance. Because love does not take care of itself, the Spirit is always close at hand to help us do the work. Our biggest difficulty may be in recognizing that he is there and speaking to us in the circumstances.

October 27
A Wonderful Thing about Friendship . . .

is that you do not have to name all its good qualities, not even to yourself. There is something in that quality of effortlessness which catches the intrinsic liking that is the healthiest of our good responses. This is the type of experience that just happens and can never be forced. It is probably wise to count as something other than friendship any relationship which you would describe as too much work. When you say of someone, "It really tries me to be a friend to X," or "Friendship with Y demands more than it gives," maybe these are not friendships at all. When the relationship needs that much work—and all on your part—then you need to find out exactly why things are going this way.

October 28
Satchel's Rules

You are probably familiar with the famous sayings of the great black baseball pitcher, Satchel Paige. They are at least as worth reflecting on as many of the things that get on banners these days. I think they give you a freer feeling about yourself.

1. Avoid fried foods which angry up the blood.
2. If your stomach disputes you, pacify it with cool thoughts.

3. Keep the juices flowing by jangling around gently as you move.
4. Go very light on the vices, such as carrying on in society, as the social ramble ain't restful.
5. Avoid running at all times.
6. Don't look back, something might be gaining on you.

October 29
Waiting

Waiting is a mysterious theme that recurs in the Christian symphony and that we remember as we think about hope. These notions are intermingled in our experience and we cannot imagine or understand them separately. Waiting challenges the surge of an age which has long since lost its feel for the turning of the tides or the changing of the seasons. To get there, to deny aging, to have the gratification now instead of tomorrow, to lose a sense of time and its passage—these are footnotes to a contemporary species of progress that has bewildered more than enlightened man. It is strange that we have wandered so far from an understanding of the waiting that comes inevitably to each of us and with which we must come to terms if we are to be human at all.

But waiting fills the Gospels just as it does the life of the Spirit. It is a gentle mystery of life, a kind of invitation into ourselves and the far reaches of our experience, where passage can be made only if we are willing to wait and listen to the meanings that come to us in whispers. Waiting is something we cannot do well if we are on the defensive; it is a spell broken by a crouched and armored figure. Waiting is a revelation for the person who is open in existence to all that is not yet and that can only be caught in hints and shadows rather than trumpet blasts and headlines. The mystery of waiting to understand ourselves, or for love to grow, or to grasp the right moment to do something—these are the most significant aspects of our existence and they are almost always tied up with other persons. The problem is that if we are in too great a hurry, or if we demand final answers before the first syllables of meaning are even half-formed, then we destroy the very vulnerability that we must maintain if we are to hear and understand the promise which God sows in each of us. This is why we have quiet seasons of preparation, such as Advent and Lent. They are times to learn the hard lessons of waiting.

Waiting allows us to feel in our own being something of the overwhelming longing of all creation for fulfillment; it is the ache that cannot be soothed or drugged away, and it tells us that there are processes in living which can neither be hurried nor falsified. A sense of Christian expectation about ourselves and others makes it possible for us to understand hope as the virtue that yields its meaning to those who gently wait. Blessed are those who wait for they shall be filled. It is part of a wisdom as deep as that of the farmer who can feel the right moment for planting his crops or beginning his harvest. It is while we wait that we grasp a little better the complexities of life's deeper levels, and of the thundering currents that have not and cannot be charted but which we must ride to find our destiny.

October 30
The Christian Life . . .

has always made room for waiting, for standing back from creation in order to see and understand it better. This is why the Christian can go into the desert or stand on the mountain top; he is not farther away but closer to the heart of the world when he does these things in response to the inviting Spirit. The Christian can always take time to pick flowers or to wonder at the simple beauty of clear water and abundant valleys. Waiting is a part of all this— it is an attitude toward God and the universe through which we can recognize and accept his best blessings and gifts. We can feel the quiver of all creation in ourselves when the Spirit stirs the waters of our souls.

October 31
It Is Not Passivity . . .

that excuses the self from activity in life. Such a blank attitude of expectation is a sign of death rather than of life. The secret of waiting is grasped best by those who have gone furthest into the heart of life's experiences. These are the men and women who know the secret places of the heart because they have not been afraid to love. Through loving others sensitively they understand the active quality of waiting that relates it so closely to hope. Only friends and lovers come up against the demands that hoping in and waiting for life together make on them. The experiences that give us a sense of godliness always take time— they are spun out through time, as well as being conditioned and deepened by it. They never pass in an instant the way quick and exciting pleasures do. Love and sharing, keeping faith and hoping—these fail if we do not understand how mysteriously waiting must be part of each of them. It is the active and loving person who can learn how to wait even when he or she cannot plumb the depths of its meaning completely. The loving Christian learns to live with this mystery of waiting that ultimately sensitizes each of us to all that is not yet, to a future with God where the ache of waiting will end at last. It is, in fact, this particular moment that stirs our expectancy now, that helps us to realize that we will never understand hope if we do not commit ourselves to waiting.

November

November 1
Decisions! Decisions!

The campaign banners flap, the leaves fall, and we all face a decision in the voting booth. For some the decision is easy; for others it is made along party lines of good old-fashioned prejudice. The uncertainty that lingers in the souls of many, however, reminds us of the choice points that line up across our lives like a series of railroad switches. The perennial need to choose is one of the pressures on the spirit through which we face up to ourselves. Look again at the two roads that diverge in the poem of Robert Frost: "And I—/ I took the one less traveled by / And that has made all the difference."

So much is decided for us by others these days. Take, for example, the blind computers that predict election results after devouring barely a fraction of the vote. These and other preprogrammed choices make us feel that our power to choose has been diluted by the circumstances or dumb luck of contemporary living. There seems no choice at all. It is easy to forget that each truly human decision is important, hard and humanly expanding. Each is important although we may be anesthetized by the parade of trivial decisions that clogs the main street of existence. These are often the plastic brand of decisions which have no roots in genuine human experience, the daily pseudo-choices that are only superficial, involuntary tics that require neither character nor sense of the self. Included, for example, are the choices between equally bland television programs or from an array of equally tasteless snacks or beverages.

Whether it is culture or food we need do no more than open our eyes or our mouths and we will be filled. In fact, many of these decisions are barely above the level of physical reactivity. They dull us to the fact that there are many daily choices that depend on our marshaling the forces of our character together; these are decisions that are important because they represent our identity in action. They are, in effect, *you* and *I* on the line in life. Each decision, when it comes from something inside of us, bears a message about who we are, what we believe, and the goals we set for ourselves.

November 2
Decisions Are Hard

To get into something more significant than the kind of breakfast food that we are going to choose means that we may have to plunge our hands into the nettles and thorns of our emotional underbrush. Good decisions are hard decisions because they make us take a closer look at ourselves; they force us, in other words, to light up corners of ourselves that we let darken long ago. Good decisions are hard because we have to sort out motives and separate them from our psyche where they may lie buried like pain in the bones of an arthritic. Good decisions are hard because we must involve ourselves totally in a confrontation with our own character. Not only that, but once the decision is made, we must live with it. The man who makes a hard decision in this manner, however, has no need to keep explaining why he chose as he did. He already knows his reasons because of the thoroughness of his difficult self-search. Making decisions, even when they are less than perfect, makes us less defensive in the face of the events that unreel as a consequence of our choices.

November 3
Rewards of Making Decisions

Although decisions are more mooned over than sung about in our culture, their nature is not just burdensome; decisions are also rewarding when we take them seriously. The process of making a good choice brings more of ourselves to life; it is through this process that we discover and actually become ourselves. Growth is a by-product of every adult decision process. Good choices are expanding because the positive changes in ourselves which they enable us to achieve can never be lost. We define ourselves through our choices; they are the essence of mature autobiography when they are the product of pursued insight rather than impulse. Difficult personal decisions are far more self-fulfilling than the counterfeit liberations we hear of so much these days.

November 4
Do It Yourself

There is enough unhappiness in life without adding the kind that comes from failing to dig into hard decisions. Some people feel unhappy, in part at least, because they have never truly decided anything for themselves. By this I mean that they have always taken the word of someone else, or followed some slogan or been swept along by a current craze or a vaguely defined inner need to be popular, married, or the member of a certain prestige profession. When these realities—what we have made of ourselves through our choices—do not really match what we are like inside, when they represent things that we thought we might like rather than things we actually wanted passionately to do, then the harvest is always unhappiness. It seems painful to face the complex process of a challenging decision; it is far worse, however, to turn away from this into the long autumn of misery that is inhabited by the undecided. Never deciding anything for ourselves is, of course, a way of staying a child, that is, dependent on other persons for the essential nourishment and direction of our lives. There is a kind of comfort in this but it is chilly if not downright cold—and it generates loneliness in the long run. Not deciding is also a failure to find and respond to the unique aspects of one's own personality. Every man need not be Michelangelo, of course—and there is nothing worse than mock creativity—but one unlocks the truth about himself with his own hands. When a person is unwilling to do this he estranges himself from his own character and his own possibilities. He even makes it harder for others to know him. There is a deadly passivity in not deciding or in letting others tell us what to do and when to do it. That's another way of letting life happen to us, not humanly, but, in the words of poet Archibald MacLeish, as it does to "sheep in a blizzard or chips on a river."

November 5
Christian Decisions

This subject usually splashes a colorful picture across the imagination. Decisions for Christ call up vast crowds of clear-eyed youths under the spell of a blue-suited evangelist shaking perspiration on his audience with every saving gesture. It sounds like a signature on a temperance pledge under the eyes of solemn-looking spinsters in rimless glasses. Christian decisions sound like Sunday school on days that were made for picnics. It is surely one of the great sadnesses of history that decisions for Christ have taken on such evangelical overtones. Decisions for Christ, of course, cannot be limited to wholehearted promises to be virtuous, no matter how innocent or well-intentioned these might be. Decisions for Christ are human decisions made by people trying to respond to the Spirit even when they are battered by the inner and outer devils of the human condition.

Decisions for Christ are essentially affirmations of ourselves in the face of life's inequities and our own inadequacies. When we are actually trying to respond to Christ we attempt to take his word seriously as a way of life rather than as a set of preachments or restrictions. We are Christian when we choose the thing that is right for us —and perhaps choose it again each day so that our commitments are purposeful rather than just forced marches. "Choose life" the Old Testament tells us and this, among other things, means assenting to life as it is, even though occasionally its unfairnesses seem to outnumber its joys. There is bitter gall as well as church-social lemonade that must be swallowed by the person who chooses to live his life deeply and truthfully. We cannot begin—cannot make the first choice—unless we realize that virtue does not lie in recapturing innocence as much as it does in continuing to make our best efforts long after we are innocent no more. People talk a lot about the gift of healing these days. Well, it does not come in ecstatic jamborees of the Spirit. Healing comes to the man who pulls himself together through the pattern of decisions that reveal the character of his belief and convictions. A man cures himself of the ills of the human condition by facing up to his job of deciding for himself even in the darkest and loneliest of moments. This man is more whole and can now be an instrument of healing for others.

November 6
Finish This Sentence

Sometimes we get a good inventory of our decision-making powers by reflecting on them in the moments when we are not under the pressures of immediate or urgent choices. One of the techniques which psychologists have used for years is known as the *sentence-completion* method. People are asked to finish sentence fragments with the first thoughts that come into their minds. Bubbling out of the less-than-conscious come notions that are very revealing even to the individual as he sees them flow onto the paper. If we want to understand our attitude toward the decision-making process in our own life—whether we are living more in the past, for example, than in the important present—perhaps we should try to finish some of these sentences. They catch some of the longing that so often hampers us in the business of meeting and dealing with the diverging roads in our own lives: "If I were a little younger. . . ." Or perhaps this would help you to understand yourself a little better: "If I had more money. . . ." And then, with a slight glance backwards: "If things had been different. . . ." You might finish with this: "I always wish. . . ."

November 7
What We Tell Ourselves

These sentences only break open the surface of our unconscious. They do tell us, however, that in the long run most of us, for one reason or another, make our lives the way we want them. We do this out of unconscious motives, or out of drives or feelings that we are not inclined to inspect very carefully, but we do it ourselves. We put up with things, delay things, choose self-punishing things to atone for our guilt—all are reasons that are available at some level inside of ourselves. We make our present and shape our future even as we prepare to regret them when they become our past. We cannot pawn that off on someone else even if we follow their advice or allow ourselves to be dominated by a parent or a friend or a nagging wife or a superior—when it comes right down to it *we* have decided to let it be that way. We give birth to our own lives, even if we will not look closely at our many-layered motivations. It is better to look deeply into ourselves and to take more responsible and conscious control of ourselves.

This gives us some insight into the way we make our

own eternity. We would prefer that the fates be its weavers; we design ourselves even as we design our environments. The more aware we become of the complex of motives that play on each decision the more we can bring them into the light and the more command we can take of ourselves. It is a step forward to listen to the echoes that come from deep inside our souls; at least these help us to realize who we are. They prevent us from kidding ourselves about our own identity, our own possibilities, or the reasons why we choose to do this or that. The truer we can make our decisions the better they will be, even though they seem to fall short of what we would like them to be. Our lives become a prayer when we listen to all that is going on inside of ourselves and try, insofar as we can, to integrate this with the best purpose of our lives. The Christian consciousness about life and people remembers that we are free and says that increased and self-decided freedom is always worth fighting for. It is through its exercise that we finally become ourselves.

November 8
Facing the Enemy Inside

Being unable to make a decision ranks near the top in the all-time ratings of uncomfortable situations. That longing for the relief of finally making up our mind, of getting something settled, is as intense and restless as anything the human heart knows. Observant men who have thought about these problems have described the moments of dilemma in ways that may be helpful. Thus, we are not invaded by mischievous phantoms squeezing a paralysis into our minds and wills. The enemy is not a stranger; in fact, he has our face and if we look at him more closely, we may rob him of his power to restrain us. When decisions won't come, when we find ourselves pacing back and forth or going all jelly in the knees just as we think we have finally decided something, we are probably experiencing conflict. To understand this better we should turn to the descriptions of conflict made famous by two psychologists, John Dollard and Neil Miller. We are in conflict when there are two responses which we can make that are mutually exclusive. In a sense, the responses compete with each other for our attention; choosing one necessarily rules out the other.

The Approach-Approach Conflict: This garden variety kind of conflict occurs when we must choose between equally attractive alternatives. Of course, if the possibilities were not equally attractive, the choice of one over the other would be relatively simple. We have all been in this kind of conflict on many occasions. For example: At times we are faced with the choice of doing two things which are equally enjoyable—staying home to talk with close friends or going out to a show we really want to see. Time and space just do not permit us to do both. As a result we hang back, although some call this hanging loose. After all, it has become fashionable to "keep your options open." We tend not to decide, in other words, hoping for some break in the situation that will make one course of action more preferable than the other. In fact, to resolve such a situation we must disturb the balance between the alternatives. During this time, we tend to do nothing except feel the discomfort that goes with an unresolved decision. Luckily, since both options are attractive, we often avoid having any regrets no matter how our choice turns out. It is sad, however, when a person ends up doing nothing, when he backs off and just does not decide at all.

November 9
A Classic Hangup . . .

is the **Avoidance-Avoidance Conflict.** The setup in this situation is the same, except that we are caught between two alternative responses which are equally unattractive. We have two things in conflict and we do not want to do either of them, yet circumstances dictate that we make a choice. The classic textbook example is that of a child at the table who is told to eat his vegetables or go to bed—choices that rate about the same on his undesirability scale. You can probably think of many situations like this in adult life as well. Many people have positions of responsibility which require them to make difficult decisions that affect the lives of others and involve them in conveying bad news, confronting people for their shortcomings, or going to meetings which they know will be abrasive and difficult. When a person, child or adult, is caught in this conflict he classically tries to escape it, he attempts to seek some third thing which will make the choice unnecessary.

November 10
For Example . . .

the child plays with the vegetables or tries to distribute them on his plate so that it looks as if he has eaten some of them; the adult may suddenly invent some other important engagement ("I am sorry I won't be able to make it today. I've just been called out on important business"). However, the unkind truth is that there is no third way; sooner or later, we must return to the undesirable alternatives and, by examining them more carefully, get them enough out of balance so that we can go ahead with one rather than the other. It is never easy to do something we do not enjoy; it is only a temporary reprieve, however, to deal with a disagreeable dilemma by looking in a different direction.

November 11
Then There Is . . .

the **Approach-Avoidance Conflict:** We may recognize this as an old friend, a familiar kind of adversary with whom we have had some fierce and well-remembered battles. In this situation the alternatives are not separate from each other. There is one situation which possesses positive and negative aspects. In other words, in itself it is partly desirable and partly undesirable. The conflict comes because we want the good part of the situation and we also want to avoid the bad part. Careful study of this phenomenon illustrates some truths about it that we should know before we get too mixed up with it.

It resembles the old situation in which the individual desires to speak to the person in authority and yet at the same time feels uncomfortable about it. Studies have shown that the tendency to approach and the tendency to avoid vary in the strength of their influence on us. In other words, the conflict arises in an approach-avoidance situation the closer we get to the difficult part of it. It is relatively easy in the beginning to make a decision to go forward; this is related to the distance we are from the boss. The tendency to avoid only asserts itself as we draw near the authority's office. Many a man has bravely started striding toward the boss' door only to slow down his pace as he got closer to it. He may even raise his hand to knock only to find it frozen in the air, paralyzed by the effects of conflict as invisible as a science fiction ray gun. And what does he do? He turns around and heads back down the hallway. Of course, the farther away he gets, the less threatening the authority becomes. He feels he can approach once more. He turns around again only to be caught in the same conflict as he draws close to the threatening inner sanctum. This is the classic picture of a person who vacillates in the midst of conflict, the individual who feels the anxiety of being both encouraged and discouraged at carrying out some resolve.

November 12
Did You Ever Have the Feeling?

What can a person do about this situation which has been memorialized in the old Jimmy Durante song, "Did you ever have the feeling that you wanted to go, that you wanted to stay?" The first thing to remember is the difference between the tendency to approach and the tendency to avoid, the latter being strong, more intense and more localized to the magnetic field of the situation. This tendency to avoid characteristically clamps an arm lock on our spirits at an embarrassing moment. Think of the jaunty fellow who begins to climb to the high diving board only to find fear resting on the upper rungs so that he must retreat redfaced to the safety of the ground below. What are the lessons to be learned from this scientifically demonstrated truth?

First, and most importantly: Never underestimate the power of the disagreeable aspect of a situation. Count your stones, as the scriptures tell us, before you build a tower just as you count your soldiers before you start a battle. Few phenomena are as discouraging as starting on a project only to find that it cannot be finished because of some unexpected conflict that overwhelms us at some point in the venture.

Second: Never force another person to do something if he or she is obviously experiencing an intense amount of threat. Un-thought-out advice and hearty encouragement do incalculable damage in the reality of this conflict situation. In other words, you do not help a person through a difficult decision by pushing him to get closer to it when everything inside him wants to pull away. It is like pushing a person who cannot swim off a pier. Well, you might say, he is in the water at last. He may, however, be paralyzed with fear and unable to help himself—perhaps even dangerous to those who try to rescue him. To put it simply, don't force people when they are clearly not able to move into conflict by themselves. They may be overwhelmed and permanently harmed by the punishing nature of the experience.

What do you do then? In such a conflict, it is better to deal with the quality of threat that makes us want to avoid the situation. Only when this negative part can be lessened —perhaps by securing more information or preparing ourselves better in some other way—can we confidently and sensibly move toward resolving the conflict. This takes a little time and a measure of patience as well as a mature willingness to wait while we get the situation more clearly into focus. But these are the elements of which good decisions are made.

November 13
What about Bad Decisions?

Bad decisions have always been difficult to judge, especially from the foreshortened perspective that our private vision of life allows us. Father Flanagan claimed that there was no such thing as a bad boy. It is even clearer that there is no such thing as a bad decision if, in fact, a person has reflected deeply on himself and the cluster of motivations which crowd him most of the time in life. A decision that is not hasty nor merely impulsive, a decision that, in effect, represents ourselves, can never be a bad one. One of the reasons—and it is far from a sentimental one—is that each decision demands some measure of faith on our part. Choices constitute a test of whether we can trust ourselves or other persons in a certain situation. The most important decisions we ever make concern those who are closest to us. So our supply of belief in others is under constant pressure. Even a decision that does not turn out in quite the way we hoped is a good one when it has required us to make an unblemished and unconditional act of faith in another person. Trusting others is like flying blind—a very difficult chore when we know that the choice we have made rests, in part at least, on those who are loved and who love us.

November 14
How Do You Measure It?

That we lost money on it? That someone with more superficial values counts it as loss? These latter are the people Jesus is constantly meeting in the Gospel, those who hedge their bets and judge everything in terms of accruing self-interest. That kind of self-contained concern has always been a bad indicator of whether we have chosen rightly or not. Perhaps a better measure would be whether what we decided, even if it failed, enlarged our lives or the lives of those around us. Perhaps the decisions in which we give up something we could easily retain—ones that lead us to being hurt—will prove to be the richest and most life-giving decisions we have ever been a part of.

November 15
Prudence, Where Have You Been?

Prudence sounds like an old-fashioned word, a dusty virtue entombed in the winding sheets of old theology manuals, a notion that seems more starchily reserved than vitally human. All this is in our imagination because prudence actually refers to how we pull ourselves together at decisive points in time. Prudence is the word we use to describe that instant in which we integrate the elements of our personality—intellectual and emotional—fusing them so that we act for ourselves at this particular moment. It is the virtue of operational responsibility, the marshaling of the self that enables us to say, as truly as ever we can: "I choose to do this; this is my action."

Prudence is a virtue particularly suited to human beings because it describes the way we behave when we are at our best, when we have looked deeply inside ourselves and reviewed the many factors that play upon any moment of choice in our lives. Prudence means that we are being fully human rather than just impulsive, that we are being honest rather than deceptive, open rather than blind to all that is going on inside ourselves. The prudent person does not just come to a stark intellectual conclusion; instead, he feels

311

throughout his being the rightness for him of a certain course of action. He has as clear a grasp of his motives as possible, taking into account his weaknesses as well as his strengths.

Although prudence never operates perfectly in a faulted world, it remains the lively human experience through which we commit ourselves one way or the other. It is the power through which we define ourselves in relationship to our own possibilities and to the good of those around us. It goes along with freedom and the informed self. Prudence means we know what we are doing even though we may have experienced a long struggle to get everything clearly into perspective. Prudence means we act for ourselves, that our decision is a moment of growth rather than of regression, a step forward rather than backward. Prudence matches the nature of the man who dares to be freely and completely human, blending risk-taking and healthy self-confidence as he makes the decisions that are his own in life.

November 16
But Remember

People who do not look deeply into themselves or who cannot sort out their emotions finally decide some of the most important things in their lives for the oddest and most mysterious reasons. They buy, sell, get married, move, take a new job, or try to fashion a new image on whim, regret, or some other unnamed impulse. This is the opposite of prudence—a failure to grow, a missing of the opportunity to make good and life-giving decisions. We should pay attention to those signs, either in ourselves or in others, which indicate that there are processes at work which notably interfere with prudent decisions.

312

November 17
The Right Kind of Help

If you find that you can never resolve the simplest of conflicts, if you find yourself obsessed by them as a scrupulous person might be obsessed with the careful telling and retelling of sins, then there are emotional difficulties which require some professional assistance. Brooding and worrying endlessly about choices is not so much a sign of great concern as it is of inner complications which need attention if the person is to be freed for a fuller and more decisive life. Pay attention to the signs of exaggerated difficulty in making decisions. A little professional assistance at a timely moment can make an enormous difference for the rest of a person's life. Getting the right kind of help for ourselves or others at the right time is a decision we will never regret.

November 18
Do We Choose to Love?

Love will always be a mystery, of course, but we know that it is something we can do only when we are in touch with the truth about ourselves. The person who listens to what is going on inside himself, the person who is able to factor out the selfish urges that are as common as heartbeats inside us, the person who can face the elements of conflict honestly—this is the person who can say *yes* to love. Such an individual is ready to love because his self-possession means that he can give something of his real personality to others in a decisive kind of love. The words "I choose you" spoken in marriage say aloud something about the inner truth of the loving person. The individual who owns himself has no mortgages to pay or to levy when he gives his heart away. This moment of choice merely signals that the individual is indeed fully present, rather than the victim of his fancies, as he gives himself to another.

It is also true that a person can choose not to love, that a man can block off his self and barricade his heart against love's invitation. This sometimes happens when the individual is not truly in touch with himself or when he is timid about the risks that come with the decision to share life with others. Choosing not to love seems a safer path to some and yet, in the long run, it means that all the other decisions of life will be harder because they will be unshared and more lonely. Love comes to be the best thing we can ever choose, the event we build toward with all the good decisions that help to bring the fullness of our personality into being. Choosing life means choosing ourselves, preparing ourselves for the love that opens us now to the moments of the life that is eternal.

November 19
How Do You Say Thank You?

It may not be on the top of the list of the world's problems but it is clear that man has difficulties with giving and receiving thanks. The process, in whatever direction it moves, seems to generate embarrassment for those involved; at times, the act of thanking someone becomes an embarrassment in itself as, for example, at testimonial dinners for some civic or religious leaders who have carefully managed to keep their light unobscured by the biblical bushel while their public relations people make sure that their good deeds are well-known by many. If, as it sometimes happens, they are crooked or hypocritical into the bargain, then thanking them puts a layer of cynicism on the noblest heart. Even aside from these public events, however, saying thanks has never proved very easy. The reason is that men often think the validity of a thank you is measured by length or weight when any sensible person knows that it is the depth that counts.

314

You may, to cite another example, find yourself slightly uneasy during the pious custom of giving thanks before meals. Maybe the old hurried ritual was worse but the way some people go on and on while the food grows appreciably colder makes even the most tolerant man yearn for a return to silent prayer. Too often, nowadays, thanksgiving before meals is turned into a forum on a series of lofty Christian topics ranging from making love to making war, and the only thing I am grateful for is when it comes to an end. There is some alien force residing in the task of giving thanks that goads and dements men who seem reasonably adjusted otherwise. It is the same force that moves a man to postpone his thank you letters or notes as though the writing of them would drain away irreplaceable life energies. Husbands are fond of letting their wives handle the thank you notes; religious orders sometimes entangle you in so many spiritual reassurances and subtle requests for future donations that you begin to doubt the wisdom of having made the original gift; some members of the younger generation, noted for other virtues, seem to regard thank you's as cop-outs unworthy of their true and beautiful personalities. Those of us who are not compulsive let the thank you notes pile up at the back of our desks while we wait for the right words or the right mood to come.

November 20
Most of Us Know . . .

from personal experience, however, that a thank you, whether it is in prayer or in friendship, need not be either perfunctory or overdramatized. In fact, a thank you at the right time can mean a great deal to people, not just so that they can check off their list of people who owe them gratitude, but because, if it is genuine, it is an important human transaction, one that rounds out a life experience, giving it a wholeness that it would not otherwise have. Thank you's like this are all too rare; where they exist they seem to have some qualities in common, and we can all learn something from them.

November 21
The Quality of Thank You

Good thank you's are, first of all, simple and to the point; they are directed to the message of gratitude and do not contain other requests or expectations. Secondly, they come from what the individual is truly feeling rather than from what he pretends to feel. The more we can put something of ourselves into what we write, the more surely we will succeed in saying the right thing. This, in a way, is the abiding genius of the Lord's Prayer, which, when we put ourselves into it, still touches deep and enduring aspects of our human experience. In prayer and thank you notes, being real cannot be improved upon; we will even feel better about getting those notes written when we are freed from feeling that we must manufacture unreal emotions. A simple thank you states and appreciates that depth beats length any day.

November 22
Where Do We Stand?

We get to asking ourselves this question in November after the rustling leaves and the All Souls services have let into our hearts long thoughts of the burnt-out autumn. No matter what climate we live in, the end of the year, knotted into holidays, waits for us as inevitably as the hard earth does for the pole-vaulter. We look back, even for a moment, and wonder how we compare, say, to the way we looked last Thanksgiving. Well, you say, just how did I look a year ago? It's been so rushed I cannot quite remember.

This very recollection gives us an answer and some insight into our common blessings and burdens. Blessings and burdens always come intermingled; this is a law as old as man himself, a deep Christian truth that is good to remember at Thanksgiving. If we look back we may well remember the blur rather than the sharp features of the receding year. This means that we are normal, that we are indeed alive, and that we are blessedly free from the leisure needed for self-pity. We should count it a good year, then, if we have the feeling that life is a perpetual-motion machine and that those longed-for periods of complete rest always seem to elude us. The vision of a life spent in a hammock on a tropical beach does not match man in this life or the next. It sounds good in desperate and aching moments when we no longer want to deal with the complexities of our individual lives—at those trying, Garbo-like interludes when we want only to be left alone. Endless ease and a healthy human being could only be paired by a crazed matchmaker who does not understand man's nature at all. It is a union that never works for very long and, as we carve our turkey this year, we can be thankful for that.

Man, we can be thankful, is made to ask questions rather than to give answers. He is curious, despite the fabled fate of the cat, and this seems to be a self-justifying activity. We explore our environment constantly for the very enjoyment that goes with searching. That man thereby discovers a great deal about himself and his world —knowledge which he can turn to practical purposes—is a tribute to the wide-eyed and distractible quality that is as much a part of him as his central nervous system. He just likes to poke into things and he craves visual and auditory stimulation; when he is denied these opportunities, he slides slowly into an imaginary world of his own. Man just does not enjoy environments that are overcontrolled or papered with a false perfection. He is better with loose ends and unfinished tasks, with something yet to complete about his own growth and that of those around him.

November 23
Man Throws Himself Out of Balance . . .

disturbing his adjustment constantly in order to seek a new
and higher level of personal integration. It is true that bio-
logically he tries to keep things in equilibrium within himself—such as his body temperature, etc.—but on the level
of his total personality he continually disrupts himself in
view of larger accomplishments. Only the man who is already mostly dead or emotionally defused finds it comfortable to sit on his laurels. "To have done," Shakespeare
tells us, "is to hang like a rusted sword in monumental
mockery." Were it not true that man purposefully
unbalances himself he would never grow, or discover anything, or even become his true self. Worse still, he would
never love or have any idea of what true loving is all about.
Healthy men take risks in order to transcend themselves
and to feel firsthand the rough beauty of their existence. It
is exciting and, although not very restful, gloriously
human. And it helps man to understand something of the
Divine.

November 24
A Law of Life

There is a law which is akin to Murphy's famous dictum
that whatever can go wrong will go wrong. It is a familiar
variant to anyone who has ever been slightly curious or
thrown himself out of balance in the pursuit of life. It
reads as follows: The solving of problems generates larger
problems. You recognize that one, right? Finish one chore
and instead of peace or even a plateau of restfulness a
larger challenge suddenly looms into view. This is true in
all areas of human activity including friendship and love.

These are, of course, some of our most gratifying and strengthening experiences; indeed, they make the rest of life bearable. But they have an inner economy of their own that demands that friends and lovers always give more of themselves to the relationship. Love is not a solid mass, an unmoving and unmovable rock on which we can contentedly build our lives once we have discovered it. Love is alive and responds to the laws that govern all dynamic activities. We must, in other words, constantly work at love, investing more of ourselves in it in order to deepen and broaden its freshness and meaning in our lives. As advice-columnist Ann Landers once wisely remarked: "Marriages may be made in heaven but the maintenance work is done here on earth." So lovers, even those who are very close to each other, find that each crisis of understanding strengthens them for the next challenge to listen and to really hear each other, for the most complicated human situation in which they must reach out ever more sensitively to be with each other. If you think this is easy, you may never have been in love.

November 25
Thankful for the Lives We Lead

It is only as we understand these truths that we can be thankful for what our lives are like when we feel crowded by events and pressured by the daily realities of a world that hardly ever slows down to enable us to get a better look at ourselves or at each other. We can be thankful that we are trying—as best we can—to lead the lives that are described on the contemporary banners of Christianity. The faith that people sing about is beyond our understanding unless we keep faith with our curious, distractible selves. We profess our faith in Sunday credos but also in the changeable weather of our uncertain and unpredictable lives; faith is tested in blind alleys and dead ends as well as

319

in our richer and deeper discoveries. And it is a part of our faith to keep asking questions even when there are those around us—whether they be psychologists or theologians—who tell us that they have all the answers.

Hope has no measure unless we unbalance ourselves in order to become more ourselves. Hope can have no meaning for the persons who feel that *status quo* security sums up the meaning of religion and life. You cannot even imagine hope unless you have taken the risks that mean that everything can go wrong instead of right. The unsettled nature of the hopeful person does not rob him of the gift of peace; that comes because his energies are engaged, because he cares enough about himself and his life to place everything in peril in order to find more of himself. Only the hopeful, then, can face death unafraid. They have already yielded themselves to a thousand deaths in their daily lives; they know, in a wisdom beyond science or conventional piety, that the darkness cannot envelop them forever.

And who knows love firsthand except the person who has felt its grip on his heart, the ceaseless drain on energies and understanding which stokes love's fire ever brighter. Love leads not to security, although lovers can count unquestioningly on each other. Love leads along a steep and winding road where there is no turning back and few rest areas along the way. Love gives everything but it asks everything as well. And what it asks is always a little more than it asked in the previous moment. To feel the truth of that is cause for thanks—a thanks that the persons who think love comes out of marriage contracts or out of the blue can never express. It is better at Thanksgiving to be on the inside of faith and hope and love as they are really found than to stand on the autumn heights waiting for winter with an unbroken but very cold heart. The person who finds it hard to get a few quiet moments to sort himself out at Thanksgiving has by this very discovery something to be thankful for. He or she is alive and involved and makes a difference to somebody else. What other blessings are there if this one is lacking?

November 26
Thanksgiving

Wisdom seems to come to men more from disappointment
and hurt than from knowledge and kindness. And, as men
track their way across the burnished plains of autumn,
now trimmed and braced for winter, they wonder about
the reasons for giving thanks. A man should be grateful
for whatever light there is, God knows, but where is the
light coming from and what does it reveal? So often it
seems to come from those fires that man starts himself—
fires that burn rather than warm, fires that light up scenes
too cruel to look at. Such light as there is seems more like
that of the Jerusalem desert, which challenged sculptor
Jacques Lipchitz and his plans for a monument there. In
an interview, he noted ". . . I must come back and struggle with this enemy, this light. It kills and caresses. You
see only wildness in this light." So it seems for many men
—they experience doubt and pain gazing into the glare of
their own lives. They look up at Thanksgiving time and
they can only see wildness; they want to be thankful but
there is no spontaneous gift of it in their hearts.

Thanksgiving bids us to see with the light that we have
even if it causes us to blink and to back away. The light of
truth reveals terrible monuments to the ways in which life
can disappoint us but there is also beauty in the shadows
that make perspective possible. Maybe it is best to approach Thanksgiving like the man Christ holds up as a
model, the man with enough light to reveal his own sinfulness, the far from perfect man whose best prayer was,
"Have mercy on me, a sinner." This is sufficient light—
better, in fact, than the glaring illumination that gives
every surface a glossy and deceptive perfection. Those who
expect or demand perfection from life, themselves, or their
fellow men are all blinded and cannot see or have a feel
for the values and experiences that are understood by
those who are willing to live in the shadows.

It is strange that what is truly beautiful about man is revealed only if we are strong enough to look at his scars. There is, in fact, no way to understand strength without understanding weakness, no way to live life whole unless we face up to its hard truths. The light we have is that which comes from the Spirit; it must, of course, lose some of its brilliance as it filters through human experience, but it is still the only light we have. And this is what the Christian is grateful for: God does not dwell on the mountain top, not, in other words, at a safe and majestic distance from us, but in the heart of our everyday lives, revealing himself as our strength when we honestly give ourselves to the faulted condition we so aptly call human. The secret is that God does not reveal himself to those who try to look away from life here and now; he is not present at all for those who despise the world or disdain human relationships. God lives, not for those who claim to long only for him and his heaven, but for the courageous ones who affirm life in this tragically beautiful world. As the famed student of mythology Joseph Campbell recently said: "Both artist and lover know that perfection is not love. It is the clumsiness of a fault that makes a person lovable. . . . Balance comes as a result of leaning on your faults. . . . Where you stumble and fall, there you find the gold." At the holiday season the Christian can be grateful for at least beginning to understand this, for having enough light to see that redemption is the prize for those who are vulnerable to life.

November 27
This Thanksgiving Season . . .

is perhaps as important as any we might remember; seldom have we been so conscious of our woes or so tempted to plaintive despair. The Christian, well aware of his scars, is sometimes afraid to count on real friends because of the loneliness that might lie on the other side of the number; for some, life is a matter of holding one's breath and not pushing too hard on the surface of one's beliefs for fear that, like a backlot set from the old Hollywood, those beliefs might collapse into disillusionment. It is a hard time, especially for the sensitive and the loving, because the light, a strange half-light at times, allows us to see the wildness where a man could easily lose himself for good. At Thanksgiving, especially, we might remember that it is only as we look into that light, and feel the tightening in our chests that tempts us to say that people are no damn good, it is only then that we sense the small perennial miracles that make life bearable and beautiful. They are like the "broken bits of summer," which according to Richard Jefferies, "can be found scattered far into the shortening days of fall"—the signs that give us hope when we remember to look at them, the signals that say there is still something to believe in.

November 28
And Pain as Well

Some incidents are almost always linked to pain, to what can go wrong when people live at close quarters with each other, when, in other words, they try to love each other. For example, there is the kind of hurt that only individuals who are very much in love can inflict on each other, and it is the very thing they want most to avoid. Half the time the pain comes because of forgetfulness or for some other indeliberate reason, but that makes the wound greater rather than less. What is important, however, is the fact that people, tasting the bitterness of these experiences, can still forgive each other and that they can do it freely and fully, without holding on to any ideas of getting even later on. There is more of a miracle in that kind of healing than there has ever been at most Christian shrines, and more faith too. People heal each other only because, faced with life's cruel odds, they retain the power to believe in each other. The same can be said for a person when he has kept faith in another way, in a time or a place in which he might have failed, but instead remained true—to his spouse, to his word, to his own promises. Maybe a man grows only when he feels the chill of the valley of temptation in his bones, when he could easily give up, or take something—money, love or whatever—just for himself, but chooses instead to do something better and more loving. There is wonder yet in our capacity to die to ourselves for what we believe is right. It is not very different when we give ourselves wholeheartedly to some cause or to someone's problems without thinking much about ourselves, when, in other words, we respond to a need without hesitation or calculation. We get a glimpse of the best that is in man when redemption for ourselves and others is truly found. But we would never see it at all if we shielded our eyes from the light that reveals the wildness of life. Like the sculptor we must return to it—again and again perhaps—to fight with it for the sake of our souls.

November 29
Some Simple Things

If the blessings we can count at Thanksgiving are so close that we hardly notice them, so too are the joys that counterpoint the stresses of our everyday experience. We always hear of the skies and the stars and how free and glorious they are. True enough, one might say, but think for a moment on other hidden joys, simple and beyond purchase, the little touches of life that make it all worthwhile. If you have ever watched a favorite movie on television and found that someone had edited out the most charming parts in order to preserve the story line, you will know what I mean. The little touches are what count, especially if the story line of our lives is fairly ordinary. For example, what is better than the beginning of a trip? It has a quicksilver magic but there is nothing quite like it. That is when we can sense the excitement, the completion of plans and the opening of new worlds to us. Sometimes the magic does not last a hundred miles, what with crying kids, flat tires, and unexpected detours. A trip, even a vacation, can quickly get to be work, especially as the dew of morning yields to the scorching midday sun. But who has not felt younger, or seen the world as more blessed in that golden moment of getting underway?

Making a new friend, or deepening a friendship that one already has, is another hidden joy. There is something bittersweet about this experience because secrets about ourselves are never shared without pain. But how wondrously different we can feel—and under what a new spell the world turns—when we share the sight of it with someone else. We never get too old to be warmed by what even a little bit of love does for us; we only get less lonely. It is a gift to receive and to give away as well.

November 30
The Reward of Integrity

There is no feeling like it and it can never be taken away from us. It is the reward for being faithful to what we have promised, the deep peace that comes when we have done something as honorably and with as much honesty and integrity as possible. It may be sticking with someone through an illness or a difficult period of mourning or unemployment. It may be in remaining truthful when there are lots of easy reasons to lie; it may be in finishing a job that has taken everything we have in the way of genius or energy. It may be—as it sometimes is for lovers—in keeping in touch through a time of estrangement or misunderstanding. Sticking with it, seeing it through even when the ending seems sad; these are the experiences that make us adults.

These are the touches that make for the well-rounded Christian life, the perennial mixtures of joy and pain through which we begin to understand the dying and rising that mark the lives of true believers. Indeed, true believers can best be identified through their sensitivity to the small touches that fill out life; they believe enough to see the

325

fuller meaning of their experience. They have been there and back, and they can tell the difference between those who only talk about life and those who have really taken it on. Thanksgiving is the time to thank God that he does not edit our lives just so that he can get the main events in. The believer knows that the real meaning of the Christian life is found as much in the small moments as anywhere else, and that salvation is already at hand for all who realize this.

December

December 1
The Picture We Have of the Person

A person's picture of what he or she is like is fundamentally important for the way we live our total lives. The way we view ourselves will determine our attitudes and feelings toward our own personality and also shape our relationship to ourselves. This latter relationship, as psychologists and philosophers are continually pointing out, becomes the model for all our other relationships. In other words, what we think and feel about ourselves is the basis for the way we think and feel about other persons. In the scriptures we are enjoined to love our neighbors as we love ourselves. Some people have always been perplexed by the fact that the Bible says we must love ourselves first; this is an ancient wisdom that recognizes what we sometimes consider a modern truth—our manner of loving ourselves provides the pattern for our love and friendship with others.

For example, if a man is not very comfortable with himself or with some aspect of his personality, he will demonstrate traces of the same uneasiness in his friendships and personal associations. The untrusting individual finds that the same fears he has about himself will usually keep him from trusting his neighbor. Similarly, the individual who feels generally at ease and self-confident with himself will have the same fundamental attitude toward others. The far-reaching implications of this truth are enough to make any man re-examine the picture he has of his own personality—his self-concept or self-image, as the experts put it. The self-concept is, incidentally, closely related to the self-denial which will be as realistic or as unrealistic as a man's view of himself. Distorted notions about the self are projected into an equally distorted and inappropriate self-ideal. Getting an accurate picture of himself becomes essential if a man is to achieve any kind of growth and relationship. In fact, the man who wants to learn more about himself merely has to take a look at his relationships with others or at his attitude toward his ideal self. These both reflect rather accurately his basic attitudes toward himself.

A man's idea of himself, however, can also be radically affected by the ideas about man that are prevalent in his culture—the powerfully formative images that shape his education, work, and even things as personal as his house and his furniture. Man's things have always been precious to him because they are so expressive of him. The world around us reflects the notions of man that are in the air, the ones that are sketched into the arts and drawn carefully into the blueprints for tomorrow's technology. A look at some of these images of man sensitizes us to them and provides a basis for a self-examination of the model that affects our own self-perception most deeply.

December 2
There Is the Divided Person . . .

who is the heritage of numerous explanatory philosophical views of man. Although this designation may be an oversimplification of the theoretical antecedents of this position, many personality models reveal a divided man; the split is usually between spirit and flesh or between intellect and feeling. Once man had been divided in this manner, philosophers and psychologists were confronted with a great problem: how the antagonistic elements of man's personality work in harmony with one another. There has never been a very satisfactory resolution of this duality but there has been a harvest of practical consequences for those who have chosen to believe that man is either mostly spirit or mostly flesh. One can recognize the logical extremes of ultramaterialism and ultraspiritualism which have dogged man's understanding of himself throughout history. It might be noted that this riven image of man was embraced by certain schools of ascetic theology which, as they tried to free the spirit from the coils of the flesh, also reinforced this mistaken understanding of the person. It is no accident that in their ordinary conversations men have come to describe their mostly unconscious efforts to heal the division which has been imposed on their personalities. People speak of "getting their heads together" or "getting it all together," implying the need to make a unity out of themselves and their lives or to get a more integrated view of human personality. These phrases, in fact, tell us something about man's deep instinct to heal himself of long-time hurts.

December 3
And the Mathematical Model . . .

which is a direct descendant of divided man, the natural outcome of man who could be conceived of as material and therefore defined in quantitative terms. Although great advances have come from classifying and systematizing, something vital and human is lost when man is reduced to being identified as a number. But numbers dominate his life these days, from those that describe school grades, IQ, and college board scores to those that tell his Blue Cross number, Social Security number, and the size of his bank account. Certain numbers, especially the amount of a man's wealth or holdings, confer power and esteem in an almost magical way. In other words, certain values which are ultimately inimical to the full understanding of man's humanity become associated with the mathematical model of man. Perhaps that is why, as psychologist Charles A. Curran notes, people get very uneasy when someone speaks of "getting their number." He ends up, Father Curran claims, "getting their goat," that is, provoking an animal reaction.

329

December 4
A Handful of Images

Spiritual Man bobs in and out of history with great regularity, especially when people become disillusioned with other models of man and desire a simpler vision or one that can free them from the burden of being part flesh. In general, this notion exalts the spiritual element of man while frequently debasing the other aspects of personality. One gets to "spiritual" man by way of one of the forks in the road drawn by those who first divided the human person into flesh and spirit. This model sometimes gets confused with the authentically religious man; there is more than a hint of it in the venerable ascetic phrase, "the spiritual life," which gives unconscious testimony to the image that God is present in only one part rather than in the whole of man. The spiritual image of man is closely related to the intellectualized view of the person which drains him of feeling and cleanses him of earthiness. Neither of these, of course, really reflects man as he is. Many movements directed to the notion of man as spirit result in the discovery that he is flesh as well. The attraction of this model is that it creates distance between man and his true personality and allows him to deny or at least look away from what he really is. The inevitable result, however, is incredible strain as the individual tries to become what he can never be.

Sensuous Man (and sensuous woman) is our century's answer to the overemphasis on superrational, overintellectualized, or spiritualized man. This model eroticizes man and his occupations, using pleasure as the yardstick for his actions and promising him an unending orgy for liberating himself and his basic animal powers. "Sensate man" is a more general term for the image that stresses gratification here and now. History has a closet full of philosophies to explain and justify this approach to life which, in this mildly depressed age of plenty, are as popular as ever.

There is something disturbingly smooth yet inherently appealing about the press agentry that goes into this image of man. However, the media usually omit the pain and emptiness that many feel when they have tried to live according to this model; in the end they feel as if they have not lived very much at all.

One-Dimensional Man, as described by the philosopher Herbert Marcuse, combines some of the types already discussed. Marcuse speaks about a culture that diminishes man because of its false sense of values. One-dimensional man inhabits the civilization in which the least important needs of man can be responded to in abundance, while his most important needs are hardly responded to at all. For example, a man in contemporary culture can choose from a widely varied assortment of leisure-oriented items, everything from campers to sports cars to color television. These commodities liberate needs that are not nearly as important as those which bespeak something deep about man and his nature. Man needs a decent education, a roof over his head, and the opportunities to fully develop his personality. When a culture cannot adequately respond to these basic human yearnings, then it has focused on a very narrow image of what man can be.

Alienated Man is, perhaps, better described as a whole tribe of alienated men roaming the face of American culture. Some of them, as characterized by Rollo May, are the estranged who despair of ever being able to communicate genuinely with themselves or with others about the deepest longings of the human person. Dr. May says that the alienated have lost touch with the verbal symbols they need to express their feelings about friendship, love, and close communication. As a result they feel cramped in a computerized world that runs on numbers. Offering little consolation to the alienated man is the nonhero, who has been elevated to a place of prominence in our civilization because of what he lacks as a man rather than because of what he possesses. Nonheroes may be popular because they never disillusion us. We do not expect much from them and we are not disappointed when they fail to meet an ideal. This model of man saves us from a certain measure of pain but does not carry us very far along the road of life. The cult of the nonhero gives us an excuse for holding back, for making little of the challenges which we must accept if we are going to grow as mature human beings.

There are countless combinations of these images of man; we ourselves may shift from one to another at different times in our lives. An inspection of our current images of man will reveal more than we may expect to find about the convictions, beliefs, and values we hold about the human person and, therefore, about ourselves. The traditional Christian vision of man, which is closely linked to the Hebrew attitude toward the person, views man as a unitary being whose body and soul, intellect and emotions, are meant to operate in a harmonious and integrated fashion. Man discovers himself only when he achieves a view that includes all the aspects of his personality in their proper relationship to each other. Then he senses the true depth of his being and can free himself from the restrictive effects of those partial images which ensnare him. The Christian sees man as fallible, as flawed but not intrinsically evil. Man is not a combination of noble spiritual elements that are being attacked constantly by the inner hounds of his fleshly inheritance. He is multidimensional and destined for continuous growth, for the full development of all his powers. The Christian life and the power of the Gospels call upon us to affirm man and to assist him to achieve his fullness. More than anything else modern man needs those who will believe in him again. Through this kind of faith Christians can make man whole.

December 5
Bottoming Out

It can happen to individuals and to groups, to political parties and baseball teams—that long spiralling fall from grace during which we cannot seem to do anything right.

Each day offers more of the same grim diet of near misses and bad luck, and we have all we can do to hold on to our self-confidence until this rainy season of the psyche blows itself out.

Sportswriters are traditionally merciless toward plummeting teams even though championship flags may have snapped brightly over the stadium a few months before. "When you're hot," the popular saying goes, "you're hot," but who has ever had kind words for an unbroken stretch of lukewarmness? The world treats us like the sportswriters, or so it seems, when we are on the way down. The quality of mercy is quite strained and we can only hope to bottom out of our problems as soon as possible. No wonder some people turn to horoscopes and good luck charms; we will try just about anything when we are in the grip of downhill days.

The days seem endless when we cannot seem to get into stride; we can skim close to the chasm of despair, wondering if our best days are forever behind us while we nurse the remnants of our courage. A demon seems to be loose for which no exorcism has yet been written, a demon with a power that is clothed in many disguises.

There is writer's block, for example, that dreaded phenomenon that causes authors to stare for hours at blank pieces of paper or, worse still, to fill their wastebaskets with crumpled sheets of failed themes and unfinished sentences. The writer who cannot engage in the very activity that defines him tastes the same bitter cup as parents who can't get along with their children, athletes who are suddenly all thumbs, and holy people who cannot seem to pray any more. Some dark force checks the very impulse of essential self-expression and a choking kind of frustration results.

There can be stretches when we cannot seem to get along with anybody, not even with our best friends. Everyone seems edgy and prepared to make the worst interpretation of our words and actions. These are usually short in duration but, since they strike at such a sensitive part of our lives, they make up for that in intensity.

There are silly mistakes, bad moves on fundamentals where we should know better and for which demons seem the only logical explanation. We should know better, for example, than to arrive home and take out the pent-up fury of the day on an unsuspecting family. That is a misplay on a basic situation but we may be in the middle of it before we realize how we dug the pit of our own evening. There is general or persistent dissatisfaction with our own behavior or achievements, a discouragement with our own personalities because we keep falling short of some ideal or because we cannot quite overcome some problem or other. This attitude may be tinged with guilt and a diminished sense of our own value. It is the kind of feeling that makes us wonder whether the daily struggle to grow or to be good is really worthwhile.

These are just the problems that remind us of patience, that special brand we require whenever we are face to face with our own varied harvest of failures and unfulfilled ambitions. Being acceptant of ourselves does not mean that we endorse our bad points; it does gain us extra finger room when all we can do is hang on and wait for the bottom of the situation to arrive. It always does and, while we are waiting, we can think of some other things . . . .

December 6
What Did You Expect?

That may seem a hard and unfeeling question but it is a realistic one. We are always coming up against the old spectre of perfectionism; it is the common denominator demon of many of these problems. It is the infection that heightens the fever of our self-disregard because it leaves little margin for error and feeds on non-forgiveness. While we are waiting to bottom out we might feel a little better— and prepare ourselves more constructively for the next like experience—if we could re-insert ourselves in the fallible human context. That does not solve everything, of course, but it gives us breathing room, allows us to readjust our ideals more in accord with our possibilities, and allows us to be more sympathetic to our fellow humans when they are discouraged. Nobody ever promised us a rose garden, either, and the special pains that come in dark nights of the spirit help us to understand and inhabit our humanity more fully and wisely.

December 7
Are We the Common Denominator?

Occasionally, when the world seems to be ganging up on us, we might take time to check out a very simple condition of our distress. Is everybody else fighting or being mean with us . . . or are we the common denominator in the situations that have us down? One can allow that we are often enough without guilt in our dealing with others. Are we, however, really ready to cast the first stone? It takes a little standing back and a lot of truthfulness to admit that sometimes things are going wrong because we are making them go wrong. We may be punishing ourselves at some unconscious level or we may be taking out our unresolved grudges on everyone around us. Whenever we discover that we are the ones who always seem to be embattled it is worth finding out if we are the aggressors rather than the victims. Our mood—and perhaps our lives —can change for the better if we can admit it and attempt to get to the bottom of whatever is really bothering us. Sometimes we find the bottom of our troubles closer to home than we expected.

December 8
The Many Sides of Forgiveness

In the currently popular *Hope for the Flowers* (Newman Press, 1972) one of the story's caterpillars, caught in a throng of fellow creatures climbing up a pillar, asks the question, "How can I step on someone I've just talked to?" Maybe a veteran subway rider would be able to handle that question easily; in fact, mass transit riders frequently end up stepping on and talking to other people at the same time. For most of us, however, the question is better phrased in another way, "How can I talk to someone I've just stepped on?"

Learning how to forgive and to allow oneself to be forgiven are two of the hardest and most important parts of the Christian life. It may be easy to love one's enemies in the abstract but it is very hard to forgive them face to face. The problem may be found in its most serious form when we must face and forgive our friends or our family, the people with whom we most regularly exchange hurts.

Sometimes the situations in which we step on others are those we would rather file and forget, pretending either that they never happened or that we did not mean them in quite the way they came out. We may be tempted to do that or, on the other hand, we can overreact to overcome the guilt or shame we feel at what we may have said or done. Neither of these attitudes deals straightforwardly with the occasions, many of them minor, on which we wound or are wounded by other persons. Turning away from it does not make the situation go away and overreacting may be aimed at clearing up our own feelings rather than healing those of the offended person. It takes a steady eye and a firm heart to come to terms with ourselves and the issues that are involved in the challenges of forgiveness.

Forgiving and being forgiven are part of the way the Lord teaches us to pray and also part of our everyday lives. Mastering the dimensions of forgiveness may be a task that we never fully complete; it is like love, something that we get better at but not perfect no matter how long we work on it.

December 9
What Do I Mean When I Say "I'm Sorry"?

That is a phrase that can be uttered in a quite perfunctory manner, much in the way a train conductor punches a ticket, and with a similar intention. It is a way of securing passage rather than a way of re-establishing relationship. When "I'm sorry" is said in an impersonal tone it does not really deliver the transforming message of human forgiveness. These words always depend on how much of ourselves we put into them. There is no magic unless we are there. That is a traditional challenge, of course, and it applies to any of the important statements we exchange with each other. Hurt is transmitted personally; likewise, forgiveness must be communicated with as much of ourselves as possible involved in the exchange.

December 10
We Never Know What Hurts People

Perhaps the worst emotional wounds we inflict are those of which we are least aware. When we focus on ourselves and our own concerns, the rights and needs of others can become obscured in our own eyes so that we hardly notice when we step on them. Sometimes people are hurt without sufficient cause; sometimes they lead with their chins so that they cannot help but be hurt. In many circumstances, however, a hurt comes because of a blunder on our part, a failure to take the other person's feelings or interests into account. Perhaps if we think of some of the small things that hurt us, we will become more sensitized to our own capacity to hurt others without even recognizing it.

December 11
Making a Relationship Whole Again

The rituals of absolution and forgiveness—those gestures through which we make a relationship whole again—are powerfully important and cannot be disregarded. They are part of our human language and, as a people, we are poorer when we let them fall into disuse for whatever reason. This is a particular danger in an era in which remaining cool has been exalted as the height of human behavior. Those who prize coolness will never be able to express forgiveness symbolically because they must give too much of themselves away in the process. They cannot easily say *I love you* and they will only be surprised when loneliness finally catches up with them.

Just as we must learn to use the language of symbols, so too we must be able to understand it. Sometimes the best another person can do is make a small gesture that has a large meaning in our regard; a widow's mite of a symbol but still the best the other can possibly do in a given situation. To reject it or to ignore it—to demand unconditional surrender on our terms—may make us feel self-righteous but it can also be a very hollow victory. Read the small gestures that seek forgiveness correctly and your life will be enlarged as will those of the persons who make such gestures to you.

Forgiveness is one of the few things we can give to other people freely. It is also something that can neither be purchased nor demanded, and its only service is to other persons. Forgiveness, in fact, can only be given away. If we make other people pay for it or if we use it as a psychological weapon associated with emotional manipulation rather than a genuine change of heart, it fails. Forgiveness is something precious because through it we can make each other new once more and open each other to the freshness of life again. Sometimes genuine forgiveness is so powerful that others refuse it, simply because they know that they will have to change in order to accept such a loving gift. This does not make us abandon our efforts to forgive or to seek forgiveness but it does alert us to the fact that this is a precious human commodity that can make the difference between life and death both for us and for those who live closely with us. It is also one of the signs of the Spirit at work in the world, the Spirit of healing and understanding, the Spirit who gives us unmeasured joy when we are big enough to be forgiving.

December 12
Rules to Remember

Things go wrong all the time: There is absolutely no exception to this rule. You can apply it in any place or in any set of circumstances. No matter how much preparation has been made, no matter how many countdowns or check lists have been run through, most things tend to go wrong. This happens in families, business, and even in that antiseptic and supposedly feelingless world of mathematics in which ill-fed computers regularly frustrate the most scientifically pure hearts. That things regularly go wrong is a basic truism of the human condition. Our trouble arises when we are unrealistically optimistic, still hoping for perfection when experience tells us that we should know better.

If things did not systematically go wrong, at least in small details, we would never have crabgrass, lovers' quarrels, or disappointments. We would never need love nor would we ever have the chance to experience the kind of growth that takes place in us when we approach each other with genuine forgiveness. Part of what goes wrong, you see, is us; we are still capable of betraying our own best intentions or resolutions and, like St. Paul, of not knowing quite why we do these things. We may never figure out quite why, nor plumb the depths of our psychological motivations completely. This is why it is vital for forgiveness to be at hand, both for us to receive and for us to give away.

Good people get to understand and to tolerate us: It is amazing, in fact, how, with real affection, our family and friends get to know and to forgive us for being the imperfect specimens we are. Life would be absolutely intolerable if this loving capacity were not present in those around us. This is something good people do without thinking about it very much, a reaction compounded of healthy instincts and an openness to the Spirit.

December 13
It Goes Beyond Putting Up with Us . . .

because it includes a kind of patient acceptance that tells us in effect, "We understand and care for you even when you are very difficult to get along with." Families probably would not survive if they could not create this buffer zone around the temperamental, the distraught, or the just plain ornery members of the group. It is a zone of blessing in which others suspend judgment while the offending member has time to come to terms with and reintegrate himself or herself with the group. This is done silently and symbolically most of the time and it is a sure cure for sulking, feeling sorry for oneself, or the other hazards that are involved in growing up or in remaining grown up.

December 14
A Sense of Humor Helps

It always does, of course, but perhaps in no situation is it more important than in that of forgiveness. We cannot stand on a pedestal of distorted self-regard if we really care about forgiving and being forgiven by others. We cannot remain on a lofty platform and maintain our illusions about ourselves when forgiveness demands, first of all, a sense of realism about both our limitations and our possibilities. We need not ridicule ourselves in order to be able to laugh in a healthy manner at our own foibles and shortcomings. Nothing clears the head of vanity better than a general and smiling confrontation with our own fumbling selves. When we can accept the cracks in our own character structure without being unnecessarily mad at ourselves because they are there in the first place, we are far more able to accept those which we will always find in others.

December 15
Self Treatment

If we begin by trying to forgive ourselves for our failures, our mistaken judgments, or our overestimations of our own powers, we take a big step toward being able to give that same forgiveness to other persons. There is no substitute, in other words, for facing the truth about ourselves. It helps to have that sense of humor we just mentioned but only if we use it as a gentle light that enables us to acknowledge more of ourselves. We cannot laugh off the wrongs we have committed if we are going to talk to those we have just stepped on; we begin by facing the true dimensions of what we have done. That is not an easy task but there can be no forgiveness from ourselves or from others if we do not put an honest name to the injury we have caused. And that's just the beginning.

Don't nurse the hurt. This applies in those situations in which we feel that we have been wrongly treated by someone else. One of our most familiar human temptations is to hold on to hurts that we should learn to let go of. It is far better to get our injury exposed to the air than to let it fester in angry brooding through which we isolate ourselves and make ourselves more miserable than the human condition really demands. It is understandable that we want to nurse our wounds because at times there doesn't seem to be anything else we can do about them. We can, however, at least admit that we are doing this and try to accept our wounded selves with the kind of forgiveness we are not quite ready to give to others.

Forgive others as you would have them forgive you. This is one of the better translations of the Golden Rule or of the scriptural instruction that we must love our enemies. If we try to offer forgiveness as we would like to receive it we will necessarily begin to try to see into the world of the other person. Seeing something of another person's viewpoint almost always improves our own way of looking at things. We become more tolerant and through understanding we heal far more wounds than we do by argumentation about who said what or for what reasons. Disputing how the fight got started in the first place only makes things worse and it is exhausting besides.

December 16
Hurt Collectors

A famous psychiatrist once described a certain class of persons as "injustice collectors," people who make a lifestyle out of being offended. There are no real reasons for their being offended, of course, so they invent them, reading into the behavior of others in fanciful ways so that they can finally accumulate enough evidence to accuse them of imaginary hurts. This is a strange way to relate to other people, a sad and diminished way to live in general, and there are two reasons why it is very difficult to deal with forgiveness with these people. First of all, they have not really been hurt, and secondly, they don't want anything to do with forgiveness. They get through life in this unhealthy fashion, offering friendship to others as bait for a trap which they finally close when the other least understands or expects it.

December 17
They Tell Us More . . .

about their own troubles than they do about anything else.
Most good people do not want to offend others and they
are taken aback when they seem to be accused by one of
these "hurt collectors." They should not lose confidence in
themselves but try to see this as part of the pattern of the
other's behavior; they should neither be dismayed nor manipulated by the offended attitude of the other. That is
playing the game according to his rules, which is just what
he wants you to do. It is better to be acceptant and understanding—and to restrain oneself from trying to straighten
the situation out rationally. The meaning of the problem is
emotional and it cannot be described or treated by intellectual means. The believing Christian must accept these
people even if he or she can do little more than that. We
can, however, realize that if we could look deeply enough
into their life histories we would understand them better
and know why they have forged such a sad and shabby
way of getting on with others. In short: understanding,
yes; involvement, no.

December 18
Being Sensitive

A man or a woman pays a high price for being sensitive,
for feeling all the aspects of what occurs in their own experience, or for sensing and caring about even those
tragedies which do not touch their own lives directly. It
hurts to pay attention to life and to look at its cruelties
and injustices, its small deceits and its big disappointments,
and to try to keep faith with it rather than to turn cynical.
It is difficult to see other people as persons rather than
members of a crowd or a mob, and it is genuinely hard to

343

remember that each individual has feelings and meanings all his or her own that must be appreciated and respected by others. Sometimes life just seems to hurt too much to look squarely at it and yet, if we give up on this, we blunt ourselves to the meaning of our existence and, in the name of missing some of its sorrows, we deprive ourselves of any feelings for its joys. Only the person who is open to life in its bad parts as well as its good can possess the kind of happiness that is the special prize of the open heart.

This sensitivity to the feelings of others also allows you to be honest about yourself and your own life experience. Best of all, even the reverberating echoes of our own hurts tell us that we have touched life and meaning, that we have not stayed on the sidelines and that we have not run away out of fear. Perhaps the contemporary meaning of "turning the other cheek" involves us in opening ourselves to the pain of the whole world and in not shrugging it off or in trying to distract ourselves from it. It is better to be alive with this kind of feeling for mankind than to be dead to it because we have become estranged from compassion for our fellow pilgrims. Those who mourn are those who are comforted and those who can share the world's pain are those who finally triumph over it.

December 19
Of Love and Loneliness at Christmas

The winds start to blow at the top of the world at Christmas time; sometimes they glaze our hearts just when we think that the season of joy should be warming them. We know that we have found the light of the world; but the blackness beyond it—the darkness that closes over the past and still shrouds the future—is filled with questions for us, questions for which Christmas has an answer. In the space around this holiday a man cannot help but wonder about the meaning of his life; the year's end is a time for counting up the losses and gains of his soul, a moment of quiet truth in wondering at where he has been and where he might be going. It is strange indeed that at the edge of celebration a man can feel suddenly and profoundly alone. It seems a bad state but, in reality, it is not and Christmas is as good a time to face ourselves as we are likely to find.

In essence Christmas invites us to the feast proclaimed by Jesus and, in a wonder surpassing most miracles, we can come as we are. The celebration is for human beings who find few ways in life that are clear and straight, for persons who store up heartbreak and loneliness, for the men and women astounded by love and puzzled by death, for everyone who has ever been alive enough to know that, as Boris Pasternak has written, to live to the end "is not a childish thing." The mystery of Christmas is not that it eliminates doubt but that it makes doubt intelligible; Christmas does not take away all pain but it does make pain meaningful; Christmas does not give all the answers but it does understand all the questions. Christmas has never been an invitation to escape this life; it has always told us that the way to follow Jesus is by entering more deeply and purposefully into life.

December 20
The Incarnation . . .

has the power to stir us to fuller life because it is the mystery that affirms us in the flesh of our existence and acknowledges the tragic dimensions of our vocation to become fully ourselves through living in Jesus. The trouble is that for so long men have interpreted this mystery according to the stern ascetic code which secretly despises life and which can only condemn, but never warmly embrace, its flaws. We are recovering from this misreading of the Gospel, from this distortion that made grimly puritanical news out of the Good News itself.

345

December 21
The Gospel of Jesus . . .

asks us to continue to grow toward becoming men and women and not to be discouraged at the constant evidence that we can never be gods; we are reminded at Christmas that we are called to become human together, bearing one another's burdens and becoming brothers as we grow better at giving freely the gifts of faith, hope and love to each other. It is this simple truth that helps us recognize that our searching is not a sign of estrangement but a hint of our longing for deepened relationships with men and God. The Christian who, at times, feels the pain of all creation is the person who has properly located life in Jesus in the cracks and crevices of time and history rather than in the glossy blue of the too distant sky.

December 22
Why Keep Christmas?

Why celebrate Christmas, one might ask, when the blessings it sings seem as far out of our reach as ever? The answer, of course, is that we keep Christmas not because life is nice but because it is cruel and harsh, because all too often it is not fair and comes out uneven. We keep Christmas because it tells us that despite all that is wrong with us, we have the help and forgiveness to be set aright, that Jesus has come for all the ordinary people who keep company everyday with the pains of living.

A few years ago Abraham Maslow, a sensitive psychologist, asked the kind of question that perplexes us at this time of the year: "Why are people cruel and why are they nice? Evil people are rare, but you find evil behavior in the majority of people." At Christmas you need not look beyond the family for enough hurt to fill an entire lifetime.

The story of the holy family seems far away as we witness around us the anguish of families shuddering under the impact of a life they cannot quite manage to share together. The child in the crib at Bethlehem is gentle and loved but recalls images, which are burned into our memories forever, of today's battered children. And the tenderness of Mary and Joseph toward each other is contradicted by the marriages in which men and women make war with each other in scenes that make everyone afraid of Virginia Woolf. Then there are the children who disappoint their parents, leaving wounds that never heal. Such multiplied misery has brought Dr. Israel Chaney to speak of the "myth of happy family life," the setting in which everything that should go right seems, with a horror beyond telling, to go wrong.

Of course, all of this is seen against the background of a world that has known only a few days of history free of wars, a world that seems to be possessed by the unjust rather than the meek, in which the innocent suffer and virtue regularly goes unrewarded. Now we make a romance of godfathering, excusing terror and murder when it is seasoned with the species of loyalty and charm that is portrayed in current gangster movies.

We see men choosing power instead of love, betrayal instead of trust, and self-interest instead of dedication to each other. Christmas finds us curiously far from the goals of a basically decent human life. There are those who say that at least we can now view life without the superstitious weight of religion, that we are well rid of believing in the kind of God who could let such a world go on. For these people the holidays only underline the desperate loneliness they see as our ultimate bitter lot.

December 23
These Are the Reasons . . .

we keep Christmas. We would hardly need this feast were the world any different. It would be superfluous if we were already fully grown, or had mastered the lessons of love, or knew the combinations which automatically insure that tragedies would no longer occur and that the children of today would inherit tomorrow a world in which lambs fraternize with lions. There would be no point in Christmas if we did not know the taste of loneliness or the special suffering of hurting and being hurt by those closest to us. If the world were not in agony the birth of Jesus would have nothing to say to us. We would have no need for a God who lived our life, spoke our language, and knew first hand all of our heartbreaks.

December 24
Christmas Is a Gentle Tale . . .

whose power comes from weakness, a story that tempers our rage because it confirms and redeems our humanity. God's becoming man tells us that life resides in our becoming men and that the enormous difficulties involved in that process constitute the essence of a faithful existence. We need Christmas because we are as yet half grown; Jesus tells us that we can make our way, not by the light of a wondrous star, but in living the truths which he spoke to us. Christmas is the season in which we can confront all that is wrong with us because Jesus knows and understands it. Jesus says that being human and tasting life as it is will reveal the meaning of Christmas. This is the way, he says; this is the road I took in the world that I knew, the road I pointed to when I said, "I am the way." We need Christmas in the midst of unrelenting and unforgiving life because it affirms again that our shadowed days are not empty but filled with meaning. We keep Christmas because it says that God is near and that our own struggles with the evils of our self-growth are at the heart of Christian living.

348

December 25
Christmas Stars

We are not a race of supermen and, in the stillness of Christmas night, we can admit this to ourselves. We see ourselves better by the light of the Christmas star. It is a wondrous light not because it generates miracles but because it allows us a view of our real selves. Christmas is not fantasy; rather, it is the one time of the year when we need not pretend at all. Jesus is man, ransoming our human vulnerability by his own. His sinlessness does not shame us because of our large and small evils. It gives us hope and light where we, left to our own inclinations, might harvest only despair and darkness. Christmas is not a demanding feast in that it asks the impossible of us. The real miracle of Christianity and the central meaning of this feast lie in this: We can respond to Christmas not by going beyond ourselves in the quest for impossible dreams but by discovering our true selves and living that reality more deeply.

The light of Christmas is bright and steady enough to reveal us all as blind and crippled in one way or another. It deepens our appreciation of being less than angels and awakens us to be men who belong to the same glorious and flawed family. Christmas allows us to see beyond our pettiness and small vengeances and to stand above the unpredictable tides that sweep across our souls. The truth about Christmas is that it knows the truth about us—that we are imperfect and unfinished; that we have only begun our great journey toward the fullness of time when we will have fulfilled the promise of Christmas in history itself; that there is still hope for all who dare to be human. And this is why we need Christmas.

December 26
Remembering at Christmas

Perhaps the best gifts we have at Christmas are our memories of individuals who live out the faith in a simple but intense way and who change us through our experience of knowing them. I have come to understand fidelity better because of something I saw for only a few seconds through an open hospital door during the past year. An old woman, sitting by the bedside of her desperately ill husband, was holding his hand very gently. Neither was speaking but they were truly present to each other. Something about the loving way in which they looked back and forth told the story of all that they had looked on together over the years.

And I remember a solidly built working man, against the blackness of a Belfast night, folding his muscular arms and blinking back tears as he talked about his murdered son, a victim of the violence in Northern Ireland only a few months before. "He was a terrible good boy, only 17 and never a bit of trouble to us. He just went up to the corner. It was only 6:30 in the evening and I just sat down to watch a film on television." The man's wife held his arm as he went on: "I said to him, 'Now be careful,' and he looked at us and he said, 'Oh sure, you know that I will,' and off he went. He was up at the head of the street and a car of young fellows pulled over and asked him for directions. When he raised his arm to point out whatever they wanted to know they shot him three times. And the next thing I know they are running in saying, 'Sean is shot!' and I run up the street and the ambulance is there and I get in and I say to him, 'It's all right, daddy's here'—but he only groaned, and then he died."

The man looked across the room at a picture of his dead son and then looked back to me: "I thought a lot about it and I don't hold it against the Protestants that my son is dead. I have no anger toward them at all. We had no peace until the other children and their friends got together and scraped up some money selling chances to send me and the wife to Lourdes. There was no miracle but we found peace there. I'm not full of revenge or anything." He and his wife looked deeply into each other's eyes and then he turned back to me, "But we miss him bad. . . ."

Christmas is a time for remembering, for drawing on the strength of all those who have known and loved us during the past year, for finding all the good that sometimes seems hidden by the bad. These are the births and rebirths of our lives that overcome the seemingly endless dreams. Christmas is the time to count the gifts of love we have received in the small and silent ways in which they are best given.

December 27
Lessons Never Finished

We never really master the art of saying thanks—not to God and not even to our family and friends to whom we owe so much. This is probably why we keep working at it and why we are grateful for the poets, even when they work for Hallmark cards, who manage to say it for us. Saying thanks is a prayer as well as good manners and there are few moments of real life in which it is not appropriate. We are never finished in our efforts to pray better. This is appropriate because we are forever deepening our realization of all that God has given to us. There is a truth to be found in the insight that a heartfelt thank you is something which becomes more meaningful each time we utter it. We can improve ourselves by applying the golden rule notion, asking what we consider the best thanks from others when we give something to them.

The best expression of gratitude resides in taking what others give to us as though it were a forward pass. We run with it, trying to use it and the moments at our disposal for some greater achievement. In the Gospels we read of the stern master who gives varying sums of money to his servants only to be outraged by the one who buries his gift in the ground, keeping it safe until the master's return. There is an inevitable measure of risk—of throwing ourselves out of balance—if we are to be true to the gifts of nature and grace which we find in ourselves. God has not given us life to hoard for ourselves, no matter how grateful we are for it. He asks that we share our lives generously— at Christmastime and throughout the year—as the best sign of our gratitude and the richest prayer we can offer to him.

December 28
Love Is Always a Struggle . . .

its lessons yielding only to those who keep their hearts open to the painful process of learning them. The life of Jesus teaches us a good deal about the mixture of tenderness and closeness with the pain and separation that are inevitably a part of the love that gives life to others. The best of it comes when we are willing to deal with the worst of it. And Christmas tells us that the path to what is divine is not separate from the long human road of learning how to love. Life has no fears for the Christian who remembers at Christmas that Jesus is the way and that he leads to love —love at the last.

December 29
The Condition of Slaves

We read in the scriptures that, in becoming man, Jesus took on the condition of a slave, making himself a servant for all of us instead of clinging to his powerful kingship. We read and marvel that he "emptied himself" because this action points so directly to a central mystery and experience in our own lives. The meaning of our existence eludes us unless, in some practical, operational way, we choose to empty ourselves as slaves rather than aspire to possess power. The imitation of Christ has always depended more on this intuition than on such outward behavior as custody of the eyes or a monastically-gaited walk which we thought appropriate to holiness. No, the essence of the Christian response has always been an interior mystery; what we surrender is inside of us, in our feelings and attitudes toward others. The Christian's inner life is not, however, just a calming form of transcendental meditation; it is the living experience of emptying ourselves of that selfishness which keeps us from being servants to each other. This is done, not by numbing ourselves, but by feeling the pain which is involved in love that is real rather than sentimental. We come alive in Jesus whenever we do this; the rest of our lives takes shape around this demanding commitment.

Emptying ourselves of selfishness does not mean daydreaming about some great event during which we will join our names to the lists of heroes by sacrificing our lives for the multitude. The best of us may at times enjoy the fantasy of such a glorious moment but, alas, it actually comes to very few. We cannot wait for a distant and luminous instant in which our generosity will be realized. Emptying ourselves is a simple and plain thing; no day goes by that does not offer an opportunity to us. It is part of our overall response to life and is found, for example in listening to others—even when we are busy with a thousand dreams of our own. If we think about it for a moment, we will realize that we are all looking for someone who will listen to us. And real listening is far different from just hearing what another person has to say. Listening is not nodding the head and making periodic grunts. We cannot really listen to another person unless we give up something of ourselves in the process. It may be as simple as emptying ourselves of the kinds of distractions which crowd our minds at most moments; it involves suspending our thoughts about what we are going to do later in the day; it demands at least the effort to surrender these considerations in order to listen while another speaks to us.

353

Others, after all, are not just trying to tell us some facts about their experience. They are seeking a confirmation of themselves through sharing something of their lives with us. Much of the mystery of life is involved in feeling that someone else has heard us and, by that action, has made us realize our own existence more fully. There is little friendship and no love at all without the mystery of emptying ourselves that touches each of our lives every day.

December 30
Being Obedient to the Spirit Asks Us to . . .

go more deeply into ourselves than our whims or superficial feelings would ordinarily allow. There are so many occasions in which we shrug off the possibilities of further self-knowledge by saying something like, "Well, that's the way I am," or "I don't want to talk about it." The loss involved in these statements is more to ourselves than to others because we actively resist a better look at the foundations of our own personality. It is never easy to search deeply into ourselves and yet, in the long run, it is important to do this at least intermittently if we are going to achieve any kind of maturity. Sometimes those devils which seem to bother us most disappear when we look carefully inside ourselves and can accept what we find there. It may seem as cobwebbed as a haunted house, filled with things we have little taste for seeing; a good look blows away most of what seems fearful and makes us wiser at the same time. A sense of identity is vitally important to each of us because without it we can neither be nor share ourselves with others. And if we can't do that, life doesn't have meaning or charm. We never find our identity, however, until we empty ourselves of the minor vanities that make us uneasy about our true selves. What we get rid of is well discarded when we are looking for the roots of our identity. There is even a bonus attached to this—we begin to like ourselves and others better in the process.

those who hurt us in life. Emptying ourselves of unnecessary defenses is the name of this very Christian game. In order to keep our relationships from reaching a dead end, and to avoid living with others merely by truce or cease-fire we must empty ourselves of those resistant feelings, the ones that make it hard to forgive and forget. Some people make a career of living off past hurts, recalling them decades and generations later, clutching them to their heaving breasts as though they were sacred and life-justifying relics. It is a diminished life if that is all that a person has to hold on to; it is, indeed, a life that can only move toward a lonely and bitter end. We begin a process of forgiving and forgetting by emptying ourselves of nursed grudges and prized wrongs. This is not easy, especially when the hurt has been deep, and we will never accomplish it perfectly. The remarkable thing about human beings, however, is that the medicine we need for healing is very powerful even when it is taken in very small doses. We really do not need much in the way of attention or forgiveness to come back to life. We revive on small amounts of the really human. We respond to love and to the efforts to forgive which are made in its name. Emptying ourselves of the memories of hurts frees us—as much as it does our neighbor—for a fuller and more blessed life.

OTHER IMAGE BOOKS

OTHER IMAGE BOOKS

OTHER IMAGE BOOKS

OTHER IMAGE BOOKS